W9-AAO-792

ISRAEL'S DILEMMA

Why Israel Is Falling Apart
And How to Put It
Back Together

ISRAEL'S DILEMMA

Why Israel Is Falling Apart And How to Put It Back Together

Ezra Sohar

Shapolsky Publishers
136 West 22nd Street
New York, NY 10011

A Shapolsky Book
Published by Shapolsky Publishers

For any additional information contact:
Shapolsky Publishers, Inc. 136 West 22nd Street, New York, NY 10011

10 9 8 7 6 5 4 3 2 1

Library of Congress Cataloging-in-Publication Data:
Sohar, Ezra, 19__-
Israel's Dilemma / Ezra Sohar.
p. cm.

Includes bibliographical references. Index.

ISBN 0-944007-59-7

1. Israel---Politics and Government 2. Bureaucracy---Israel.

I. Title.

JQ1825,P3S64 1989 89-10796
320.95694---dc20 CIP

EZRA SOHAR, is one of Israel's most respected social critics. He is the author of eight books, including the Hebrew-language best-seller, *In the Pincers of the Regime*, (1974). Sohar is editor-in-chief of *Meurav Yerushalmi*, a popular weekly news magazine.

Ezra Sohar, M.D.

- Educated at Kibbutz Mishmar-HaEmek
- M.D., Geneva, Switzerland
- Lt. Col. (Res.) Medical Corps, Israel Defense Army
- Commander of the Army Field Hospital in the Sinai during the Yom-Kippur war
- Head, Dept. of Medicine, Chaim Sheba Medical Center, Tel-Hashomer, to 1982
- Head, Heller Institute of Medical Research, to 1987.
- Professor of Medicine, Tel-Aviv University Medical School
- Founder and First Chairman of the Israeli Society of Ecology (1970-1972)
- Chairman of the Committee (appointed by the Ministry of Health, 1977) to propose reform in Israeli Medicine
- Published more than 200 scientific papers and chapters in medical textbooks on genetic-metabolic diseases and on physiology of man in hot climates

Books

Sohar, E., *Man and His Food*, 1971.
Sohar, E., *In the Pincers of the Regime*, 1974.
Sohar, E. & Shapiro, Y., *The Body and It's Functions*, 1977.
Sohar, E., *The Desert*, 1977.
Sohar, E., *Yanshuf* 1977.
Sohar, E., *Man and Climate*, 1980.
Sohar, E., *Health Without Superstition*, 1987.
Sohar, E., *Sedom or Chelam*, 1987

CONTENTS

CHAPTER ONE

ROOTS OF THE CRISIS

The roots of Israel's socioeconomic morass reach back to the beginning of the century, when the early Zionist pioneers were laying the foundations for the future Jewish state. From 1905 until the outbreak of World War I, some 35,000 young Russian Jews settled in Palestine. Although deeply sympathetic to the revolutionary ideologies current in turn-of-the-century Russia, these youthful pioneers were persuaded by the sheer force of Russian anti-Semitism that their contributions to socialism would have to be made elsewhere. Palestine became their experiment station. The party they established in 1919, Ahdut-Ha'avoda, or the Union of Labor Zionists, served as the political expression of their socioeconomic philosophy.

"Russia's political culture differs from that which dominates the West," according to Yonatan Shapiro, chronicler of the early days of Labor Zionism. "As the ideas of individualism and free enterprise gained ground in the West, absolutism was being maintained in Tsarist Russia. The government interfered in all spheres of its subjects' lives.... This collectivistic political orientation was sustained in Soviet Russia, where politicians continue to control and manage the economy.... This political culture, acquired by the leaders of Labor Zionism in Russia, guided their efforts towards the establishment of a political organization that would administer the entire economy. This was the explicit aim of Ahdut-Ha'avoda upon its establishment in 1919."[1] Within a single decade, 1919-1930, the Labor Zionists succeeded in transforming themselves from a splinter faction in the Zionist movement into the dominant force in the economic and eventually, political life of Palestine Jewry.

Governmental institutions such as police, army, and the judiciary were in the hands of the British Mandatory authorities. The only way Labor Zionism could secure the allegiance of the Jewish proletariat was through hegemony in the economic sphere. Labor Zionist leaders regarded control of the economy by politicians as both legitimate and desirable. To achieve this goal, they established the Histadrut, or General Federation of Labor. The Histadrut was not merely an expanded version of a labor union. It was intended from the start to embrace all pursuits of the Palestinian Jewish proletariat: agricultural settlements, cooperative societies, urban workers groups, the Sick Fund, Bank Hapoalim (the "Workers Bank"), schools, workers kitchens, corporations such as the Solel Boneh construction firm, cultural organizations, and sports clubs. It is no wonder, then, that some seventy percent of the Histadrut's target membership joined within five years.

At the second Histadrut Convention, the leadership founded Hevrat Ha-Ovdim, the Corporation of Workers, to control all economic activity. It was placed under the supervision of the Histadrut Executive Committee. The Executive Committee had the authority to approve budgets, hire and fire directors, collect dues, fix prices of Histadrut-made goods, and set wages; it was also given sole authority to negotiate with non-Histadrut institutions. To secure complete control of agricultural settlements, the Executive Committee proposed to establish a shareholder company, Nir. It was to become the settlements' legal owner, and would be subordinate to the Executive Committee. Each settlement would hold one share. Many settlers objected to the idea, but they found themselves pitted against iron willed Labor Zionist leaders like David Ben-Gurion, who believed that the maintenance of "our movement's economic unity cannot depend on moral convictions alone. Legal authority is needed to coerce traitors."[2] In the end, Nir was set up according to plan. Agricultural settlements were no longer permitted, for example, to sign contracts directly with the World Zionist Organization. This was done for them by the Histadrut. The politicians became the absolute rulers of the Histadrut economy. The control politicians gain over the economy also affects the structure of a society's economic organizations: the economy becomes part of the political institutions, and considerations of power and control take priority over economic considerations of productivity and efficiency. The economy in turn serves to multiply the power of the politicians who control it. M. Djilas points out that the intent of all economic decisions in the Soviet Union is to enhance the power and the privilege of the bureaucracy. Matters developed similarly in Palestine, where the economy became subordinated to the needs of politicians.[3]

The Histadrut encompassed a number of parties, of which the Labor Zionists were the largest. The leaders of Labor were also the leaders of the Histadrut. Naturally, they appointed party activists to fill all important administrative positions. True to their views, the Laborites sought control not only of the economy, but also of education and culture. The Teachers Association – which was not part of the Histadrut – defied the leaders and demanded that the educational system remain autonomous. In 1930, Ben-Gurion threw down the gauntlet at a teachers conference. "...We are now going to form one united labor party, which will direct the population's political, educational and cultural activities." He exhorted the teachers to participate in this enterprise under the auspices of the party. Eventually the teachers did as told, and taught the principles of Zionism as Labor interpreted them.[4] Financial support for a large cultural network – newspapers, periodicals, theaters and more – brought many intellectuals and artists under the Histadrut umbrella. "The key to the success of Ahdut Ha'avoda and its leaders in becoming the dominant political factor in Palestine's Jewish community," according to

Shapira, "was their success in gaining control over economic resources."[5]

The Histadrut was constituted in such a way as to guarantee self-perpetuating elitism. All Histadrut members elect delegates to the Convention. The Convention then elects a Council, which in turn elects the Executive Committee, that is, the leadership. The Council is supposed to supervise the Executive Committee. The delegates to the Convention are not elected directly but rather by members voting for national slates of delegates nominated by the leaders of each party. This system deliberately puts distance between elector and electee. The Histadrut's elected delegates owe the voters nothing.

The Convention affirms, usually by acclaim, a list of Council nominees previously negotiated by the leaders. By this stage, little remains of the voter's intention. The Council is a relatively small body governed by individual interests. Many of its members are – or strive to be – appointed by the Executive Committee to the party bureaucracy. The leaders who comprise the Executive Committee can influence members of the Council by promising them jobs, promotions, and more. In other words, Council members depend on the Executive Committee in a virtual employee-employer relationship. Since most members of the Executive Committee also belong to the Council, their automatic re-election is assured. Ultimately the Council's "supervision" of the Executive Committee is a farce. As the eminent political scientist Maurice Duverger notes, indirect elections are "an admirable tool with which to abrogate democracy while claiming to administer it."[6] To this day, elections for the Histadrut and for all Israeli political parties are indirect. This permits a caste of politicians to seize control of the party bureaucracy and rule indefinitely.

In the early 1920s it was decided that all Histadrut members would receive the same base wage; any additional payments would depend on family size. Thus wages were determined by politicians, irrespective of a worker's productivity or an employer's profitability. Such a decision could be taken only in a subsidized economy, in which spending has nothing to do with profits. Meanwhile, the bureaucratic elite was enjoying a long list of "benefits" or "amenities" on top of salary. Managers and party functionaries were reimbursed for "expenses" for travel, automobile upkeep, "representation" (out-of-pocket hospitality expenses), food and board, and more. Many Histadrut and party officials received loans for various purposes, including the construction of residences, and repayment was often waived. This was an inevitable consequence of the equal-wage principle. Even as base wages stayed the same, a covert wage scale developed, out of the public eye and different from one person to another, depending on the individual's status and connections. Ultimately, Histadrut leaders and directors fared far better than the hapless working masses.

The Histadrut became the de facto government of Palestine's Jewish workers, embracing a wide variety of functions in its bearhug. Such a complex task required it had to assemble a massive bureaucracy. In an important sense, these increasingly powerful bureaucrats played a key role in the political leadership of Palestine Jewry: in return for the bureaucrats' support, Labor Zionist leaders would adopt no resolution contrary to Histadrut interests. "Ben-Gurion's leadership was not of the charismatic sort," Shapira notes. "He did not recruit his followers by force of personality, but he needed the apparatus to control them. Whenever he tried to appeal to his followers without the bureaucracy's support, he failed.[7] (Forty years later, when Ben-Gurion tried to circumvent the party's bureaucrats and marshall popular support for his positions, he was expelled from the party.)

An entity as powerful as this obviously aspired to improve its standard of living. Some functionaries went at it by illegitimate means. Instances of party favor and "protectionism" were discussed in various internal forums as early as the 1920s. Not that such behavior was held in disrepute. To the contrary, Ben-

Gurion went so far as to state, "The expertise of Histadrut functionaries is not in business administration but in devotion to Zionism... The question is not whether our comrades are honest and experienced, but whether they are good Zionists."[8]

In the Western world, a political party is an association of people who share similar beliefs. The benefits the party members seek to attain are on a national and not on a personal level. Things were different in pre-Israel Palestine. Emulating the Histadrut, more parties set up economic and welfare organizations and vied for funds from Diaspora Jewry. This had a devastating influence on the very nature of the political parties, which became substitutes for government and channels for funneling economic support. The parties – or the organizations they established – founded agricultural settlements, launched housing projects, set up employment bureaus, offered medical aid and dispensed loans. They fulfilled most of their members' daily needs. Schools, too, were divided along party lines. Even sports was a party affair. Immigration permits were distributed by the Jewish Agency according to party. Ben-Gurion was once asked why he joined the Zionist Executive, which included representatives of the "bourgeoisie." He replied that by doing so, he was able to prevent the immigration of 10,000 members of Betar, the youth movement of his rivals, the Revisionist Zionists. In other words, the strength of a political party determined the number of its followers it could bring over from Europe.

This state of affairs goes a long way toward explaining the difference between Israel's political parties and those of the West. This is the background for the polarization and brutal struggle waged by the parties against one another. The ruinous schism that besets Israel today is rooted in the country's peculiar party structure. The Israeli socialist slogan "Hegemony of Labor," voiced to this day in Histadrut circles, was born in the hearts of the early socialist pioneers and soon adopted by the burgeoning Histadrut apparatus.

By the time the State of Israel was established, in 1948, Histadrut-style socialism dominated economic life and the Laborites held sway in politics. The combination insured that socialist principles would govern public affairs in the new Jewish state.

Railway ownership passed from the Mandatory authorities to the Israeli government. Urban and interurban bus transportation was taken over by monopolistic Histadrut cooperatives. A policy of restricting use and ownership of private cars was introduced. Much of the trucking industry belonged to Histadrut cooperatives; a government trucking company was established later. Air transport was entrusted to a governmental monopoly, El-Al; the merchant marine was handed to Zim, jointly owned by the government and the Jewish Agency. Postal services, including telegraph and phones, remained in government hands, as under the Mandate.

The Israel Land Authority was set up and granted ownership of all lands not privately owned – 93 percent of all land in Israel. Control, planning, and supply of water was entrusted by law to the Ministry of Agriculture. Agriculture itself was handed to a government-Histadrut-Jewish Agency troika. It set up agricultural settlements and decided how much land and water each would receive. Consequently, only socialist-oriented cooperative settlements – kibbutzim and moshavim – were established, until 1980. Production quotas were determined by the government. Naturally, the government also decided whom to subsidize and to what extent. Monopolistic production boards were put in charge of the marketing of agricultural produce. Farmers were forced to buy their supplies through purchase and credit organizations, which were controlled by political parties.

The Ministry of Housing and Construction was empowered to house everyone in apartments, apart from the wealthy, who built on private land in the major cities. The ministry determined who would receive an apartment, where, and at what cost. In the "development" towns its control was absolute.

The Israel Broadcasting Authority was granted monopoly status in the mass media – first radio, later television too (TV was introduced in 1967). The Authority's board of directors was composed by party representatives in accordance with the number of seats each party held in the Knesset. Owners of radio and television sets have to pay a "license fee" of about $100 yearly.

Some 200 government corporations were formed, each controlled by the appropriate ministry. Half of them are full-fledged economic enterprises. They extract mineral resources (including those of the Dead Sea), refine oil, and generate electricity. The government also owns construction companies and various factories. Many enjoy monopoly status. The Israel Aircraft Industries, the country's largest industrial enterprise, comes under this rubric. The armament industry is also government-owned.

The Histadrut's clammy grip was felt even in health care. Almost all Israelis have health insurance, and 75 percent of them obtain it through the Histadrut sick fund. No one can be insured by this fund without paying Histadrut membership dues. Two thirds of the dues support the sick fund; the rest sustains the Histadrut apparatus. New immigrants are covered free for six months, and many thereby become Histadrut members. Many public-sector employers compel employees to choose the Histadrut's sick fund over its rivals. Licenses for new sick funds are not granted.

A major proportion of the country's industrial enterprises are still owned either by the government or by the Histadrut. The establishment of private enterprises is de facto limited to entrepreneurs whose ventures qualify as "Approved Enterprises." In that case, most of the capital they need is bestowed upon them by the state, followed by tax exemptions and other benefits. With an intricate web of price and wage control, import and export licenses, individually tailored subsidies and so on, no industrial plant of consequence is viable without government aid. Many of these "approved" industries are also sheltered from competing imports; others are appointed as sole importers of what they manufacture. Some enjoy monopoly status. Directly or indirectly, the government is the exclusive importer of basic commodities such as meat, sugar, fuel, grain, edible oils, and more. Import of many other commodities requires a licence.

Energy is government controlled. The Israel Electric Company, privately owned during the Mandate period, is now a monopolistic government corporation. Until very recently, the fuel market was divided among three companies that formed a cartel. Most of their shares belong to the government and the Histadrut. Each company was accorded a fixed percentage of the market. These companies are also the sole importers of oil, operating under "cost-plus" arrangements with the government, which owns the refineries.

Possession of foreign currency is prohibited by law. Banks have virtually no freedom of action. Loans, savings plans, and similar banking activities must be government approved. Banks, insurance companies, and pension funds are required to keep most of their assets in government bonds.

Taxation was high to begin with and has increased with time. Income tax is characterized by exceedingly high rates on relatively low incomes. A complex set of exemptions and credits serves as a tool for overt government subsidy.

The government has taken control of the hotel industry. One needs a permit to build a hotel. All large hotels are "Approved Enterprises" that get practically all their financing from the Treasury. Prices are controlled. There are three public education systems. The Ministry of Education determines all elementary schools' curricula and publishes most textbooks. The Ministry also supports theaters, museums, and assorted cultural and sports activities.

Immigration was traditionally handled by the Absorption Department of the Jewish Agency. Then the government established an institution of its own: the Ministry of Absorption. The two are absorbed in spending lots of money and energy on constant feuding. That comes at the expense of the immigrants, who are utterly dependent on petty officials and often find themselves in a bureaucratic maze. Every immigrant is entitled to housing, but its location, size, and other attributes are determined by absorption officials.

A far-reaching network of monopolies and cartels has gradually developed, ranging from oil refining and cement production to the marketing of citrus fruit. The web also embraces insurance premiums and prices of medicines. By requiring businesses to obtain import licenses, abide by production quotas, and conform to other sundry constraints, the government can turn the manufacture or import of any item into a monopoly.

The number of permits required by Israeli citizens for mundane pursuits is surely a record high in the democratic world. To open a business in Tel Aviv, for example, one needs eleven permits (and it takes many months to obtain them). Often several permits are required for the very same purpose.

In every area of Israeli society, in every aspect of daily life, governmental interference has straitjacketed the Jewish state, forcing it to succumb to the application of the most rigid socialist ideology in the Western world.

CHAPTER TWO

THE POLITICAL ESTABLISHMENT

In the first Israeli national elections in 1949, a special assembly was elected to write the country's constitution and prepare elections for the Knesset, Israel's parliament. Instead of doing so, the assembly appointed itself as the first Knesset. Because Israel has no constitution, the Knesset's power is absolute. It can enact anything a majority of its members fancy at a given moment, unhindered by checks or balances. It can pass retroactive laws, and has done so more than once in order to nullify High Court rulings. Furthermore, there is no separation between the legislative and executive branches of government. All these vast powers of state are concentrated in the hands of the Knesset and the cabinet – which is composed of Knesset members.

One of the first acts of the Knesset was to enact the Law on the Privileges, Obligations and Immunity of Knesset Members. It abounds with regulations governing immunity and privileges, but says almost nothing about obligations.[1] It does forbid an MK to draw a salary from any source other than the Knesset, but allows him to receive other kinds of income such as personal expense accounts, use of automobiles, and more. The law therefore does not prevent MKs from exploiting their status to further their financial interests. In many cases, election to the Knesset becomes a lucrative sinecure.

Israel's parliamentarians enjoy the broadest immunity in the democratic world.[2] The law stipulates that "An MK shall not be responsible, criminally or civilly, for any action taken in the fulfillment of his duty or for the purpose of fulfilling his duty." That covers just about everything an MK might do on the job. Criminal immunity is likewise absolute, even when the offense has no bearing whatsoever on the MK's work. This immunity may be revoked only by a resolution of the Knesset plenum. Not that MKs have never been accused of criminal acts. The first to be indicted for bribery was Yitzhak Rafael. He was followed by MKs Rechtman, Abuhatzeira, Flatto-Sharon, and others. In such cases, the Government's legal adviser may lodge a motion for the revocation of immunity.* The Knesset usually tries to obstruct these requests. The most flagrant episode occurred in 1985, when MK Shlomo Amar was accused of wiretapping and the Knesset Committee rejected the request to lift his immunity. The government's legal adviser revealed that a number of MKs pressed him to rescind his motion, even hinting that his perseverance might hurt his career.[3]

Many jurists naturally perceive the Immunity Law as an expression of the schism between the people and their elected representatives, and as part of the corruption that envelops the political establishment. Even the government's own legal adviser has warned that "The present system regarding MKs creates an unprecedented state of inequality before the law. Equality before the law is not only a principle of law; it is the very soul of the legal system. In Israel, the law applies to all except to the lawgivers themselves."[4] The High Court itself has described the Immunity Law as going "beyond what is necessary, justified, and acceptable in most countries governed by parliamentary rule."[5]

In early 1982, the Knesset voted to uphold the immunity of six members who had committed traffic violations. A public

---

* In addition to the Attorney General and the Minister of Justice, the government has its own legal adviser. He decides in what cases legal action should be taken against MKs, civil servants, and lawyers.

outcry forced reconsideration of the case, culminating in a Knesset decision that immunity would not apply to traffic violations – unless the offender asked the Knesset Speaker to extend it to him! Dr. Ze'ev Segal, a jurist, denounced this 'revision' of the Immunity Law as "no more than a parliamentary trick by which the Knesset pretended that it has responded to the public's wishes."[6]

Back in 1971, the Speaker of the Knesset commissioned Prof. Claude Klein to prepare a comparative study of immunity laws in democratic countries. In due course the professor presented him with his report, which showed that Israel's immunity law is unparalleled in its largesse. The Speaker locked all 120 copies of the report in a safe. A year and a half passed before Klein was allowed to reveal his findings to his students.[7]

The Immunity Law mirrors the status of the political establishment. Since the prerequisites of government and parliament are more sweeping in Israel than in any other democracy, it is only natural that MKs grant themselves the same. Traffic violations involving ministerial limousines are typical. Not long ago, the Minister of Police was caught speeding at 87 mph (in a 55 mph-zone). Identifying the passenger, the policeman apologized and let the chauffeur off with a warning. Any ordinary citizen would surely have been slapped with a heavy fine and several months' suspension of his driver's license.[8] When queried about the incident by a reporter, the minister expressed surprise that the media should be interested in such a 'trivial matter'.

Although themselves immune to prosecution, the politicians do not hesitate to interfere in the legal system and manipulate how it treats average citizens. The Office of the State Prosecutor, the Attorney-General and the granting of clemency are three favorite targets of the political establishment. It is the Attorney-General who determines whether or not to present indictments on a long list of offenses against lawyers, elected officials, and national or municipal bureaucrats. This gives him a great deal of power.[9] A large proportion of the important criminal cases, and most of those that turn into stormy public issues, funnel into the Attorney-General's bureau. Inevitably he comes under heavy pressure from cabinet ministers and Knesset members. Cases are sometimes held up with the Attorney-General for months or even years.

Between 1981 and 1985, the Attorney-General was presented with 15,000 applications for stays of proceedings – and acceded to no less than 30 percent of them. "...The order for stay of proceedings is substantially flawed, because it gives appointed officials the power to call off, by their own discretion, a criminal proceeding in an ongoing trial under Court authority," notes MK Uriel Lynn. "The Attorney-General is entitled to invoke this power any time after the indictment is presented and before the verdict is handed down."[10] After one of its senior executives committed suicide, Bank Hapoalim became the target of an investigation concerning alleged foreign currency offenses. The Histadrut's holding company, the "parent" of Bank Hapoalim applied directly to the Attorney-General, circumventing the police. By pigeonholing the file for more than two years, the Attorney-General effectively shelved the investigation.[11]

The Attorney-General has repeatedly closed cases against mayors and other establishment figures.[12] Members of Knesset eager to peddle influence were involved in all these cases, of course. Some of them were lawyers, acting in their clients' interests, according to former Jerusalem District Prosecutor Michael Kirsch.[13]

The State Prosecutor works in much the same way, and is therefore known as a "preliminary judge." In a number of cases, the prosecutor declined to prosecute public figures despite the recommendation of the police.[14] The Prosecutor routinely argues that "lack of public interest" justifies a decision not to prosecute. But if an offense was committed, why should there not be a trial? Who has the right to determine whether the public has or lacks an interest in this question?

The third area in which the political establishment meddles in law and law enforcement is that of clemencies. Clemency is the prerogative of the President of Israel, according to the recommendation of the Minister of Justice, and clemency orders must be signed by both officials. Clemencies are so commonplace that the process has been called a "clemency mill"; about 25 percent of all requests (presented by the convict him/herself or by relatives, acquaintances, or others) are fully or partly approved.[15] In many cases, prison sentences are exchanged for probation – after the courts had explained in their verdicts why a prison sentence was warranted. In some cases clemency is awarded on grounds that were previously rejected by the court. Between 1981 and 1985 the President pardoned 456 drivers whose licenses had been revoked, including one who had been tried and convicted for 26 traffic offenses.[16]

Not long ago, a Jerusalem merchant was sentenced to a fine and three months in jail for a serious income tax violation. The prosecution appealed, and the Supreme Court increased the punishment to six months, despite the defendant's claims of poor health. Twenty-four days later, under pressure of various higher-ups, the President and the Justice Minister reduced his prison term back down to three months because of his health. The President of the Supreme Court wrote:

> Everything that has happened since the Court issued its ruling in this matter shows that the Court's judgment has been replaced by that of the persons who handle clemency applications The courts have been dealt an unjustified and grave affront... Thus practiced, jurisprudence becomes pointless and even ridiculous...[17]

Although this case made headlines, neither the President's Bureau nor the Justice Ministry regularly report on clemencies, thereby keeping such matters out of public view[18] and reducing the possibility of public protest.

Persons convicted of "white-collar" crimes are much more likely to be pardoned than ordinary prisoners. Justice Ministers have said that Knesset members apply heavy pressure on them to pardon such people.[19] "Rank-and-file people have virtually no prospect of gaining clemency," says jurist Haim Misgav. "But convicts who find their way, any way, to the Ministry or the Minister of Justice find that their chances improve beyond measure." According to MK Amnon Rubinstein, clemency is "used as an instrument to serve the cronies of persons in power..."[20]

In keeping with long-standing tradition, Israel's cabinet ministers do not assume responsibility for their errors. The concept of "ministerial responsibility" does not exist. No minister would think of resigning for mistakes committed by the bureaucracy under his charge. In rare instances, government does appoint investigatory committees. But their recommendations concerning ministers' responsibility are generally ignored; at times, they are instructed in advance to disregard the ministerial level altogether. In the aftermath of the Pollard affair (when Israeli officials recruited an American Jew to obtain classified U.S. military data), the Knesset formed a committee to examine the responsibility of the four senior ministers involved – Shimon Peres and Yitzhak Rabin (Labor), and Yitzhak Shamir and Moshe Arens (Likud). The committee, which was composed of Labor and Likud MKs in equal numbers, and chaired by Labor's Abba Eban, found all four ministers responsible. Peres was blamed more than the others, because he was prime minister at the time. The government took no action on the report. Labor Party leaders viewed the matter with utmost gravity. Abba Eban came under severe criticism, and was treated, as reporters put it, "as a union would treat a member who disclosed union corruption."[21] Peres pointed an accusing finger at Eban: "You sit in the [Knesset] Foreign Affairs Committee not as a judge, but as a Labor Party representative."[22]

Knesset members come from a wide range of professional backgrounds. The Knesset is full of lawyers, economic consultants, company owners, directors, and mayors. Nothing prevents their retaining their jobs while serving in the Knesset. Lawyers and economic consultants benefit most. Their clientele swells quickly after they are elected. They meet clients in the Knesset cafeteria and represent them in hearings with government offices and (according to some reports) the all-powerful Knesset Finance Committee itself. Corporate officials in particular are willing to spend lavishly in order to be represented by lawyers who are MKs. Some MKs resent this practice, privately asserting that such things are unheard of in other Western parliaments.[23] "You see your colleague fighting in the Finance Committee for this cause or that, and suddenly you realize that he's being paid for it," one MK told reporters. "MKs obtain vast economic advantages for those who enlist their service," a second remarked about his colleagues. "It's a moral scandal sanctioned by the norms of the Knesset."[24] The scope of MKs' business activities "has reached scandalous dimensions," an editorial in the daily *Ha'aretz* noted in 1983. "If MKs wonder why their public image is not the finest, one of the reasons is that quite a few of them appear to 'be hacks,' who are being paid to intercede with the authorities...the situation is not improving but deteriorating."[25] MKs seem to have another way of exploiting their status. Minister Gideon Patt once said that "Every other MK is an importer of soft drinks."[26] What he meant was that MKs find it much easier to obtain import licenses than other citizens. If they do so in partnership with a businessman, they can line their pockets with very little effort.

The roster of MKs includes directors of large enterprises that are directly affected by Knesset resolutions. Since they are not allowed to receive salaries, their companies or employers provide them with...limousines (often with chauffeurs), unlimited expense accounts, overseas travel, and more.[27] In turn, the corporate officials-turned-MKs strive to further their companies' interests in the Knesset. "Decisions taken by officials and ministers transfer vast sums from the public coffers to private pockets," writes Shimshon Erlich in *Ha'aretz*. "Such decisions are influenced by the elected representatives of the people. Seven-digit expenditures in development loans, grants, "encouragement of capital investment," export subsidies; millions as "deferments" of tax and social security payments; postponement of court proceedings; construction permits, insurance company licenses, low-interest loans and similar decisions, are worth vast sums to the clients and cost the public a fortune. Putting a stop to MKs' intervention on their clients' behalf would prevent the flow of these Government funds into private bank accounts....[28] Influencing government decisions through payments to elected representatives would be a grave offense in any country. In Israel, where the government has a virtual hold on the economy, it is catastrophic.

Ministers, Knesset Members and government bureaucrats alike covet trips abroad, especially at public expense. Obviously some Israeli officials must go abroad on occasion to meet with other countries' ministers and officials, to appear at international conventions, and so forth. There remains, however, the question of good taste and proportion. It is no secret that many government delegations ostensibly undertaking "fact-finding tours," or trips meant to "explain Israel's views," actually spend much of their time catching up on their shopping and attending to personal affairs. Having made such a mess out of Israel, members of the politico-bureaucratic elite naturally seek to vacation elsewhere, preferably in the greener pastures of Western Europe and the United States. So eager are they to flee that MK Sarah Doron has suggested that the most effective punishment for MKs who do not show up for Knesset meetings would be to bar them from going abroad in parliamentary delegations.[29] In 1981-82, according to official statistics, Israeli cabinet ministers spent 11.5% of their time abroad. Each minister departed, on the average, once every 73 days on a trip lasting 8.4 days.[30] Since the government has between 20 and 25 ministers, and because each minister often travels with an entourage of high officials, these journeys cost the Israeli taxpayer quite a pretty penny: in 1975 alone the government spent $14 million on VIPs' overseas junkets. There is a ministerial committee which decides on officials' travel. On one occasion, the committee decided that three VIPs were to attend a UN trade and development convention in Nairobi, and another four officials a housing convention in Canada. In the end, 10 went to Nairobi and 14 to Canada.[31] With regard to overseas travel, as in other domains, the political establishment seems to feel that what applies to ordinary mortals need not apply to them. Israeli governments have spent years trying to limit citizens' travel abroad, even imposing a travel tax of $150-$200 per person. While ordinary Israelis are compelled to endure such taxation in the name of patriotic "belt-tightening," VIPs are busily tightening their own belts – the seatbelts in their first-class airplane compartments.

The life of an MK, then, is one of endless privileges, unprecedented power, and very few obligations. Under these circumstances, it is no wonder that some of them find it hard to distinguish between right and wrong. MK Aharon Abuhatzeira was sentenced to three months in prison for corruption, but never saw the inside of a jail cell. Instead, all he had to do was check in twice daily at a Jerusalem police station. He promptly moved into a hotel in the capital and charged the expense to the Knesset. When publicity about Abuhatzeira's billing habits caused a stir, his party undertook to foot the costs. Evidently, it never occurred to anyone that Abuhatzeira ought to pay his own hotel bill!

Equally characteristic of the establishment's disregard for the public's feelings are the sumptuous weddings of affluent Israelis, always attended by the same prominent politicians who lecture ordinary Israelis on the need to "tighten their belts." Neither do some consider it in bad taste to throw conspicuous parties of their own. In the midst of the Lebanese war, one cabinet minister hosted 2,000 people at his daughter's wedding at the

King David hotel in Jerusalem.[32] At about the same time, another MK threw a giant wedding celebration for his daughter at the Tel Aviv Hilton; the MKs, ministers and thousands of other invitees merrily consumed 20,000 bottles of wine. The surrounding streets were closed to traffic from 6:00 that morning.[33]

Wages in Israel are determined by painful, protracted negotiations between the Treasury and the unions. One major problem in these talks is the inevitable demand for "linkage" between various occupational groups. When one sector succeeds in obtaining a raise, all others clamor for the same. One group of Israelis, however, is exempt from all this: MKs and other lucky members of the political elite, including the President, cabinet ministers, deputy-ministers and judges. The Knesset adjusts their salaries periodically, using the average salary as a guideline. In other words, if one pressure group succeeds in getting a raise -- for whatever reason – the salaries of the ruling class jump automatically.[34] Back in 1965, the salary of an MK was about twice that of the average salary; by 1982, it was almost four times as high. In real terms, the average salary rose by about 55% during this period, while that of MKs surged by 165%.[35] In addition to salary, MKs are paid for car upkeep, lodging in Jerusalem, entertainment expenses, newspapers, and more. Cabinet ministers enjoy other amenities: rental of housing in Jerusalem, partial clothing expenses for themselves and their spouses, higher entertainment expenses, and a chauffeured limousine, to name a few.

Telephones in Israel have always been scarce and expensive. Waiting lists are long, and installation fees high. That is, for the rank-and-file. The political establishment has no such problems. Each MK can make 25,000 phone calls per year at no charge -- not only while serving in the Knesset, but for life! Other VIPs get partial benefits, according to this incomprehensible scale:

Beneficiaries	Type of Exemption or Reduction
Knesset Members, past and present	25,000 free calls annually; free telephone installation
Judges, Chief Rabbis, State Comptroller, President of the Bank of Israel, his deputy, religious court judges, retirees who filled these posts in the past, widows of ministers and Supreme Court Justices	1,000 free calls monthly; free telephone installation
Widows of judges in civil and religious courts	500 free calls monthly; and 50% of installation fees
Former Presidents, widows of former presidents	All telephone services free

These reductions and exemptions cost the exchequer an estimated $250,000 per year.[36] No former MK has ever forfeited these benefits, including two MKs-turned-newspaper editors who lead the outcry against corruption. Thus the Israeli system: A given commodity is expensive or scarce, or made to be so. Citizenry is divided into categories, some of whom enjoy exemptions and reductions to various degrees. As expected, the list is always headed by the top echelons of the political establishment and the bureaucracy.

As scandalous as these telephone arrangements may be, the health care benefits are worse. Knesset Members, secular and religious court judges, as well as their families, have to be insured through one of the Sick Funds, but are also entitled, at public expense, to every kind of treatment, in Israel or abroad, not provided by the Sick Funds. This group consists of some 3,000 people, including all the "ex"s, however briefly they held office.

A second class is even more privileged. They don't even have to pay Sick Funds' insurance premiums. They receive free medical care, abroad if necessary, at State expense. About one thousand enjoy this status, including deputy ministers, Chief Rabbis, Supreme Court Justices, members of the High Rabbinic Court, the State Comptroller, the President of the Bank of Israel and his deputy, ministry directors-general, and a long list of treasury officials. Since these benefits are for life (for both recipients and their survivors), the number of beneficiaries increases yearly as the bureaucracy swells and office-holders switch positions rapidly. The sums required also grow steadily. One cabinet minister requested hospitalization abroad at a cost of $70,000. An MK demanded $50,000 for treatment, much of it cosmetic. A high ranking official asked for thousands of dollars to have his daughter fitted with an IUD abroad.[37] A Supreme Court justice, asked about waiting in line in a Sick Fund clinic, answered "It is not appropriate for me." That may be so. But why is it appropriate for the elderly, for busy mothers, for laborers wasting valuable working time, or, indeed, for any citizen?

Israel's civil service pension laws are equal for one and all: benefits accrue by 2 percent yearly up to a maximum of 70 percent of the last pre-retirement base wage. Pension payments begin at age 65 for men and 60 for women. An MK who served a single 4-year term is entitled to a pension of 20 percent, or 5 percent yearly, even if the Knesset is dissolved before the end of its term – meaning that MKs need only a quarter of the time required of other citizens to become eligible for full pension. And the MK's pension is payable from age 40, rather than 60 or 65. For ordinary retirees wage components such as automobile or travel expenses and clothing allocations are not included in pension calculations. Pensions of MKs and their similarly privileged colleagues, however, are computed on the basis of the entire salary. That's not all. When an ordinary retiree dies, the surviving spouse receives just 60 percent of the pension. But the surviving spouse of an MK receives 100 percent. According to one estimate, the ratio between pension rights of the general public to those of the privileged is one to twenty-four.[38] The 1984 pension bill for 209 Knesset veterans and surviving spouses was nearly $5,000,000. A retiring president enjoys the additional privilege of a new apartment at public expense, if he does not already own one. Outgoing presidents sometimes engage in a flurry of pre-retirement transactions in order to exploit their economic privileges. Some have sold their old apartments in order to qualify for new ones; one purchased a luxury automobile tax-free just before the end of his term.[39] Nothing attests more succinctly to the alienation of the privileged from the people than President Chaim Herzog's appeal to the Knesset Finance Committee "to approve the following positions on the basis of special contracts: an assistant, an adviser, a spokesman, a secretary and a chauffeur – for the President, for past presidents, and for the widows of past presidents."[40]

Certainly MKs and top administrators deserve salaries commensurate with their posts. Maybe they really should be paid much more than the rank-and-file. But these salaries have to be above-board, based on universally applicable principles. The fact that a small group of individuals have voted themselves special benefits, exempted themselves from the limitations they apply to their constituents – and done so on the sly – suggests a grossly insensitive attitude. Exploitation of status for the enhancement of personal bank accounts, special salary and pension arrangements, unnecessary junkets abroad, absolute civil and criminal immunity, paucity of obligations, wanton violation of traffic laws, and luxurious lifestyles – all of these express the alienation and insensitivity of a satiated and corrupt establishment that considers itself not the people's servant but a "higher class," in the words of one MK, or an echelon "touched by greatness" according to another.[41]

Members of most Israeli political parties, especially the large ones, pay no membership dues, except perhaps a nominal sum on the eve of party elections. Instead, the party holds a "census." Members sign a form entailing no practical obligations. When three splinter parties united to form a faction called La'Am, each faction produced its list of "members," many of whom appeared on all three lists or at least on two of them.

The numerical ratio between party members and party voters is 1:10 to 1:20 in most democratic countries. Not so in Israel. One example is the "census" held by the Labor Party before its April, 1986, convention. In the little town of Or Akiva, 812 persons signed Labor's "census" forms, while only 677 persons had voted Labor in national elections a year and a half previously.[42] One suspects that those who signed the census forms were motivated by something other than allegiance to party principles. For example, when an election or a "census" is held in a workplace during work hours, turnout is usually high because of pressure by the powerful labor committees.

Intraparty elections resemble those adopted by the Histadrut in the 1920s. In his memoirs, Asher Yadlin described how Mapai convention delegates were elected in 1965.[43] He was chosen to represent one of the party's Tel Aviv wards. The ward secretary predicted that he would come in third in a field of twelve. That's exactly what happened. "Just how does this machine operate?," Yadlin wrote. "Its aim is that 90 percent of the delegates be determined in advance; otherwise the world would cave in..." It is not always necessary to use blatantly fraudulent methods; it can be done in a more sophisticated way. In a given ward 3,000 names are listed, of which all but 800-900 are fictitious. Some 700 members come or are brought to the ballot. Most of them have never even heard of the candidates, because the number of members who show up for local party meetings is seldom greater than fifty. Each voter is handed a list of "recommended" names, which he obediently casts into the ballot-box. "In the 1973 Labor party census," Yadlin recalled, "300,000 members were registered, most long departed from this world. Did the party really have 300,000 members? Far from it! There were barely 100,000 card-carrying members, none of whom paid any membership dues. So why all that fuss? [Labor party leader Pinhas] Sapir wanted 300,000 – and everyone started collecting names."[44]

According to regulations, elections for party conventions must be held approximately every two or three years. In practice, however, up to 15 years may elapse between conventions. In other cases, party leaders agree beforehand on the composition of the convention, thus avoiding elections. When elections are actually held, only a small number of party "members" participate – and they usually vote as instructed.[45] In addition to the delegates thus elected, a large number of functionaries become delegates automatically by virtue of the positions they hold in the party. When party leaders clash, these "entrenched" delegates can turn things upside down. A confrontation in the Labor Central Committee between Yitzhak Rabin and Shimon Peres is a case in point. When polled, about two-thirds of Labor voters sided with Rabin. In the Central Committee, the party apparatus ruled in favor of Peres.[46] Party elections are typically accompanied by allegations of forged results, members' being denied their right to vote or deprived of their membership cards, attempts to bring newly-registered members to the polls, and so on.[47]

The convention "elects" a council that is about one third its size. The leaders agree among themselves as to the council's composition, and the convention ratifies their decision by acclamation.[48] Predictably, the council consists largely of party functionaries. Using similar methods, the council then elects a Central or Executive Committee, which convenes more frequently. This committee elects a secretariat, which actually runs the party. This system usually insures all but minor changes in the composition of the leadership, since the makeup of all these party institutions – Council, Executive Committee, Central

Committee, Secretariat – is prearranged by the leaders, who decide how many of their respective supporters will serve on each. In a devastating critique of the system, entitled "Neither Equality nor Democratization – Party Institutions Composed of People Who Elect Themselves," Prof. (and later Labor MK) Shevah Weiss described how Labor's council was put together: "The delegates to the conventions, the members of the councils, the central committees, the secretariats, the directorates, the committees and the bureaus, are all highly dependent on the party. These bodies decide which party representatives will serve as ministers, MKs, mayors, and so forth. Since the electoral bodies of most parties are made up of people who depend on the party, they naturally elect those favored by the machine."[49] The final selection of the party's slate of Knesset candidates is the climax of all the complex activities described above. Until a few years ago, this was done by "Nominating Committees" which confirmed a list agreed upon by the party leaders. Mounting public criticism eventually forced the adoption of cosmetic changes in the system. Some parties' Nominating Committees are no longer appointed from on high but are elected by the Council; other councils vote directly or indirectly for one or more slates presented to the members of the Council or the Central Committee, which are composed mainly of party functionaries with vested interests, each of whom supports a certain leader and expects to be rewarded for doing so. Consequently the process of selecting the leaders remains completely divorced from the wishes and preferences of the party's rank-and-file, for the members of the electoral bodies are still not directly elected.[50] Even if the new methods seem more democratic, practically all previous MKs appear on the new slates. In democratic countries, a party attempting a comeback will usually present the voters with a new leadership. By contrast, Labor's slate for the 11th Knesset was virtually identical to the one that was hounded out of office seven years earlier. This can happen only in a country where there are no primaries, and where party candidates need only curry favor with the apparatchiks. This perversion of democratic procedure prevents the ascent of new echelons of leaders, independent of the old establishment. Prof. Asher Arianne, lecturing on the matter at Tel Aviv University, said that "Israeli democracy has produced oligarchies led by stable elitist cliques."[51] Former Minister of Justice Shmuel Tamir argued, "In the absence of a law governing the functioning of the parties, we are not a real democracy."[52]

A newspaperman once accused a certain cabinet minister of rewarding members of his party's Central Committee with sinecures. The minister's response: "Your article did wonders for me. Never have I been so popular with the Central Committee." One minister has defined "a member of the Central Committee" as "a shareholder – he tries to draw the greatest possible dividend." Another senior minister was reported to have remarked, "It's inefficient to have Knesset candidates selected by the Central Committee. It only leads to corruption. Material benefits such as import licenses, building permits and cheap loans are requested and granted. Consequently, the selection of MKs must be taken out of the hands of the Council and put in the hands" – not of the people, but – "of a nominating committee."[53] Apparently he could think of no other way of securing the selection of those deemed worthy. The idea of holding primaries of some kind, in which the voters would have a say, never crossed his mind.

The role and performance of Israel's political parties has not changed substantially since the 1920s. Rural settlement, employment, housing, industrial plants, loans, vital permits, synagogues, sports and many other objects of crucial importance are attained to some degree through the parties. Needless to say, party loyalty brings great material advantages in train. Hence the parties' unique place in Israeli society.

In theory, the right and left wings of the Zionist movement differed profoundly as to the social structure on which the future Jewish state should be based. The Left saw the state's future through essentially Marxist lenses, in contradistinction to the classical Liberal views of Jabotinsky and his followers on the Right. The ideological differences separating the two camps was honed by rivalry over distribution of pre-State immigration permits and financial support from the world Zionist movement. Nothing testifies more succinctly to this unbridgeable chasm than the fact that even under Nazi occupation, rightwing Zionists and leftwing Zionists in the Jewish underground movements in Warsaw and other ghettoes refused to unite.[54] Even in the aftermath of the Holocaust, the bitter rivalries persisted. In his War Diary, Ben-Gurion describes a conversation in September, 1948, with Israeli Communist leader Shmuel Mikunis, who was negotiating with Poland for the emigration of Jews from that country. Mikunis informed him that the socialist (Mapam) party was demanding that its members be given preference over other Jews.[55]

A distinction must be made between the Labor Party (initially known as Ahdut Ha-avoda, later Mapai, and currently the Labor Alignment) and the other parties, because it was Labor that, in the 1920s, established the norm of extended party activity. By implementing the Histadrut's unique political formulae, it aimed to become the country's eternal ruling party. Only Labor had the tools to do so. Until 1977 it controlled almost all of Israel's agricultural settlements, industrial enterprises, energy resources, construction firms, transport companies, banks, consumer and producer cooperatives, and the Histadrut Sick Fund, which serves close to three quarters of the population. It controlled the bureaucracies of national and municipal government, the Jewish Agency, the Histadrut and, of course, its own complex apparatus. In short, Labor was able to improve the economic lot of whomever it chose to favor.

Labor thereby gained control over most new immigrants during the mass immigration years, as newcomers were trapped under the heel of Labor's governmental bureaucracy. Jobs were apportioned by means of notes passed between bureaucrats or politicians. The same method was used to procure permits for imports, construction, land acquisition, and more. Consequently, the labor force in privileged workplaces such as the Haifa Port Authority, El-Al, the Electric Company and others was composed almost exclusively of Labor appointees. A term was coined for the procedure: "protektzia," or pull. Behind that innocent sobriquet lies a pattern of cruel discrimination that has conferred affluence on party stooges and denied it forever to others. It would take pages to list the myriad ways in which not only lower social strata but society's higher echelons as well – teachers, entertainers, artists, writers, journalists – were brought under Labor control. Labor took care of the rich, too. The right to establish an "approved enterprise" or a monopoly had the practical effect of bestowing riches upon the owner at the state's expense. Prof. Joseph Ben-David refers to Israel's regime in the 1950s as "enlightened Bolshevism"[56]; "The difference between the accepted norms of a Bolshevik regime and those prevalent here is small," writes Yoel Marcus of *Ha'aretz*.[57]

In the United States, ranking officials are replaced whenever a new administration takes over. Since the ruling party bears the responsibility of government, it has to install its own people in key positions. The British eschew this tactic in favor of a permanent, apolitical Civil Service comprised of experts in the various fields of government.

At first glance, Israel would seem to have adopted the British model. A new minister is theoretically allowed to replace the ministry's director-general, his own secretary and driver, and no one else. In fact, however, ministers fill every opening in their ministries, down to the lowest echelons, with their own people. Then they create new jobs, appointing assistants and advisers whose job it is to neutralize department managers and make life difficult for veteran officials.

Thus the government bureaucracy grows constantly despite periodic solemn promises to freeze hiring. Yoel Marcus has compared the governmental structure to "geological strata, as each regime plants its own people, and each new minister adds a layer."[58]

Since the rightwing Likud bloc owns no economic enterprises and few agricultural settlements, it compensates its faithful by handing out government appointments. This is hardly an innovation. When Labor was in power, especially during Israel's first two decades, nobody dreamed of landing a government job without party connections. "The entrance ticket to public service was a red booklet (Histadrut membership card)," Yoel Marcus notes.[59]

In a centralized economy, political appointments to vital positions provide parties with significant advantages. Applications for Social Security benefits can be processed without investigation. The Land Authority can hand out land arbitrarily at the locations, and at the prices it chooses. The Water Commission can control the distribution of a scarce, vital commodity. The Ministry of Tourism can grade hotels, decide on the extent of the financial assistance given to each, and set their prices. The Ministries of Industry and Trade, Transportation, Health, and Education – to name but a few – can do likewise.

Political appointments became a serious point of contention between Likud and Labor when they entered into coalition following the electoral deadlock of 1984. Squabbles over appointments, especially of directors of government corporations, repeatedly threatened to tear the coalition asunder. According to regulations, directorships are unpaid positions; incumbents merely receive "compensation" (a respectable sum in itself) for participating in directorate meetings. In fact, at least ten board chairmen receive salaries, use of a car, or both.[60] Of the 27 new directors appointed by Ariel Sharon during his tenure as Minister of Industry and Trade, 23 are active Likud members.[61] Minister of Energy Moshe Shahal (Labor) made a series of appointments to government economic corporations; most belonged to his party and lived in his home town, Haifa.[62] Shahal went so far as to propose to "pack" the government corporations' boards.[63] In short, each party tries to lay hands on state-owned economic enterprises for its own benefit. For some year, this was done discreetly, out of the public eye. During the term of the Labor-Likud National Unity Government, however, numerous scandals surfaced. Nevertheless, even extensive publicity about scandalous behavior has not deterred the politicians from doing as they please. It would seem that the party's well-being takes preference over the country's, since the great majority of appointees chosen to administer the 100 government-owned business enterprises were selected for reasons other than their qualifications.

Each party has at least one rural settlement movement, which administers its communal or cooperative farm villages. This is of great value to the party. The Independent Liberals, for example, have lost their appeal to the voter, failing to send a single deputy to the Knesset in 1981; yet by virtue of their agricultural settlements – a handful of kibbutzim and moshavim – they are able to staff an office in Tel Aviv, which functions as the party's center and keeps it alive. How so? Rural settlement budgets provided by the government and the Jewish Agency are dispensed through the settlement movement centers, which first deduct all sums needed for their own survival. This applies to sports budgets as well. Many of the country's national sports organizations are party-controlled. So are schools and teachers colleges. Several parties are allowed to own banks (Labor's Hapoalim, the NRP's United Mizrahi). Parties have their own youth movements and cultural institutions, which are partially financed by the Ministry of Education and the Jewish Agency. Housing projects are sometimes organized through parties, which obtain government subsidies and easy credit terms. This is only a partial list. It does not include, for instance, the Labor-controlled Histadrut economic empire. Naturally, the Jewish Agency's Board of Governors is appointed by "party key", that is, by each party's relative strength in the Knesset. Even the universities'

Student Unions are composed of groups affiliated with and supported by national political parties.

The parties own real estate and miscellaneous chattels. The public is only dimly aware of this fact, since the parties register property under names of affiliated individuals or related bodies. In the heat of a 1980 debate in the Tel Aviv Municipal Council, it was revealed that Labor owned 40 buildings, 16 lots, and 43 sports clubs in the city.[64] There is no doubt that much party-owned real estate in Tel Aviv and elsewhere was handed out free of charge or at vastly reduced prices. When the Liberal Party sought a plot for new headquarters, Tel Aviv City Hall handed over an expensive piece of land at no charge.[65] In another instance, opposition members sued Haifa City Hall for refraining from collecting city taxes on coalition parties' offices.[66] Exempting parties from taxation or granting them large discounts is probably the rule rather than the exception, although the State Comptroller has expressly ruled against it.[67]

Everyone values power; otherwise they would not struggle to attain it. Power is even more valuable under a centralized regime, and its price rises accordingly. Prof. Arnold J. Hindenheimer devised an index calculating parties' expenditure per voter in various countries. Israel ranked first, spending 45 times as much as Australia, and about 20 times as much as West Germany or the United States.[68] The data was compiled in 1963. If changes have occurred since, then they have surely been for the worse.

In the mid-1970s, the Knesset adopted a Political Parties Law which is, in fact, a Political Parties Financing Law. It authorizes enormous allocations from the national budget to the parties, far beyond similar legislation in other countries. The funds are distributed according to the number of MKs each party has; in 1984 the rate was $90,000 per MK for a total of nearly $11,000,000.[69] Expenditures are subject to supervision by the State Comptroller. The law permitted the parties to raise outside funds totalling up to half the government allocation. Actually, the parties seriously overspent in 1981. Before the Comptroller could present his report, however, the Knesset asked for a stay of two months. During that period, it enacted legislation permitting the parties to collect 100% matching funds from outside sources![70] This is an example of how the Knesset legislates retroactively. This disgraceful scenario – overspending, retroactive cure – was re-enacted in the 1984, and 1988 elections. It seems that the Parties Law serves only to fill party pockets; its attendant supervision is a fig leaf.

Overspending and other violations of the Parties Law have gone unpunished. As for party funding, former Justice Minister Amnon Rubinstein had the following to say:

> The big parties passed the Party Financing Law, the essence of which is that the public – thwarted from participating in the life of the parties – is obliged to finance their functionaries.... Thus we are faced with wasteful public spending unprecedented in any democratic society. This is a case of party financing reaching epidemic proportions.... Loans from UJA, consolidation loans, Jewish Agency annual grants, payments above or under the table – anything to fill the party coffers, as needed to extend indefinitely the rule of those in whose hands rule resides. Party functionaries are independent of the voters' opinions, thanks to the public funding they have appropriated for themselves.[71]

In addition to government funding, the parties receive Jewish Agency allocations for youth movements and "immigrant absorption," not to mention generous government loans for debt consolidation, and similar allotments. The Histadrut also allocates funds to parties according to the percentage of the votes received by each in Histadrut elections. With all this, the parties are still not satiated. Alongside their legal and semi-legal sources of funding, there are various fictitious "Citizens for..." groups that pretend to be "independent" and thereby collect donations above and beyond the limitations of the law. Parties also raise funds abroad. This is legal, although it is palpably undemocratic.

Operating undercover, foreign powers transfer funds to whomever they chose to support. Obviously no one does this with official embassy cheques; they use more sophisticated methods. If an American or Canadian millionaire makes a six-digit donation, who knows where the money came from? Of the $15,000,000 spent by Labor in 1981, a portion came from the West German Social Democratic Party. This would certainly be considered illegal in other countries, but in Israel nobody was shocked. Shortly before the 1981 elections, the media reported that "Major financial agents abroad" were "channeling enormous sums to Israel to finance election propaganda."[72] Swiss Jewish millionaire Nessim Gaon was mentioned in this context for allegedly contributing sizable sums to a number of parties. Appeals to outlaw overseas solicitation of funds have been ignored, since most parties have no desire to give up such an important source of income. Thus it comes as no surprise at all that the State Comptroller's report put the cost of the parties' official 1984 campaign expenses at some $40,000,000![73]

Additional large sums spent on elections do not appear on paper. These funds are drawn from economic enterprises directly or indirectly controlled by the parties. Most industrial plants were built with government funds and depend on the government for licenses, approval of monopolies and monopsonies, subsidies, and so on. It is reasonable to expect their owners or directors to help the parties that control their fate. Since it is illegal for them to exceed relatively small contributions, they make up the balance by covering party expenses such as printing, advertising, or chartering buses on which potential voters and their families tour the country at no charge or, at the utmost, for a nominal fee. Party-affiliated companies sometimes launder money abroad and siphon it back into the country by devious routes.

The main beneficiary of all this is Labor, with its Histadrut-run economic empire. Details about Histadrut aid to the Labor Party surfaced in the memoirs of Asher Yadlin, a high-ranking Labor Party and Histadrut functionary. Indicted for accepting bribes, he argued that he took the money not for himself but for the party, and added, "Every functionary of my rank does the same." He wrote his book in prison. By aiming merely to justify his own actions, Yadlin missed the opportunity of turning his account into a "J'accuse" against the entire system. Nevertheless, his book discloses much reliable information about the transfer of funds from Histadrut economic enterprises to the Party. His claims were never denied.

Yadlin relates that after "the tremendous waste of the 1965 elections" (when about $30,000,000 was spent in the struggle against David Ben-Gurion's splinter faction), Labor's coffers were empty, "and I accepted the fact that one of my tasks as Secretary of the Histadrut conglomerate was to help replenish them." At the request of then-Premier Levi Eshkol, he arranged a meeting in the office of Golda Meir, then Labor secretary-general. All the VIPs of the Histadrut's economic empire participated, and promised, after Golda's appeal, to do their best.[74] Before the 1969 elections, Pinhas Sapir took temporary leave of the cabinet and assumed responsibility for fundraising. Yadlin describes what ensued:

> Money flowed in by the strangest of channels, sometimes through one or two intermediaries — from Israel and abroad, from Histadrut industrial funds and government budgets. State funds were, of course, the major source of income, though they were granted indirectly. Every Israeli lira received from a non-governmental source usually cost the Treasury two or three times as much. An example is the Allison affair. Allison, in charge of the Histadrut construction company's foreign operations, had repeatedly requested export subsidies and was turned down by Finance Minister Sapir. When Allison pledged $250,000 of his overseas resources to the party, however, he was awarded government subsidies worth more than $1 million.[75]

Another important source of party financing was the "United Port Services Company," (UPSC) founded during the Mandate to allow Jews to occupy strategically important posts at the port of Haifa. Over the years, the number of its employees grew substantially. It became a Labor power base in Haifa and an inexhaustible source of party funding. All this combined to produce a socio-economic monstrosity. It cast its shadow on Israel's economic life and contributed decisively to the shaping of the country's murky labor relations.[76] The UPSC, and especially its directors, received exorbitant salaries in various disguises in return for services rendered.

Yadlin goes on to tell a story about Israel's ambassador to Burma. The government gave him $70,000 to bribe Burmese officials. They did not want it, so he returned it. To his amazement, the money never found its way back to the Treasury, but somehow ended up in Labor's till.[77]

Yadlin describes a conversation between Ben-Gurion, Berl Katznelson, and David Remez sometime in the 1930s. The theme: was it permissible to exploit Histadrut economic enterprises to finance party expenditures for Zionist Congress elections? Ben-Gurion and Katznelson considered it not only permissible but downright desirable. True, the Histadrut's companies belonged to all the trade organization's members, but since 80 percent of them were affiliated with Mapai, the Histadrut should rightly help Mapai win the elections.[78]

The ruling party of every democratic country might like to raise standards of living shortly before elections, but in free market economies such manipulating is seldom possible. Not so in a centralized economy. A government such as Israel's, which fixes salaries and prices, can crassly bestow favors on the population on the eve of national elections. It is no secret that before every election in Israel's history (except 1988), the Finance Ministers did their best to endear their party to the voters. In this respect, as in so many others, there is no visible difference between Labor and Likud. Before the 1981 elections, Finance Minister Yoram Aridor of Likud slashed taxes on cars, electric appliances, and television sets. Prices of subsidized commodities were frozen. Other steps were taken in the same spirit. Gabi Kessler of the daily *Ma'ariv* computed the cost of the 1984 "election economics" at some $400 million, including $30 million worth of pre-election labor sanctions and strikes aimed at the government.[79] Capitulating to striking workers created norms which burdened the government budget and the economy for years. Prices of subsidized commodities were frozen as hyperinflation multiplied real costs, welfare cuts were postponed, and Social Security allocations for large families were augmented. If Israel cannot afford to spend $40,000,000 or more for an election campaign, then surely the indirect expenditure of $400,000,000 on "election economics" is utterly unbearable. Oversees funding of elections contradicts every accepted democratic norm, and under-the-table funding is criminally corrupt. Nevertheless, the pattern repeats itself every four years.

CHAPTER THREE

THE TENTACLES OF THE OCTOPUS

In modern society every citizen needs various permits, authorizations and licenses which must be obtained from the authorities. The more centralized the regime, the greater the bureaucracy's power and the more documents are required. Since in Israel the government and its agencies control almost every walk of life, the citizen comes into contact with the authorities far more frequently than in other democratic countries.

A complete list of all the permits and authorizations devised by the various branches of the Israeli bureaucracy would fill several volumes. Nor can one even begin to compile a list of all the forms the average Israeli must fill out in the course of everyday life.

Laws regulate the relationship between government and citizen. However, the bureaucrats are legally entitled to make exceptions to those rules. For instance: Israel's payroll tax, equivalent to 4 percent of employee salaries, raises labor costs and stifles the economy. Employers are outraged. How has the government reacted? Not by abolishing the tax, but by exempting manufacturing and other sectors. A large factory obviously engages in "manufacturing." Smaller enterprises have to prove themselves eligible for the exemption. Furthermore, to which employees does the law refer? The sandwich vendor? The bookkeeper? In 1986, the Treasury announced its intention of levying a tax of 6 percent on loans from abroad. This met with severe criticism. The Treasury responded that it would not impose this levy on credit used for equipment purchases, exports, or suppliers. Airlines, shippers, and fuel companies were exempted.[1] Consequently, bureaucrats must now authorize exemptions, enabling them to favor some that were not intended to be exempt. Once again the citizen is at the bureaucracy's mercy.

This system of different rules and regulations for different sectors prevails everywhere: from varying tariffs on phone installation and use to the right to open a foreign-currency bank account.

Take the case of the Ramat Gan family who bought a second garbage can. It turned out that to have a second can emptied by the municipality, one must request permission from the Sanitation Department, which sends an inspector to examine the situation and then appoints a committee to make the decision. It is hard to imagine this committee's criteria and even harder to presume that no favoritism is involved.

Another anecdote concerns a Tel Aviv physician. Mailmen frequently refuse to deliver journals to homes on the grounds that mailboxes are too small, this forces subscribers to stand in line at the post office during working hours. One such subscriber, a physician, protested to the Ministry of Communications. After two years of correspondence, he received a letter from the Minister himself, promising home delivery in the future. The physician happily informed his neighborhood colleagues that from now on all would receive their journals at home. It soon became apparent, however, that the Minister's promise referred only to the nagging doctor: the mailman received specific instructions to deliver his journals only.

A garbage can is hardly one of life's important issues; neither is waiting in line at the post office. The same discriminatory procedures, however, are in effect everywhere. They govern such vital areas as housing, factory and hotel construction, membership in agricultural settlements, and more. Typical is the story told by a new immigrant from a Western country, who asked the Jewish Agency whether it offered mortgages to new immigrants. The official asked his age, and upon hearing that he was 70, replied that mortgages were given only to those under 65. When the man turned to leave, the official said, "Why are you leaving? Submit an application and we will consider it." You request, we decide. Israel: a bureaucrat's paradise.

The bureaucracy has a way of flaunting its power by withholding much-needed public services. Queues in many government offices are intolerable. Officials make private phone calls, leave the office, take tea breaks, and make the waiting public feel that they are doing them a favor rather than performing their duty. One can wait several months for a driving test; at one time 40,000 people were waiting for it.[2] Dealing with the Vehicle Licensing Office can be a nightmare. Telephone repairs, even if they take no more than several minutes, are liable to be delayed for weeks. And these are only a few examples.

The public defends itself with the only means at its disposal. In certain sectors bribery is common. In 1986, 14 examiners and other officials of the Jerusalem Vehicle Licensing Office were indicted. In 1985 television viewers were treated to a "candid camera" shot, showing a telephone company employee offering to expedite installation in return for a hefty bribe. This, however, is not the most common method. Generally, people look for "pull," that is, someone who knows the right official and can put in a good word for them, or someone of authority who can speed things up or get decisions made. There is the classic tale of a man who calls his friend at three in the morning to ask if he knows anyone in the Fire Department. "Have you gone out of your mind?," the friend demands. "Why at three in the morning?" The caller's reply: "My house is on fire and I don't know anybody in the Fire Department." The "pull" factor strengthens both politicians at various levels and, of course, bureaucrats. The rich, the powerful and the influential easily obtain whatever they want by invoking their "pull," while the ordinary citizen is often ignored, treated in a condescending manner, and kept waiting indefinitely. "B. and P. are the initials of our government's two evils – bureaucracy and pull," wrote Avraham Tal in *Ha'aretz* not long ago. "There never was cause to believe that B. and P. would disappear completely, but it was hoped that they would weaken with time... In fact, the opposite is happening: they are gradually tightening their grip on the country, wrote Yoel Marcus of *Ha'aretz*."[3]

> They exasperate people. We hardly differ from a Bolshevik regime, in which people are entirely at the government's mercy. It can break into their homes any time, detain them for interrogation irrespective of guilt or innocence, expropriate their property or tax it exorbitantly, impose new decrees, and attach part of their salaries as "loans." Such a regime legislates many laws that people just cannot obey, turning every citizen into a potential lawbreaker to be prosecuted whenever advantageous. Then it arrests, nationalizes, or fines. The citizen is guilty until proven innocent. As I write, I am amazed at the similarity between the description above and what has been happening to us. Exasperating the population has certainly taken a turn for the worse. It brings back memories of the first few years of the state, when the government bureaucracy thought one of its main functions was to make life difficult. Astoundingly, income-tax "commandos" permit themselves to break into houses in their owners' absence. They are authorized to do so. Such Bolshevik practices should worry us. For months, income-tax teams have been stopping cars on the highways and confiscating drivers' registration, keys, and vehicle until they pay whatever they owe, however little. Yes, it's legal. But what kind of law grants officials the arbitrary right to behave like highwaymen or burglars?

Former State Comptroller Yitzhak Tunik once remarked that "The establishment is not sufficiently aware of the rules of sound public administration." When asked if he meant red tape, contempt, and indifference towards the people, he replied: "All of the above."[4]

The bureaucracy's behavior towards the rank-and-file is always on the public agenda. It is a favorite topic among Israelis in conversation and in letters to editors; it is the subject of hundreds if not thousands of newspaper articles and academic studies. This behavior ranges from apathy – not answering letters, refusing to arrange things by phone – to accidental or willful deception and even cruelty. Occasionally one comes across a letter to the editor praising the courtesy of a public official, a phenomenon that only confirms the unfortunate fact that Israelis cannot take courtesy for granted.

In 1986 the public services employed 459,000 wage earners. Of these, 194,000 were directly employed by the government (including 50,000 teachers and 65,000 Army and Defense Ministry employees), 50,000 by the Histadrut or its Sick Fund, 77,000 by the municipalities, and 65,000 by government corporations. The rest worked for "national" organizations such as the Jewish Agency or institutions of higher learning.[5] In other words, 36 percent of the labor force receive their salaries directly or indirectly from the government or the Histadrut. Their number increased steadily from 417,500 in 1980 to 424,000 in 1982 and 490,000 in 1983. In the two months preceding the 1984 elections, the number of public servants swelled by 7,100.[6] The ratio of these servants to industrial workers is approximately 1:1 – an intolerable ratio by any standard. Even the politicians responsible for the perpetual growth of the bureaucracy deplore it, at least publicly. In 1975, before becoming speaker of the Knesset, Menahem Savidor remarked:

> In 1952 a government-appointed committee examined the civil service, then numbering 26,000 people, and found 1,500 employees superfluous. In 1971, when the government bureaucracy encompassed 56,000 people, this committee ruled that it should be reduced by 1,500. Now that this monstrous apparatus has swelled to unbearable dimensions, numbering 65,000 employees (plus the mushrooming government corporations), the government has announced its decision to dismiss 700 temporary workers and 1,500 tenured ones. Whom is it trying to kid?[7]

It is unclear whether the reality of the last four decades has resulted from outright deceit, impotence, or both. It has certainly been an outgrowth of the political and economic system. Over the years, millions have been spent on "efficiency programs." Never implemented, these plans are gathering dust on every ministry's shelves. Of course, every minister and MK knows the truth: 20 ministries is far too many. Many departments do more harm than good, and the monstrous swelling of the bureaucracy is a major reason for the budget deficit.

Private firms can only pay so much; after all, they have to make a profit (though in Israel, as we shall see, they depend more on government support than on profit). The civil service has no such requirement; hence there is no limit to what they can make the government pay. The government eventually capitulates to workers' demands, however shameless or ridiculous. Every minister wants to be popular with his ministry's employees, and since there is no need to balance the budget, why not give in? Besides, government employees and their families are an electoral force to be reckoned with, equivalent to 10-12 Knesset seats or as much as 10 percent of the House. Who would want to alienate them? Consequently, it is not surprising that the wages earned by government employees are constantly rising, while the amount of work they perform is diminishing.

Salaries in Israel are awkwardly constructed. Civil servants' income is composed of salary; special remuneration for overtime, "on-call," and occupational hazards, plus premiums, field supplements, and reimbursement of expenses. Many of these actually belong in quotation marks, for they are nothing but flimsy excuses for raising salaries without compromising the sacred principle of "linkage" (the practice of attaching all salaries in a pre-determined ratio). The State Comptroller's 30th Annual Report states that in 1979 civil servants received over 400 kinds of payments on top of their regular salaries and reimbursements.

These payments bore such peculiar names as "antenna supplements" and "gluing supplements" in the Ministry of Communications, and "concentration supplements" in the Ministry of Labor and Social Affairs.

There are, of course, many more ways to increase salaries, such as automatic mass promotions, "personal ranks," generously subsidized loans for car purchase, travel abroad, and virtually free lunches. Defense Ministry employees once imposed sanctions and threatened to strike when the government sought to raise the price for a three-course lunch to the grand sum of one dollar! Needless to say, the government backed down. Similarly, Land Registry workers demanded a 30 percent wage hike for agreeing to computerize.[8] In the summer of 1982, income-tax officials cancelled a strike only after 100 of them were promoted.[9] A civil servant is entitled to a fixed number of sick days annually, which he may save up for the future. Monetary compensation is awarded for unused sick leave. Nonetheless, a survey has revealed that about half the sick days claimed by policemen are unjustified.[10] An "automobile maintenance allowance" is often a disguised salary raise, because more bureaucrats qualify for it than own cars.[11] In 1979, Education Ministry treasurers were paid to work 75 hours overtime monthly: 16 in their offices and 59 at home.[12] For doctors and the like, the "on-call" supplement is justified, but it has been adopted in many government ministries where there is little chance of being called after hours.[13] "Seminars" in Israeli hotels are often nothing but vacations at government expense. High-ranking officials also benefit from overseas junkets. The complete list of benefits ranges from the sublime to the ridiculous, and in some cases it defies imagination. A veteran of such activity, Shlomo Arnon, has revealed some of the details:[14]

> The salary component of the 1980 budget, excluding defense, was about 11 percent... In 1979-80, 74,524 civil servants went on strike and 82,257 employees imposed sanctions. The overtime supplement, which costs the Treasury tens of millions

of dollars each year...is usually based on false reporting... On-the-job travel: in their work, about 20,000 administrators and high-ranking officials travel 150 million kilometers a year in their cars. The state reimburses them with millions of dollars. Yet it is well-known that kilometrage reports are usually exaggerated. Some reimbursement recipients don't even own cars... To this day, the Treasury extends cheap loans to civil servants purchasing cars. These employees would not be buying cars in the first place if the state had not been covering maintenance costs. Per diem; administrators and other high--ranking employees receive $2 million yearly. It is common knowledge that most neither eat nor sleep anywhere but at home... "Supplementary-education" funds: during 1979-80, 5,403 employees "supplemented their education" abroad (93 percent) and 398 (7 percent) in Israel... I myself joined such a trip overseas. In three weeks we visited four countries and attended 12 rather shallow lectures. So much for education. The rest of the time we enjoyed the scenery and beauty of these countries... For every $1,000 we spent, the Treasury and other institutions covered $667... The term "supplementary-education fund" is a sham. A more appropriate term would be "pleasure trips abroad, on the house"...

Many of the aforementioned perks are secured by means of sanctions and strikes. Hardly a day goes by without negotiations, strikes, or sanctions of some kind in some government service. In any event, there seem to be fewer and fewer differences between ministerial employees who are striking and those who are working. For one thing, they generally come late and leave early. In 1981 a labor dispute erupted in the Tel Aviv Bureau of Standards. Management wanted employees to park their cars in the new parking lot, thus reserving the old lot for guests of the Institute; the employees claimed that their parking places, regarded as permanent for over twenty years, should not be changed now, and that the Institute guests were not to be given preference over the Institute's permanent employees. The works committee claimed that the new parking lot was far away. The arbitrator, attorney Lillian Pergament, ruled that the workers would have to park in the new lot, in return for which they would be permitted to report to work five minutes late.[15]

Many employees – sometimes 50 percent or more – simply vanish from work for hours or even days with impunity. In government buildings, it is not unusual to find entire floors of offices either locked, open but empty, or filled with idle, chattering clerks. In recent years no effort has been made to conceal the situation. In short, many government employees regard their salary not as remuneration for work, but as something the government owes them. Labor's morale and attitude can be gauged by the 38 demands presented to the Treasury by customs officials slated to work in the VAT offices:[16]

- Any employee who so requests may retire after 25 years' work, and, upon reaching age 45, be eligible for full pension (70 percent of last base wage), in addition to an enlarged grant of one month's salary per year. The latter is due to "accelerated physical depreciation resulting from daily labor."
- Employees' Social Security payments made by the employer.
- Participation in high school and college expenses for employees' children.
- Establishment of an employees' welfare grant fund.
- Redemption of unused sick leave.
- Employee loans for housing, "housing culture," and children's weddings (loans should be equivalent to the average annual wage of tax department employees).
- Meals.
- $4.00 per diem per day for soft drinks and miscellaneous expenses for computer workers on the night shift.
- Participation in costs of cultural and sports activities, outings, and so forth.

- "Indispensable official" status with respect to motor vehicle upkeep allowances for employees at or over the salary rank of 17, and reimbursement of personal vehicle expenses for those at level 16.
- A substantial increase of vehicle kilometrage to 1,200 per month, as customary in the Budget Division. Increase of clothing bonus, and increase in number of message units permitted in use of personal phone.
- Establishment of an accumulative fund with employees' participation for "advanced study" abroad.
- $1.00 per day for employees working outside the office.
- Overtime for high-ranking officials on the basis of fixed regulations.
- $13.00 per session for employees attending evening committee meetings, and immediate activation of the "guidance committee" in place of the defunct public committees.
- Increase of the committee administrator payment to $25.00 per month.
- A special 1% bonus for uncovering tax evasion and smuggling, with the proceeds deposited in an employees' welfare and culture fund.
- $25.00 per employee for every appearance in court.
- A 30% "special effort" bonus for working under conditions of manpower shortage and multiple duties.
- A 20% premium for the annual increase in budget and requisite output.
- Authorized signatory bonus.
- Sabbatical year and study abroad.
- Treasury participation in cost of courses.
- Noise bonus for customs employees at the airport.
- Risk bonus for work with violent clients.
- $12.50 monthly grant for employees who neither absent themselves from work nor come late.
- Increased vacation allowance.

- Recognizing an added work hour for employees whose place of work is especially distant from residential areas, such as Ben-Gurion Airport.
- A search-and-investigation bonus for employees whose jobs entail these activities.
- Increase in the number of hours recognized as overtime for shift employees.
- Abolition of moonlighting limitations.
- Abolition of the cooling-off period for ex-employees taking on similar work outside the Civil Service.
- Extension of all the above benefits to pensioners.[17]

In 1977 the government decided to move several of its ministries from Tel Aviv to the capital. Employees were given the alternatives of moving to Jerusalem, resigning, or continuing to work in Tel Aviv. Those who chose to move were eligible for various forms of housing assistance: a loan that would become a grant after five years; a regular loan; an "unlinked" (non-indexed) loan; or a "transfer grant." Their spouses were also given preference for government jobs in Jerusalem.[18] In addition, whoever opted for relocation would be permitted to commute to Jerusalem for two years, receiving 125 percent of overtime wages for travel time, plus Fridays off and a $7.50 per diem. Those who elected not to move were entitled to compensation amounting to 150 percent of their salary plus 15 months of salary (based on a promotion). These benefits totalled about $45,000 per worker. Journalist Elazar Levine sums it up: "Want to get rich quick?... Work for the government or the Histadrut... Once your office is transferred to Jerusalem, your financial future is secured."[19] What actually happened was that about half of those ostensibly moving to Jerusalem reaped all the benefits, subletted out their new apartments in the capital, and continued to live in Tel Aviv.[20] In 1984 the Knesset Interior Committee calculated that in the seven years since the transfer decision, 500 officials had made the move. Actually, only about half had done so. The Committee appealed to the Housing and Construction Ministry "to grant incentives and benefits to people seeking to live in Jerusalem," that is, to provide Jerusalem-bound Histadrut employees with the same benefits as those received by the civil servants.[21] Thus one abuse spawned another, and millions went down the drain.

To scale the wall of bureaucratic apathy, the public has no choice but to resort to "pull" or bribery. Bribery was relatively infrequent during the early years of the state. "Pull," through politicians and parties, was more common. Eventually, however, bribery began to play an increasingly important role. When a district court convicted an income-tax employee of graft in 1977, the verdict noted: "Corruption in the civil service is no longer a rarity. The multitude of cases proves that this plague has reached vast dimensions, and its penetration of the very fiber of public life endangers the existence of a proper democracy."

Every year officials are tried for bribery, embezzlement, and other forms of corruption. They often invoke the 'defense' that their misdeeds are the norm throughout the civil service. The mercy shown by the courts is astonishing. They often refrain from handing down a prison sentence or even from dismissing the official in question, settling instead for a reprimand, a promotion freeze, a fine, or a recommendation that the accused be transferred to a different post. Whether the crime is punching two timecards, pre-punching one, accepting bribes, embezzling public funds or engaging in fraud, the courts are quick to forgive -despite the repeated warnings sounded by individual judges. The Haifa District Court has ruled that "holding down private jobs during work hours is so common among civil servants that it is downright disgraceful."[22] Those convicted of corruption – and even those who have served jail sentences – are often not dismissed from their jobs. Thus Labor Party activist Shmuel Kishlas was convicted of taking bribes while serving as secretary of the Aircraft Industry Works Committee. After a stint in prison, he returned to work in the Aircraft Industry, where he became a candidate for a prominent post on the directorate.[23] A special disciplinary court was established for civil servants back in 1963, but by 1981 this court had handed down only 600 verdicts, many of them extremely charitable.[24]

The comptroller ranks high in the hierarchy of state functionaries. He independently employs hundreds of officials to monitor the government's bureaucracy and corporations, public institutions like the Histadrut, the sick funds, and other state-funded bodies. Every year, the comptroller issues a voluminous expose of hair-raising waste, abandoned government property, faulty maintenance, neglected stores, superfluous bureaucracy and trips abroad, favoritism, excessive suppliers' payments, budgetary overruns, disregard for regulations, and more. During the early years of the state, the comptroller's revelations aroused great interest. Widely publicized by the media, they sent apprehensive authorities scrambling for alibis. Every year, the comptroller noted the same faults but nothing was done to correct them. Gradually, it dawned on people that the comptroller was essentially powerless. Thus, the inept administration depicted in his reports came to be regarded as routine, and no longer caused a stir. Nevertheless, these reports still cause a certain discomfort in political circles. Since politicians have neither the power nor the desire to alter their unattractive image, they prefer to shatter the mirror. Indeed in 1987 the Knesset discussed the possibility of curtailing the comptroller's authority.[25]

How did the government apparatus become a bloated, rigid, exploitative, wasteful bureaucracy indifferent to its own obligations? Is everybody corrupt and evil? On the contrary, most government employees are decent people who, under different circumstances, would perform their tasks conscientiously.

The simple truth is that many government functions could be accomplished quicker, cheaper, and more efficiently by private business. Furthermore, the stronger the bureaucracy and the more extensive its authority, the greater its self-importance and contempt for the public. As one government minister put it, "A self-perpetuating apparatus has developed, which undermines every initiative for the citizens' benefit."[26]

In the beginning, employees were told to defer to and lavish favors on political cronies "for the good of the cause." Then they realized that their bosses – ministers and high-ranking officials alike – were exploiting their positions for their own good as well as that of the party. The national interest was not always their top priority. Eventually it became clear that advancement in rank was based not on hard work and excellence, but on completely different criteria. Many superfluous government workers were employed for political reasons, or because ministers sought to expand their apparatus. Considering the enormous power these officials amassed through their unions and the undesirable norms of public conduct within the political establishment, it is easy to understand how matters degenerated to the point where the civil servants' concept of "service in exchange for salary" has been completely distorted. Moreover, the strikes and sanctions have led to exorbitant salaries in the upper echelons of the bureaucratic hierarchy, while their underlings still earn much less than people in business. Consequently, officials have neither a moral nor a financial incentive to serve the public properly.

Local authorities in Israel function according to the Municipality Ordinance enacted by the British in 1934 and amended only slightly by the Knesset. The Interior Ministry uses its broad jurisdiction to approve or veto their budgets, taxes, and bylaws. The local authorities employ 77,000 people (excluding teachers and policemen, who are paid by the central government), imposing a heavy financial burden on the citizenry. Municipalities get their money from city taxes (property, water, and so on), service fees, percentages of various national taxes (luxury tax, real-estate tax, automobile levies), ministerial allocations for health, welfare, education, and culture, and a grant from the Interior Ministry to cover their deficits.

In 1983, municipal incomes totaled $1.4 billion, as follows:[27]

Municipal sources:	
Property tax	13%
Other taxes	15%
Governmental sources:	
Transfers	20%
Ministerial allocations	27%
Interior Ministry grant	25%

Thus only 28 percent of the municipal budget was funded by the municipalities themselves; 72 percent came from the government. In the mid-1980's, the Interior Ministry instructed the municipalities to raise taxes so as to lower government participation. Nevertheless, the central government remains the major source of municipal incomes – 60 percent as of 1987.

Government offices throughout the country (except in "development towns") are exempt from local taxes; so are various public institutions. In Tel Aviv political parties enjoy a 33 percent reduction on property tax. In Haifa the parties have not paid this tax for years, and the same is evidently the case in many other municipalities.[28] The Beersheba Municipality has been slow in collecting property tax from certain factories and businesses.[29] In 1976 the Haifa Municipality forfeited $250,000 in taxes "for fear of violence." Considerable tax breaks are granted to "big clients." Municipal "reduction committees" evaluate applications for tax relief, using unknown but readily imaginable criteria. When the religious party chairing the Jerusalem committee left the municipal coalition, the media reported that its members would henceforth find it much harder to obtain tax breaks.

But municipalities do more for the parties than just waive taxes. The Tel Aviv Municipality set aside a quarter-acre plot on a main street for the Liberal Party, explaining that the building to be erected there would bear the name of a former mayor. The Nahariya Municipality allotted half an acre to an Orthodox party as a reward for joining the municipal coalition.[30]

The Ministry of Interior's hammerlock on the municipalities has produced a seemingly endless series of squabbles and scandals. Pinhas Ayalon, former Mayor of Holon and the chairman of the Association of Municipalities, "Budget negotiations with the Interior Ministry involve nerve-wracking, ugly bargaining. There are no objective criteria for the allocation of funds. Mayors who run up large deficits are rewarded with large grants. Those who administer their cities frugally lose out. Wasteful, inefficient mayors are the winners."[31] The Israeli practice of treating municipalities as subcontractors of government ministries (Education, Welfare, Health, and so on) leads to duplication, waste, ceaseless arguments, and procrastination. It is simply unhealthy for one body to collect money and another to spend it. In the words of the Treasurer of the Jerusalem Municipality, in response to accusations of wasting money, "It's not our money; we got it from the government."

The education budget illustrates the absurdities this system produces. The Education Ministry has a Building Department for schools, and every municipality has its own Education Department. Teachers are paid by the government, school janitors by the municipality. The school nurse is employed by the municipality, but part of her salary is covered by the Ministry of Health. The Ministry of Education covers 75 percent of the cost of school construction as a grant, and the rest as a loan subject to approval by the National Lottery. School landscaping is paid for by the municipality, using credit provided by the Interior Ministry. Upkeep is the municipality's problem. Furniture is purchased with loans from the lottery.[32] How many quarrels over positions, costs, timing, and plans accompany this ridiculous arrangement? How much coordination is needed, and how many people devote their time to it?

As things stand, mayors are compelled to bargain with government bureaucrats over every detail. They may not collect taxes, sell plots, or even put up road signs without government authorization. They lobby aggressively to have their localities ranked as A, B, or C-type "development towns." This is of great importance, since any of these rankings determine the level of government support for local industry. Adjacent towns are sometimes classified differently, in direct proportion to the clout and political connections of their particular mayors. "I spend a great deal of time in the government offices in Jerusalem... I built relations with the lowest ranking secretaries... In the long run, they're the ones who bring the documents to their bosses, and if I'm nice to them – it pays off," says a local council chairman.[33] Others utilize threats, party pressure, and public opinion. Some take "unauthorized," that is, illegal steps. "Mayors are "subordinate to government officials, not all of whom are talented or honest," points our Ze'ev Yafet of the daily *Ha'aretz*. "These officials were not elected and owe the public no explanation. They often act in keeping with political interests of their ministers, which may be diametrically opposed to those of the municipality." After the 1978 elections, the Minister of Interior issued the mayor of Tel Aviv a veiled warning: don't exclude my party from the coalition! Such a hint, from the man who approves the municipality's budget and grants, carries a lot of weight.[34]

Government ministries routinely attach strings to the funds they allot the municipalities. Demands include grants for yeshivas, including some out-of-town; jobs for "our boys" in the municipal bureaucracy, and more. The chairman of the Kfar Tabor local council, a political ally of the late Finance Minister Simcha Ehrlich, says: "I supported [Ehrlich] in his difficult hours, when everyone else abandoned him – and it paid off. I got almost everything I wanted, and sometimes even more."[35]

To obtain government grants, municipalities are required to present their annual budgets to the Interior Ministry, for examination. This process usually takes several months, lasting well into the next fiscal year. In the interim, mayors have to take out high-interest bank loans in order to meet current obligations. Once the grant finally comes through, inflation may have whittled its value to virtually nothing. Mayors complain that this practice plunges them heavily into debt and brings many local authorities to the brink of financial collapse. The Ministry of Interior denies this, blaming municipal woes on mismanagement and asserting that "The government should not reward failure."[36] Both sides have a point. Since there are no clear criteria as to the size of grants – it all depends on the mayor's talent at persuasion and the Interior Ministry's willingness to cooperate – most municipalities feel deprived. The Mayor of Tel Aviv says he is not compensated for services rendered to residents of neighboring towns. The Mayor of Haifa insists that his city is deprived for political reasons.[37]

The grant system, in effect, invites mayors to pressure the government. When the city till is empty, salaries are not paid. City employees strike, garbage piles up in the streets and, lo and behold, the government forwards the money. Tel Aviv Mayor Shlomo Lahat (Likud) plays this game most effectively: "I was elected to build Tel Aviv," he says, "not to watch over the budget." Before the 1983 elections, Lahat ran up a mammoth budget deficit on city beautification and public relations. To induce the Ministry of Interior to cover his debts, Lahat promised in writing never to let it happen again. After the elections, he went to work on a new and even higher deficit. What about his solemnly signed commitment? "I signed because I needed money,"

Lahat declared shamelessly. When asked by a reporter whether the government would make good for his extravagance, he replied: "I never worry about the Likud government failing to come up with the funds to cover our deficit. It's a political problem, so I allow myself to spend whatever the city requires. If another government is elected some day, it will be faced with a fait accompli."[38]

Logic dictates that the hard-pressed municipalities should streamline their administrations. But they have no incentive to be efficient if they know that the government will foot the bill. The Tel Aviv municipality owns real estate, buildings, public institutions, and no fewer than 170 kiosks, which could provide it with considerable income. But the properties are administered carelessly and without appropriate supervision. "More money is spent on maintaining them than they provide in income," according to *Ha'aretz*.[39] City-owned companies are big money-makers all over the world. Not in Tel Aviv. Dov Ben-Meir, the official in charge of municipal companies, says that profit is not their purpose.[40]

Featherbedding is rife throughout Israel's local authorities. The late Deputy Mayor of Tel Aviv, David Shifman, once estimated that there were 3,000 employees who should be dismissed in that city alone. He referred to his city as a "bureaucrat's paradise."[41] Another mayor claimed that the efficiency of his administration would greatly improve if he fired 40 percent of his employees. Such a step is out of the question; the unions and the council members, who constantly press for jobs for party supporters, would never hear of it.[42] Department heads in the Tel Aviv Municipality say that only 15 percent of the employees put in a full day's work; the others, especially those with field duties, simply punch in and vanish. Hundreds 'moonlight' in broad daylight. Some department heads are satisfied if their employees work four hours a day. Parking inspectors write an average of just 25 tickets each day. In 1975, one out of every 30 residents of Tel Aviv was on City Hall's payroll. Work norms conform to those of the least efficient workers, and the unions make sure no one is ever fired.[43]

Among municipal council members, only the mayor and his deputy are legally entitled to salaries; the other members serve on a voluntary basis. Thus it often proves impossible to assemble a coalition without appointing several deputy mayors. At one time Bnei Brak had no less than five deputy mayors, each with an office, a secretary, and a car.[44] Mayors and deputy mayors enjoy generous severance pay, preferential salary conditions, and even doubled salaries. Many councilmen get some sort of monetary compensation, including use of a car. In Tel Aviv, one municipal official collected three salaries for administering three municipal companies.[45] City employees also get cheap loans (usually before elections) and often pay reduced city taxes.[46]

One of the most sought-after benefits is a trip abroad at the public's expense. When the Bat Yam Municipal Council debated a motion to dispatch eight councilmen to Germany, fistfights almost erupted. A plan to send Tel Aviv councilmen to Romania – at the invitation of Romanian Chief Rabbi Rosen – was deferred for two years because of disagreements as to who should go. The Likud representatives were furious – not at the blatant waste of taxpayers' money, but at the mayor's supposed discrimination against them. During a raucous council debate on the subject, one said: "Mr. Mayor, why don't you throw *us* a bone once in a while?"[47]

To do just about anything in an Israeli town, one must obtain permits in breathtaking variety and number. In a letter to the editor, a resident of one large city described the months of run-around and harassment he experienced when he decided to build a roof to protect his car from the sun. He finally named the shelter "Kafka." Here are some illustrative excerpts from a Tel Aviv Municipality leaflet on how to obtain a business license:

> Every business so defined in the Business Licensing Ordinance requires a license.... Any change in an existing business, as in nature or ownership, requires a new license.... The procedure takes between three and five months, since the approval of several agencies must be obtained.
>
> How to Obtain a Business License:
>
> 1. Present an application to the Business Licensing Department
> 2. Obtain approval of the Planning and Building Department
> 3. Obtain approval of the Fire Department
> 4. Obtain Approval of the Ecology Department
> 5. Obtain approval of the Veterinary Service
> 6. Obtain approval of the Public Health Department
> 7. Obtain approval of the Police
> 8. Obtain approval of the Ministry of Labor
> 9. Obtain approval of the Ministry of Health
> 10. Obtain approval of other agencies, as warranted
> 11. Pick up your license
>
> This leaflet does not purport to list all the requirements in detail; it is meant to help the citizen understand the subject.

It is hard to understand why a process that should take a few days has to last five months. It is harder to fathom why even six months of wrangling is often not enough. Israeli's are compelled to hire go-betweens, whose business it is to obtain licenses and who know how to talk to the bureaucrats.

Taking out a business license is nothing compared with obtaining a building permit. In Tel Aviv, that requires 74 separate steps and 20 separate licenses. The average application take five years to process.[48] Inevitably, hundreds of buildings are erected without permits. In Rishon Lezion, a contractor has to pass through 15 stages to receive a "certificate of completion." Since it is impossible to get the 15 signatures during a reasonable period of time, most contractors do without it.[49]

Who needs building permits at all? Municipalities could publish precise instructions of what is permitted and forbidden in each zone, leaving the police to deal with violations. This, however, would pull the plug on the Town Building Committee, whose business it is to make exceptions to the rules. Otherwise, how would it be possible to let major contractors overrun zoning percentages by 50 or even 100 percent? The rank and file face endless difficulties when trying to close in a balcony, while large areas of additional building space are approved for those who know how to apply pressure. It happens every day. A study on town planning and building-law enforcement found that "Political pressure is often of greater influence than pure planning considerations."[50] Of the many cases of preferential treatment of the wealthy and influential, a case involving hotelier Chaim Schiff stands out. In return for retroactive approval of excess construction in an apartment hotel he had built on Tel Aviv's Ibn Gavirol Street, Schiff undertook to lay the foundation of Liberal Party headquarters on nearby city-owned land.[51] By law, every public building has to come with parking space, according to a fixed index. In practice, owners pay the municipality a relatively small "ransom" and come away exempt from this expensive chore.

When it takes years to obtain a building permit, and when local building committees practice blatant discrimination, illegal construction is inevitably rife. Two thousand illegally constructed buildings await court disposition in Jerusalem. In Tel Aviv there are some 5,000 demolition orders, of which about 70 are executed every year. The Jerusalem city comptroller described his city's situation as "a sad picture of inaction and lenience in the face of law violations... Offenders go unpunished and ultimately profit from their misdeeds." In 1974, former Supreme Court President Shimon Agranat bluntly asserted that "Demolition orders issued by the courts are ignored – this is the root of the evil."[52]

Since more than 10,000 demolition orders have not been executed, the few who comply with them feel like victims of discrimination. The State Comptroller described how Tadiran (a major electronics company owned by the Histadrut) overran its building permit by 80,000 square feet in its magnificent office building just outside of Tel Aviv, and the local committee approved the plans retroactively. No wonder municipal employees meet with violent resistance whenever and wherever they come to tear down illegal structures. In one instance, a head of household brandished a gun and aimed it at the police while his house was being torn down. He was killed in the ensuing shootout.[53]

CHAPTER FOUR

THE HISTADRUT -- GUARANTOR OF LABOR'S HEGEMONY

"The Labor Party views governmental assistance to Histadrut enterprises as its main objective, even when this is directly opposed to the national interest or that of the employees, who are Histadrut members." Prof. Yehoshua Porat, 1986[1]

"I believe in the hegemony of the workers movement in Zionism." David Ben-Gurion, 1928[2]

The Histadrut is not simply an expanded trade union. Initially, its founders did not intend to establish trade unions.[3] The Histadrut came into being in 1920 because David Ben-Gurion and his Labor Zionist comrades feared that the workers would not be loyal to them unless dependent upon them. Therefore, the Histadrut was designed in such a way as to guarantee party control over the workers and, later, over the entire Palestine Jewish community. The Histadrut did indeed play a leading role in the struggle for the establishment of Israel. But after 1948, the Histadrut did not relinquish its national functions to the government. On the contrary, it was given even more power, in order to ensure "workers hegemony," that is, Labor Party rule.

The Histadrut is today Israel's largest organized body. About 60 percent of all Israelis are members. The following is a list of its activities:[4]

Mutual Assistance

Sick Fund

17 hospitals, 1,242 clinics, 19 convalescent homes

Insurance and pension funds

Social benefit funds

Trade Union

Country-wide labor unions

Thousands of works committees on the job

Economic Activity

A holding company, Hevrat ha-'Ovdim ("the Workers' Corporation"), which employs 22 percent of the country's labor force. It includes the cooperative sector with its agricultural settlements Regional Workers' Councils

72 councils that supervise and coordinate local and district activities.

Culture and Education

Cultural, educational, art, and propaganda activities, including schools for Histadrut functionaries.

Vocational Education

27 vocational high schools, 11 trade schools.

Na'amat, an organization for women and working mothers, maintains a network of daycare centers and nursery schools.

Youth and University Students

Establishment of youth clubs and assistance to university students with respect to work and payment.

"Union of Working and Studying Youth"

Educational and social activities for adolescents.

Sports

Close to 1,000 chapters of Hapoel (literally, "The Worker") engage in 19 different sports.

Consumer Authority

Consumer protection

Industrial Democracy Division

Encourages labor participation in management

Labor Legislation
Immigrant Absorption
International Liaisons
Including an International Institute for Cooperation, Development and Labor Studies.
Journalism and publishing
Davar daily newspaper and Am Oved publishing house.
Religious Needs Department

The list of Histadrut activities is awesome in its range and scope. Even a brief glance discloses that this is no mere trade union. What connection could there possibly be between a trade union and economic enterprises, newspapers, educational networks, or agricultural villages (all of which employ workers)? Many of the Histadrut's endeavors duplicate government activity. It is common knowledge, too, that many of them are totally opposed to the needs and functions of a trade union.

What, then, is the Histadrut? It is in a sense, a vast pressure group. Some of its members depend on it for livelihood, others for improvement of their standards of living. Persons employed by the "Workers' Corporation" presumably vote for parties whom, they believe, will never let Histadrut-owned companies go under. The cooperative farm villages are showered with government benefits, procured for them by the Histadrut. In turn, the hundreds of thousands of Israelis paid by the Histadrut or its institutions are likely to vote as their employer expects.[5] The fact that many of Israel's entertainers, actors, and singers support the Labor Party is at least partly due to the Histadrut's hefty budgets allotments for "culture and art." All this is done to ensure "workers' hegemony" – a concept diametrically opposed to democracy as understood by the Western world. This is not a professional organization, but a state within a state.

Histadrut elections are still indirect, as they were in the 1920s. The only novelty is "party funding," based on the same principles as those of Knesset elections. The Convention "elects" the 501 members of the Histadrut Council, who, in turn, "elect" the 195 members of the Executive Committee. The Executive Committee elects the Histadrut Secretary-General, the directorate of the "Workers Corporation," and the 40 members of the Histadrut Directorate.[6] Because there is obviously no way 1,500 convention delegates can elect a 500-member council, they agree on a list presented by the leaders. Since Labor has always enjoyed an absolute majority in the Histadrut, an absolute majority of the "elected" functionaries are actually Labor appointees. All administrative positions are filled by appointments of the Secretary-General and the Directorate. The Labor Party has never agreed to share important executive positions with other parties. As a result, the directors of the Workers' Corporation and its subsidiaries are Labor appointees, and the benefits accruing to Labor from this situation are self-evident. The same applies to the Sick Fund (Kupat Holim) and all other Histadrut institutions. It takes hordes of officials to administer this giant complex. The nationwide institutions are concentrated in the enormous Histadrut Executive Committee building in Tel Aviv, and overflow into adjoining buildings.[7] Seventy-two regional workers' councils are scattered throughout the country. The existence of such councils is another concept unknown in the Western world. (Interestingly, the name, "workers' council" is a literal translation of the Russian term "Soviet" – and that is not merely coincidental.) Each council employs scores of people; in some large districts, they employ hundreds. Plainly it requires lots of money to maintain this bureaucracy. Whence this fortune? The Histadrut's leaders knew and still know that voluntary membership dues would never suffice. Health care provides the lifeline.

Israel has all it takes to provide excellent medical service: the highest number of doctors per capita in the Western world;

an internationally recognized level of professional expertise; a surfeit of medical equipment; enough hospital beds; and 9 percent of GNP pledged to health care. Nevertheless, service is cumbersome, discontinuous, and irritating. Bureaucratic red tape entangles every citizen. Resources are underexploited. And since the mid-1980s, the entire health service system has been steadily deteriorating.

Health care is a public service, based on a system of social insurance, (payment of a percentage of income) and government support. Since the Mandatory period there have been four major Sick Funds, each established more or less along party lines: Histadrut, General Zionists (later known as United Sick Fund); Maccabi (set up by middle-class circles); and National, belonging to the Revisionist Movement (later Herut). All were founded before Israel was created; since then, no new sick funds have licensed. Though not obligatory by law, nearly all Israelis are members of a sick fund.

At first glance, everything looks proper. There are four competing sick funds, and the most efficient is sure to attract the largest membership. But reality differs. The Histadrut Sick Fund insures close to 80 percent of the population, and all the others scramble for the rest. To understand Israel's inability to exploit its medical resources, one must comprehend how important the Histadrut Sick Fund is for the survival of the Histadrut.

Until 1937, Histadrut membership dues and Sick Fund payments were collected separately. Since then, a "Comprehensive Tax" has been levied, with two thirds of the tax going for medical insurance and the remainder for the Histadrut. In other words, the immense Histadrut bureaucracy is sustained in part by dues paid by citizens who simply want to belong to the health insurance plan. (The labor union of the National Religious Party ((NRP)) insures its members with the Histadrut Sick Fund. They carry blue membership cards, as opposed to the red ones of the Histadrut. From their dues, approximately 30-35 percent are deducted for the NRP apparatus. This is one of the NRP's major sources of income. According to a law proposed by the Likud government in 1978, Social Security was supposed to collect health care premiums, thus severing their linkage to any other dues. NRP leader, Yosef Burg, blocked the bill on the grounds that such a measure "is not healthy for the NRP.") In a poll of a representative sample of Histadrut members in 1974, about 52 percent admitted that they had joined the Histadrut only for the Sick Fund's services. Some 15 percent said they worked for institutions or companies where membership was compulsory. Amnon Barzilai of *Ha'aretz* has described the Sick Fund as "the Histadrut's lifeline...guaranteeing its financial basis and survival." The late Labor Minister Mordechai Namir once said that "If the Labor Party in England had a sick fund, it would never lose elections."

In 1976, the Labor government presented the Knesset with a bill basing health care on the existing sick funds. "The bill guarantees to wipe clean the Histadrut Sick Fund's past, present and future deficits and debts (about $200,000,000)," wrote Amnon Barzilai. "It also gives the Histadrut complete control of the health services... This law does not purport to solve Israel's medical problems. In the guise of a health insurance law for the people, Labor Party functionaries strive to ensure their parties' health indefinitely and perpetuate their rule by means of the health services... Paragraph 83 guarantees the Histadrut Sick Fund representatives an absolute majority and control in the Health Council, the new administrative body meant to circumvent the Ministry of Health, while adding another bureaucratic yoke on the State... The Histadrut controls the Sick Fund only in theory. In fact, the Fund is directly controlled by the Labor Party, whose leaders appoint its directors without any public supervision... Paragraph 39 prohibits Histadrut members from joining other Sick Funds.[8] This bill, which Yoel Marcus of *Ha'aretz* called "a caricature of a law,"[9] was never enacted because of a change of government. The Likud, despite repeated promises, never presented an alternative law. In late 1985, the Histadrut announced that it now favored National Health Insurance administered by the Sick Funds, on condition that the government footed the bill...[10]

From the perspective of the Histadrut, the Sick Fund is not merely a welcome vehicle for mutual assistance, but also a major power base for Labor's control of the State. The Sick Fund has funneled hundreds of thousands of politically unaffiliated immigrants into the ranks of the Histadrut membership.[11] This process is facilitated by the Jewish Agency, which pays the first six months of sick fund dues for every new immigrant; for many years, everyone was automatically registered with the Histadrut's Fund unless he or she specifically asked to join another fund. Those who did so were a negligible minority. The small sick funds spend the membership dues they collect on health, while the Histadrut uses part of the money to maintain its own apparatus. By making up the difference, the government actually sustains the Histadrut bureaucracy.[12]

Strange as it may seem, Histadrut dues ply a regressive scale. Deductions are 3.9 percent of earnings up to $300 monthly, 3 percent from there up to $730, 2.2 percent of the next increment up to $1,100, and 1.6 percent up to 1,600. How the Histadrut reconciles this with the Labor Party's socialist views is anybody's guess. In 1986 the Histadrut defied the government's demand to raise its dues, so as to collect an additional $60 million and thereby reduce the government's subsidy. Journalist Abraham Tal:

> We live in an age when chutzpah in public life is an accepted norm... The Histadrut Sick Fund's income cannot cover the service it provides, so it demands governmental support of tens of millions of dollars annually. What the Histadrut's actually saying to the government is: please do not interfere in our affairs. Just sign the check.[13]

In 1977, the Histadrut employed about 1,000 dues collectors; all the other sick funds together managed this task with some 500. Social Security offered to collect dues for all the sick funds, employing only 40 additional workers – forty instead of 1,500! The proposal was rejected.[14] Uri Laor, a high-ranking Treasury official, informed a Knesset committee in 1976 that "it would be cheaper to pay the 1,000 employees of the Histadrut's Collection Bureau their salaries and keep them at home.... They let hundreds of thousands of members get away with reporting lower salaries than they actually earn....[15] They give kibbutzim, which are entitled to a 16 percent discount, additional cuts.[16] The losses they incur annually amount to $25 million, while their salaries are $10 million...." He recommended that Social Security collect dues. In the meantime, the Histadrut Sick Fund continues to run up mammoth deficits – $450 million in 1980-1985 alone.[17]

The Histadrut Sick Fund maintains about 1,000 neighborhood clinics in urban areas. They are expensive and unnecessary. In some of the other sick funds, doctors see their patients in their private offices – a convenient and economical arrangement. Patients are understandably sick of the red tape and time-wasting they endure in the clinics; all they want is to see the doctor as quickly as possible. To this, a prominent functionary once replied: "We want the worker to come to the Sick Fund, that magnificent institution of mutual assistance, not to the doctor's office. That way he'll realize what we're doing for him."[18]

In the neighborhood clinics, one ostensibly chooses between two or three doctors. In practice, however, most patients have no choice, because if one doctor is booked up, the clinic clerk automatically refers them to the other. In some clinics, patients take numbers at 8:00 a.m. and face a lengthy wait in line (Dr. Ram Yishai, chairman of the Medical Association, has alleged that there is a black market in clinic waiting-line numbers).[19] The clinics are open every day from 8:00 to noon, on Sundays and Tuesdays from 4:00 to 6:00 or 7:00 p.m., handle 'urgent' cases on Mondays and Thursdays, and are closed on Wednesdays and Fridays. Clinic physicians work a 28-hour week, including a morning tea break and other interruptions. The fact that most receiving hours are in the morning, of course, costs the patients heavily in lost days of work. For instance, the case of S.R.:

> For more than three years I've been taking two types of blood pressure pills that I get from the Histadrut Sick Fund, Jerusalem South branch. On March 26, 1986, I went to the clinic, and waited 65 minutes for the doctor. Then I waited three minutes in the clinic office (to buy the stamps I have to give the pharmacist in order to get my medicine) and 35 minutes in the clinic's pharmacy. There I was given only 25 pills out of 60 for the first drug, and they didn't have the other medicine at all. They told me to come back.
>
> About a week after I ran out of pills, I went back to the pharmacy. This time there was a substitute pharmacist, who was not sure how things were arranged. I stood 52 minutes in line. To my good fortune, they gave me the second drug this time. I was told to go back to the doctor for permission to buy the first drug in a private drugstore. The doctor had already gone home, so I had to come back the next day. This time I came early, so as to be among the first admitted. I waited only 20 minutes, and bought the pills in a private drug store. For this I paid NIS 41 ($27), and I wanted immediate reimbursement from the Sick Fund. But they told me to come back the next morning, because they have afternoon hours only on Sundays and Tuesdays.
>
> If this was an exceptional case, I would accept it understandingly. But I walk this Via Dolorosa each and every month, and I cannot take it anymore. In 1985, only on three occasions did I get all the drugs in one visit to the clinic. I used to find out at which of the Sick Fund's pharmacies I could get the medicine even if I had to cross town, but for the past several months they say I'm supposed to get the drugs at the pharmacy of my branch only.
>
> I sometimes get the impression that my blood pressure goes up every time I visit the Sick Fund. It's not clear to me why the Sick Fund of the Histadrut, which ostensibly represents Israel's workers, serves the sick only twice a week in the afternoon...

The newspaper columnist who presented S.R.'s case adds: "This is a real story. Anyone who needs medicine at the Sick Fund, anyone who needs a doctor at the Sick Fund, anyone who needs any service at this institution, can confirm that there's nothing exceptional about the harassment that S.R. of Jerusalem has had to face."[20]

The Israeli family physician (General Practitioner) directly handles only a small number of ailments, mostly banal. Children are examined by pediatricians. The general practitioner refers any case that exceeds his limited authority, however trivial, to a specialist. Thus of the scores of patients lined up for the doctor at 8:00 a.m., most conclude their affairs quickly and the clinic is almost always empty by 11:00. It is no exaggeration to say that on average the rooms in these clinics are used no more than three-four hours per day. Once referred by the G.P. to tests or specialists, patients apply to the clinic clerk. Such clerks are very powerful people. They determine when and where the tests will be carried out, and set appointments with the specialists. In some locales a patient may wait no more than a few days for this stage of care. Elsewhere, the "line" can last weeks or even longer. The difference has much to do with the clerk. He can move people's appointments up or down, send patients to this lab or that. That's real power. Needless to say, the more exalted a patient's status, the greater his chances are of getting to a specialist quickly. A phone call from the Secretary of the Labor Council or somesuch political operative is very helpful. There are other sick funds, to be sure. In two of them, Maccabee and Meuhedet, patients consult any doctor they desire, doctors receive patients on their own premises, appointment are frequently set by phone, and visits are scheduled by day and hour.

Specialist clinics exist in all parts of the country. Their hours and use of facilities are similar to those of the neighborhood clinics. Most of them have labs, X-ray facilities, and so on. Here the specialists frequently repeat the tests already administered by the family physician. When surgery is indicated, the patient is referred to a hospital. In other words, these clinics have surgeons, orthopedists, opthalmologists and ear-nose-and-throat specialists-- who do no surgery. After being told when to report to the hospital clinic – again, a matter liable to take quite a long time – the hospital specialists re-examine the patient and usually do the X-rays and tests all over again. The specialist clinics are fundamentally unnecessary. They are the Sick Fund's way of throwing out money in order to show their clients that their medical system is complete. Most hospital clinics work only in the mornings; only few stay open until two or three in the afternoon. Because every region of the country now has its own central hospital, the logical step would be to have the hospital clinics (which are no more than 20 minutes away from 90 percent of the population) co-opt the clinic specialists in a second shift. This would eliminate the redundancy of tests, unnecessary appointments, and non-utilization of resources. It would not only save a great deal of money, but would substantially improve service. Professor Dan Michaeli, while serving as Director-General of the Ministry of Health, explained why the reform has never been introduced:

> The Histadrut Sick Fund and the other funds consider the specialist clinics an institution that adds prestige. This prestige costs the fund member and the tax-payer lots of money... The Sick Fund has a conspicuously political motive in keeping the regional clinics going. In Haifa, where there are three hospitals – only one belonging to the Histadrut Sick Fund – the Sick Fund has a regional clinic to which all patients in Northern Israel are referred. Its doctors are the ones who decide to which hospital to refer them. It seems that the doctors of this regional clinic refer patients whose care is considered prestigious to the Histadrut hospital... The two government hospitals in Haifa depend on the Sick Fund for their supply of patients, and this makes the Sick Fund very powerful.[21]

In short, these clinics are an obstacle to quality medical care. They often interfere with the system's sound performance, refer patients to hospitals on the basis of extraneous considerations and make minimal use of their own rooms and resources. Many of these clinics are situated in expensive downtown locations. Simple medical logic requires that the clinics be sold off and integrated into the regional hospitals. Here, however, as in other areas, political requisites call the shots.

The most serious problem of the medical services is hospitalization. Although there are enough beds to meet needs – with an oversupply of about 1000, according to Professor Michaeli – almost all the hospitals are seriously overcrowded,[22] with beds in the corridors, doctors' offices, and even bathrooms. The wait for hospitalization is long, and can reach or exceed a year for surgery. Emergency cases are handled well, even if they may have to wait many hours. Any Israeli hospital provides care of a quality considered conventional in good European and American hospitals. Until this care is delivered, however, patients are frequently made to walk the Via Dolorosa.

The case of Elazar Goldberg is typical:

> Elazar Golberg, 60, a temporary employee in a canned-foods plant, needed some orthopedic surgery. After waiting about a year, the operation was scheduled for last September. A few days before his appointment he was notified that he would need to undergo a series of pre-surgical tests. Mr. Goldberg, an obedient citizen and patient, did as told. On the appointed day at 8:00 on the button, he reported to the hospital. After waiting about an hour, a clerk said: "Wait; they'll call you." He waited. He was summoned to the doctor about two hours later. After a few brief questions, the doctor reached the conclusion that his patient should have kidney X-rays and urological tests before surgery. "What about my appointment for surgery?" asked Goldberg. "First do the tests. Then come back for a new appointment."
>
> Racing to and fro for a month, Goldberg succeeded in taking the tests and even setting up a new appointment for his

operation: February. When he received his summons for surgery, he found clipped to it a demand that he repeat the original pre-surgery tests a week before the operation. "But I already did the tests," he told the clerk. Her answer: "That was in September. Things might change by February."

Elazar Goldberg went through the entire process again, and reported to the hospital on the appointed day at 8:00 on the button. This time the clerk did not keep him waiting long. Sorry, she said: the queue for surgery was too long and they could not take him. "Why didn't you tell my by phone?" the patient asked. The clerk shrugged her shoulders and said that she would send him a new appointment for some time in April. "Will I have to do the test over?" "No, no," the clerk snapped, already motioning to the next in line.

On the appointed day in April, Goldberg reported as usual at 8:00 on the button. At 11:00 his wife called the department where her husband was to be hospitalized, but only "for administrative purposes."

Mrs. Goldberg did not understand. "Look," the nurse explained. "We signed him up as if he is hospitalized, but because we don't have enough doctors, we sent him home. Tell him just to wait patiently until we call him."

Goldberg's wife was close to despair. Three times her husband had informed his boss that he was going in for surgery. Three times he had come home without a suture to show for it. His boss didn't believe him anymore, and this temporary employee had lost three days of work. And he still had no way of knowing when he would be operated on. In her anguish, Mrs. Goldberg told the tale of woe to one of her husband's friends. Lo and behold, this friend had "pull" at the hospital. Using it, he straightened the matter out within two weeks. Goldberg underwent his operation and is now recuperating.

Add it up. Things like this happen not to one patient per year, nor a few dozen, nor hundreds, but to many thousands.[23] For them, however, the end of the story has two variations. Either one has "pull," as in Goldberg's case, or one goes to the doctor's home (as one can with many doctors, if not all), pays cash, and thereby circumvents the queue.

Why this outrageous inefficiency, which so demoralizes the public and wastes its resources? It's a combination of the centralized administration of the Ministry of Health and Sick Fund and political power struggles. One reason for the overcrowding in hospitals is a shortage of beds for the chronically ill. It is much cheaper to hospitalize such patients in institutions specializing in their care than in general hospitals. Israel has lived with this problem for thirty years or more. During that period, general beds have been added but the shortage of beds for the chronically ill remains unresolved. So they clog up the expensive general beds.

A second factor is the use of X-ray facilities, labs, operating theaters, and other ancillary services on one short shift only. Most such facilities operate six or seven hours a day, and the operating rooms of several hospitals are utilized only 40 percent of this short shift.[24] As a result, hospitalized patients sometimes wait more than a week for X-rays or surgery, taking up beds in the meantime. Because some surgery departments are given access to an operating table only once or twice a week, patients pile up in lengthy queues. The idea of putting these services on a second shift has surfaced in media reports for two decades. In 1971 there was talk of "running hospital ancillary clinics on two shifts – and alleviating the hardships of hospitalization." In 1975 reports had it that "the Health Ministry is studying the possibility of putting the X-ray department and various labs on two or more shifts, so as to boost the hospitals' output and reduce hospitalization days; all the experiments in this regard came to nought because of X-ray technicians' resistance." In 1982: "The Health Ministry views with favor the activation in the afternoon of operating theaters, X-ray facilities, and labs." In 1983: "The Health Ministry is considering the possibility of running operating rooms and X-ray facilities on a second shift." Reports in 1984 spoke of "the second-shift barrier."[25]

Hospitals are paid by hospitalization-days. Thus they are given a powerful incentive to prolong the hospitalization of patients doing as little as possible every day. The great expenses of hospitals derive not from providing hotel service but from medical procedures such as X-rays, surgery and tests. Hence it is in the hospitals' interest to overbook and underperform.

An additional problem is the salary issue. Israel's socialist system decrees that all doctors at a given rank receive the same salary, regardless of their expertise or output. An internationally renowned heart surgeon or similar specialist is paid the same as a dermatologist or an internist. A doctor who puts in long hours earns no more than one who does little, spends few hours in the hospital, and is frequently absent. A doctor in a large central hospital once said: "Before the great strike, the doctors in my department saw 80 patients per clinic day. Now we don't want to see more than 30."

The practice of scrimping on doctors' pay has consequences more ominous than those described thus far. Increasing numbers of department directors are falling for the temptation to sell beds. This is a most enticing prospect, with restless patients on the one hand and low pay on the other. At first only a few department directors engaged in this. Over time, the practice has spread. Today, many departments are all but inaccessible unless one first visits the director at home or offers a hefty bribe, especially for surgery. Health authorities turn a blind eye to the phenomenon. It's an easy way of reducing doctors' pressure for wage hikes.

Health service officials are aware that private patients are given preferential treatment. Things have reached such a state that the director of one of Israel's large hospitals recently remarked that no industry is as corrupt as medicine. The Minister of Health said: "Black-market medicine is spreading through the hospitals."[26] "The doctors are getting rich at the workers' expense," according to Histadrut Secretary-General Yisrael Kessar. "We'll take legal action against doctors who use Sick Fund hospitals for private business."[27] It fact, no action, legal or otherwise, has been taken against corrupt doctors, even though the hospital administrators undoubtedly know who many of them are and could catch them in the act without difficulty.

Meanwhile, there have been repeated strikes by nurses, administrative workers, X-ray technicians, ancillary service employees, and, of course, the doctors. With every such strike, service is reduced to the Sabbath format, queues become longer, and treatments are postponed. Worst of all was the four-month doctors strike in 1983, which caused inestimable suffering and ended only after the doctors embarked on another strike – a hunger strike. The nurses strike of 1986, likewise caused untold suffering to innocent patients. Late 1987 and the first half of 1988 were marked by serious labor disputes in the health services, including constant strikes and faulty, incomplete service for months on end. (Sometimes care is postponed or inadequate due to technical malfunction; for example when patients awaiting eye surgery at the Histadrut's Beilinson hospital were compelled to wait two weeks due to a shortage of thread for sutures.[28] Could this conceivably happen in a private hospital that had to show a profit?)

Even when striking – let us state to their credit – the doctors and nurses behaved responsibly, handling all urgent cases as warranted and averting disasters. But the lengthy queues and sundry delays in care have unquestionably taken a toll on the public's health.

When the government slashed the health budget in 1985, many hospitals tottered on the verge of functional collapse. A new record for dehumanization was set when the Health Ministry held up its negligible support payments for those among the chronically-ill elderly who were hospitalized in private institutions for long-term care. In a heart-wrenching scene, these hospitals picked up their patients bodily and deposited them at entrances of government hospital emergency rooms. Even though they were trucked back the next day after the Minister promised to tender payment, it was an episode that shocked Israeli society. The political establishment, with its slogans about equality, human dignity, and progressive society, had shown its true face. Even as it came up with tremendous sums for unnecessary cosmetic medical care abroad for politicians and bureaucrats, it dumped the indigent elderly ill into the street. It was not only a moment of disgrace for a government in which a majority of ministers view themselves as socialists; it was the direct result of socialism as practiced in Israel.

Is it any wonder that Israel's politicians and senior bureaucrats seek to exempt themselves – and their families – from Israeli health care? "Equal medicine" is well and good, but not for them! This is not because they have to wait in line or be hospitalized in a crowded ward; a quick phone call to the hospital director would straighten that out right away. But that isn't enough. A long list of politicians and bureaucrats (and their families) enjoy private care, in Israel or abroad, and hand the bill to the government. At first, this perk was offered only to cabinet ministers and Supreme Court justices. Slowly, however, the Knesset added others to the list. Now this is one of the many fringe benefits accruing to ministers, judges, Moslem qadis, rabbis, Knesset members, and ministry directors – thousands of people in all.

Must it be this way?

Of course not. Israel could save a fortune and improve service significantly by implementing some simple overnight administrative modifications:

A. Let the Social Security Administration collect health care premiums. This alone would trim more than 1,000 workers from the public payroll, and would result in realistic collection that would augment revenues by hundreds of millions of dollars. It would enable the government to halt its regular subsidy of active medical services, and would allow the Health Ministry to engage in preventive medicine and supervision.

B. Place the government and Sick Fund hospitals under one administrative authority.

C. Run the hospitals' medical services on two shifts.
D. Let the specialists operate their clinics and ancillary facilities in their homes or in the hospital clinics on a second-shift basis. Thus the system could sell off its unnecessary buildings and instrumentation.
E. Pay hospitals for what they do, not for how long they hold onto patients.
F. Let people choose their family physicians, and pay them by the number of families listed with them. At the same time, close down the neighborhood clinics and let the doctors receive their patients on their own premises.

All these are initial, simple steps. They require no additional investment and only a change in methodology: the Histadrut would have to stop using its Sick Fund as a means of exploiting the medical services. Under the existing regime, however, even this is out of the question. In the long run, Israelis have to give up the idea that the Sick Fund should not only insure against illness but provide medical service by itself. Provision should be made for establishing new sick funds, competing with each other on the open marketplace. At present, the system is coercive: the Histadrut Sick Fund, ten times larger than all the others, is capable of providing better service, and many of its members belong to it as the result of de facto coercion. The hospitals should be either private or public-independent, and should have to compete. Their directors should be free to hire whomever they want (today, department directors are appointed by committees on which the hospitals are not represented!), pay them as their value and output warrant, and fire them if they so desire. Hospitals should be paid not by the patient but by the Sick Funds. Under these conditions, Israelis would get the best medical care the country can provide – and that's a lot. Medical service would be significantly less expensive than it is today, and would operate efficiently and without malfunctions – as it does in countries where these methods are practiced.

Instead of watching its doctors emigrate on a large scale, Israel could take in many thousands of patients from abroad. They know of the reputation and quality of Israeli medicine, and would want to come to Israel for care if the conditions permitted this. "Therapeutic tourism" could become a major export industry securing the jobs of thousands of health care employees, including hundreds of doctors, and bringing in more foreign currency than many other export activities.

As in many other fields, the problem in Israeli medicine is not lack of possibilities or ability. The problem is a socialist regime, politicization, power struggles, anachronistic methods, and a fossilized political establishment.

In 1921, David Ben-Gurion suggested the establishment of a "Workers Corporation" (Hevrat Ha-ovdim). It would create an economy shared by all workers and would permit public supervision by the Histadrut. The aims of the Workers' Corporation were the planning, administration and, organization of the labor force, production and marketing, Histadrut ownership of products and means of production, concentration of employment and jobs in Histadrut hands, centralized supply, and equalization of standard of living.[29] In 1923 the Histadrut convention authorized the establishment of the Workers' Corporation. The "Central Consumer Cooperative," the "United Office for Public Works" (later the notorious Solel Boneh construction company), and the Workers' Bank (Bank Hapoalim) were brought under the auspices of the new corporation.

The Workers' Corporation is a holding company with two main branches. One comprises directly-owned enterprises (the industrial concern Koor, the construction companies and the financial institutions); the other consists of "voluntary" affiliates, including the farm settlements and the consumer and production cooperatives. The term "voluntary" is misleading. The agricultural settlements are firmly tied to the Histadrut and its institutions through Nir Ltd. and the powerful agricultural establishment. The settlements were founded and are supported with national capital; the cooperatives as well. The bus companies, for example, totally depend on the Histadrut for their monopoly, subsidies, and fat salaries.

The branch under direct Histadrut ownership was established with national capital placed at the Histadrut's disposal. It received billions of dollars in loans, which the banks granted knowing that the government would never let the "public sector" economy collapse. The Workers' Corporation presides over a vast economic empire which produces about 22 percent of GNP. Koor alone comprises scores of companies including monopolies and monopsonies (cement, oil production and exploration, steel), electronics and armament industries, and many others. As of 1987, they employed 35,000 workers. Until its collapse in the early 1980s, one Histadrut construction company alone (Solel Boneh) employed 20,000 people. The Workers' Corporation controls Arkia Airlines, which dominates domestic air transport. It holds a share in Zim and thus controls Israel's merchant marine. It owns the country's largest insurance company (1,000 employees), a marketing company that supplies the nation's farmers, a chain of department stores, and various kibbutz industries that employ more than 13,000 workers. It controls or has a share in all three fuel companies. It controls a citrus orchard maintenance contractor with about 10,000 employees. It owns 46 percent of the mammoth Klal conglomerate. It owns a citrus marketing company that boasts a 45-percent market share. It has 32 packing plants. Its financial arms are Bank Hapoalim (10,000 employees) and Ampal, which raises money in America. The 22 percent of GNP controlled by the "labor economy" embraces about 75 percent of all agricultural produce, almost 100 percent of public transportation, 33 percent of insurance, and 25 percent of industrial output.[30]

Most of the investment for Workers' Corporation enterprises came from the State Treasury. The government provided heavily subsidized loans, directly or indirectly (such as guarantees to foreign investors). One of the great windfalls was when the Histadrut received approval to use pension funds for its own purposes – although the funds are ordinarily obliged by law to keep close to 90 percent of their assets in government bonds. The Histadrut's pension funds were permitted to keep only 50 percent in government bonds; the rest was channelled to the Workers' Corporation via the Worker's Bank. Then the government insured these funds against inflation! This fundamentally undemocratic waiver of law allowed the Workers' Corporation to amass billions of dollars to finance new enterprises and buy up others. Only in 1980 was the arrangement cancelled. Another bonus given to Histadrut institutions, including the Sick Fund and the Workers' Corporation, was the right to forward withholding tax after 60 days, and not after 15 days as the law of the land stipulates. This gave Histadrut enterprises large amounts of free money for 45 days. This cozy arrangement was not cancelled until 1984.

Two goals motivated Histadrut leaders before Israel was established and immediately thereafter: a) establishing enterprises which, they believed, were vital for the State, and b) making sure that these enterprises would be under the Histadrut umbrella and Labor Party control. Then as now, the need to show a profit was not one of the tenets of Israel's largest economic empire.

In 1986, the Histadrut Secretary-General wrote that "The Workers' Corporation is the economic arm of the Histadrut. Its aim is to provide jobs and raise the workers' standard of living."[31] Not a word about profit! The Secretary-General of the Workers' Corporation said: "[We are] an economic organization with a socio-national orientation, from which all our actions derive. This implies that our considerations are not always purely economic, but are motivated by our political credo."[32] The truth is that, "providing jobs" in economically unsound enterprises is bad for the national economy and for the workers. It inevitably result in low wages and a need for permanent Treasury support, bringing about high taxes and continuous begging overseas. Both of these combine to prevent the creation of profitable jobs.

The Workers' Corporation is the only economic empire in the non-communist world ruled by a political party. "In Labor Party thinking, the Workers' Corporation is a major achievement, a power base for the Party and the Histadrut alike," wrote Razi Guterman in *Ma'ariv*. "The Likud faction in the Histadrut has accused Labor of using the Workers' Corporation as if it were its private property, doling out honorary positions to its own people and finding jobs for every party functionary in need of an office, a car, and a secretary."[33] In 1976, the Minister of Industry and Trade (a Labor man) confirmed that "The government will continue its massive support of the Workers' Corporation."[34] Nehemia Stroessler, business editor of *Haaretz*:[35]

> Until 1977 the Histadrut had a big daddy in the Treasury. Pinhas Sapir was the prototype; he was their patron. Everyone in the Workers' Corporation understood that for survival one has to pray in his direction every day... In 1977 the tables were turned. No longer was there a patron saint at the Treasury. The shock was great and jolted Labor into doing its utmost to attract the lost electorate – all those who are paid by the Workers' Corporation but, for some reason, voted Likud. In 1977 the party leaders ordered the director of the Histadrut's construction company (Solel Boneh) to become a vote-getter. He was not to fire workers under any circumstances. He was to raise their salaries and capitulate to all the union's demands. The unions took advantage of the new situation and demanded not only salary raises but amenities like weekends in Eilat, department-store gift certificates, and more. In those years the slogan was, 'what else should the workers be given to make them understand for whom it pays to cast their vote on election day?'... Profit? Forget it.

An investigation undertaken for Solel Boneh found that in 1984/85 the company had outbid its competitors by presenting building estimates below cost. Thus they ran up debts of about half a billion dollars, which were partly covered by the Labor-Likud "national unity" government.[36]

"Steel City" was built in the 1950s to manufacture structural steel. It was a heavy burden on the economy from the very beginning. It is virtually a monopoly, protected by prohibitively high import duties. Consequently, the price of steel in Israel is some 40 percent above the world market. The Tel Aviv Chamber of Commerce claims that the government is subsidizing Steel City to the tune of $26 million yearly, or about $43,000 for each of the plant's 600 workers. In 1985, the Ministry of Industry and Trade sought to issue import licenses for a small quantity of steel, but was challenged by the Knesset Finance Committee:[37] "If steel must be imported, let Steel City do it!" In 1981, the company showed a deficit on production, which it partially covered by importing steel and selling it at windfall profits. Despite Steel City's heavy losses, huge subsidies, and obsolete equipment the CEO of its parent company (Koor) has declared that he "will do everything to prevent the establishment of a new steel factory,"[38] which just might produce at a profit.

The actual magnitude of the Workers' Corporation's losses is difficult to calculate. Koor, its industrial conglomerate, is defined as a private company and is therefore under no obligation to publish its balance sheets. Furthermore, most of the subsidies it receives are concealed: price control, high duties on competitive imports, cheap loans, subsidies on water, fuel, transportation, and so on. Despite all this assistance, Koor admitted to a loss of $250 million and debts of close to $2 billion in 1987.

As for the Histadrut's construction company, *Ha'aretz* has this to say:

> Solel Boneh is the most bloated building company in Israel. It has so many levels of administration that even Prof. Parkinson would be astonished: branches, divisions, departments, districts, subsidiaries and sub-subsidiaries. Each has its own offices, directors, accountants, secretaries, and so on. A typical example

is one of its relatively successful subsidiaries. When called to shorten a hot water pipe in an apartment, four workers in two vehicles appeared, accompanied by a foreman. They toiled all day to shorten the pipe, a task any trained worker could have accomplished within an hour. No reasonable price can possibly cover the expenses of five workers and two cars during a whole day! At Solel Boneh, they said: "That's how things are done in the public economy.[39]

As for the Histadrut company that grows, harvests, packs and markets 45 percent of Israel's citrus fruits, its own internal comptroller disclosed the realities in his report for 1984-86: inefficiency, negligence, uncollected debts, excessive payments to suppliers, amateurish management, exaggerated or superfluous fees to consultants, and more. And the result? "Economy measures" forced the company to lay off its comptroller.[40] The publication of the report is in itself very unusual, since most comptrollers know on which side their bread is buttered.

As can happen only in a political body, the Board of the Workers' Corporation gradually expanded, reaching 80 members by 1983. Such a large group is rarely capable of administering anything. This led to a vacuum, which was filled by "gangs," in the words of a former director-general of the Workers' Bank, who was driven to suicide because of internal power struggles. General Zamir, former Chairman of the Board with Solel Boneh, charged that, "The Workers' Corporation method is to grab a power base... The Corporation is actually managed by two or three people who behave as if it were their private property."[41]

The Workers' Corporation owes the banks enormous sums, estimated at $7-8 billion, most of it to Bank Hapoalim. Such a debt endangers the bank's existence.[42] Koor owes $2 billion. Solel Boneh and the Sick Fund owe some $500 million each, and the agricultural settlements another $3 billion or so. And what about all the others?

The Workers' Corporation proves that an economic empire in the hands of a political party can only be inefficient and in constant need of government bailouts. No data has ever been published on how much the Workers' Corporation costs the government and the Israeli economy. It surely runs into many billions of dollars. The Workers' Corporation is based on dangerous, anti-democratic tenets. Its aim is to create a hegemony of one political party with the help of money and preferential treatment by the government. This concept is responsible for putting party interests above rentability and payment of debts. The Secretary-General of the Workers' Corporation has said that "The concern's actions are part of our socio-political views." One might legitimately ask how a company committed to "socialism" can dole out exceedingly high salaries and hundreds of thousands of dollars in severance pay plus fat bonuses to managers, while blue-collar workers take home just a few hundred dollars each month.[43] This is certainly a far cry from BenGurion's dream of a "cooperative economic enterprise of all workers." What real benefits do simple Histadrut members derive from the existence of the Workers' Corporation? It belongs to the workers just as much as the "dictatorship of the proletariat" belongs to the proletariat.

CHAPTER FIVE

THE INFRASTRUCTURE

When Israel came into being, its government controlled 93 percent of the country's land, including Jewish National Fund lands. Three percent was privately owned by Jews, and 4 percent was owned by Arabs, mostly in villages.[1] The government knew very clearly what it wanted with its land policy, a policy pursued -- in theory, but not in practice – by all Israeli governments to this day: scattering the population all over the country, mainly by establishing "development towns"; preventing urban sprawl on agricultural land, especially on the coastal plain; and preventing illegal takeover of land. Professor Elisha Efrat, who spent years in comprehensive planning with the Ministry of the Interior, writes: "Few places on earth enjoyed such a rare combination of optimal conditions for successful planning: a new, almost empty country, a pliable population, and the availability of skilled people – architects, engineers, entrepreneurs. They were handed a golden opportunity to plan and develop a state on the basis of modern concepts."[2] To make matters even easier, almost all the land was de facto governmental. To carry out government policy, the Israel Lands Administration (ILA) was established and the lands were transferred to it. That is where they remain to this day. Sadly, not one of the objectives listed above has been attained. Population dispersion is a dead letter: about 80 percent of Israel's Jews live on the coastal plain, including about 50 percent in a narrow segment of this strip of land in and around Tel Aviv, about 35 miles long and 12 miles wide. Some of the development towns are literally falling apart. Coastal plain farmland is increasingly giving way to urban neighborhoods. Finally, thousands of acres have been taken over by Arabs in the Galilee and the Negev, and by Jews in the cities.[3]

Government land policy, combined with the deliberate creation of a private transportation and infrastructure shortage (especially with respect to highways worthy of the name) first drove the population dispersion effort into a cul de sac and finally brought it to a halt. About twenty "development towns" were founded and populated by groups of impoverished immigrants. The quality of housing and public services was poor from the very outset, as the British expert Netanel Litchfield found when he surveyed the situation on behalf of the Ministry of Housing.[4] To move from one of these towns to central Israel and retain the right to obtain an apartment, one needed a "permission slip" from the authorities. People with university educations, and those with connections, obviously had no trouble procuring it. Thus a negative selection process ensued: the people remaining behind were educationally and vocationally inferior to those in central Israel. Almost no highways to the boondocks were built, and many of the towns remained many hours' travel time from the center of the country. This was true even though with modern means of transportation, nearly all of them would be about one hour or less from Haifa or Tel Aviv. Few economic enterprises were established, and the ones that were created used unskilled labor. That kept salaries low. Because people in central Israel had more pull than those in the development towns, and because enterprises went where the government told them to go, the important enterprises went up in the center. Furthermore, only one or two of the towns reached a take-off point in terms of population size. Finally, they were dispersed in such a way as to reflect their founders' intent to put the residents to work as wage laborers in the fields of the surrounding kibbutzim.

In fact, they rather resemble the old American "company towns," except that here the Ministry of Housing is the sole builder, determining the type and number of apartments, the number of schools, shops (which could only be rented, never purchased), and more. For years, no private construction was allowed in most of the towns. There was a time when various benefits were offered to those who had been "transferred" to those towns, and to professionals required by schools, clinics, and so on. As time passed, private construction of the "Build-Your-Own-Home" variety was permitted, too. What this meant was that the ILA, in conjunction with the Ministry of Housing, placed a small number of plots (after development by the Ministry) on the market at prices that were exorbitant if not altogether absurd. On one occasion they floated 1,000 plots in Arad; they were snapped up. The ILA did not repeat this "mistake." Ever since, plots have been doled out in portions of only a few dozen. To move to a development town today, you need a license. In 1981, 250 families that applied to settle in Kiryat Shmona were turned away because they could not demonstrate that they possessed any local source of livelihood.[5] The town reportedly had 1,000 empty apartments at the time.[6]

In the free world, the process of setting up a city far from population centers begins with entrepreneurs building industrial plants, to which workers are attracted. In Israel they went about it the opposite way: they put up tenements and promised that the factories would follow. Thus these towns were doomed to failure from the outset. Distance from the center of the country, exorbitantly expensive cars, bad roads, a high percentage of vocationally and educationally backward population groups, few jobs, low-quality housing and services – these, taken together, were the downfall of the development towns. Tax breaks did not help; all they did was induce people to establish their domicile in a development town without really living there. Neither did the other sundry benefits help. Most of the development towns – excluding Arad and Carmiel, to which veteran Israelis, not immigrants, were directed – are deteriorating. Thousands of apartments stand empty, and young adults reluctantly head for greener pastures. In one of these towns that used to be a success, Dimona, many apartments in the older neighborhoods have been sealed with concrete blocks. Neglect is rife in Yeroham, and Mitzpe Ramon stagnates with its empty apartments, locked shops, and chronic out-migration.[7] All of these testify to yet another futile attempt by the government bureaucracy to implement a plan while neither ensuring the necessary conditions nor considering the population's well-being. Failure was inevitable. Another reason for the failure to disperse the population is the policy of refusing to allocate land for cheap construction in distant areas. Arie Shahar, Managing Director of the Dead Sea Works, has pointedly asked why the State should not give Beersheba residents a quarter-acre per family on which to build their homes.[8] Instead, the ILA presents one obstacle after another, red tape, footdragging, repeated applications for this permit and that, and, of course, the jewel in the crown: an exorbitant price. The same is true in the Galilee. In the early 1970s, numerous residents of Haifa, Acre, Nahariya, and other places within convenient commuting distance from the Galilee asked the ILA for land in the Galilee mountains – an area that the authorities constantly claim is in need of Jewish settlers. There, amidst rustic scenery and a quality of life unavailable in the development towns, they would build their homes. Thousands applied – yet all were turned away. Groups of university-trained Israelis employed in the armaments industries and elsewhere fought for years for the right to live in the Gaililee, but lost. Ultimately, the government established forty "look-out settlements," semi-settlements starting out with ten or twenty families, built with mammoth government investment and constant support. Most of them have grown slowly in the intervening years, meaning that several hundred families have been settled by grace of the government. Had a quality highway been built and land given to anyone who wanted to build on it, thousands of families would have moved to the Galilee. It is hard to escape the conclusion that Israel's governments – Labor,

Likud, and both together – are simply not interested in settling people who apply independently, outside the framework of the established, party-controlled settlement movements. The government prefers to forego Jewish settlement in the country's strategic border regions, and waste large amounts of money on top of that, rather than yield political control of settlement.

Land policy is also one of the reasons that industrial enterprises are established in çentral Israel and not in border areas. In countries where the market sets land prices, firms that need large amounts of land choose sites far from the centers, where land is expensive. Not in Israel. Since the Land Administration allocates cheap industrial land in the center of the country, companies have no incentive to head for the boondocks, where transportation is poor and essential services inferior. By applying the necessary kind of pressure, even the "special development area" grant can be obtained in central Israel.

If Israel had a land policy like those practiced in free countries – where land is bought and sold on the basis of its real value - and the government would concurrently build infrastructures and adopt a Western price policy on automobiles, the population might very well disperse itself in the best way. Any attempt to accomplish this by shunting defined population groups hither and yon in a manner reflecting Iron Curtain thinking, backed by an addle-headed land policy, had to fail, and in fact has failed.

The ILA may have failed to disperse the population, keep the coastal plain farms down on the farm, and prevent land theft, but in one thing it has succeeded: land prices have skyrocketed beyond all reason. In 1982, average land prices in Jerusalem fluctuated between $8,000 and $25,000 per room, depending on the neighborhood. A one-eighth-acre plot (including development) in Givat Shaul went for $150,000. In Tel Aviv, again depending on the area, you might pay between $5,000 and

$20,000 per room for land. In the suburbs of Tel Aviv, people paid between $50,000 and $150,000 for an eighth of an acre.[9]

Land prices in the cities themselves are the result of the Administration's failure to allocate land for high-quality private construction. The price of privately owned land in northern Tel Aviv and desirable neighborhoods of Jerusalem accounts for 33 or even 40 percent of apartment cost (taxation claims 50 percent of construction cost). Consider the effect these prices have on prospective immigrants – and prospective emigrants. Moreover, the process is not confined to privately owned land. The parcels around Tel Aviv and Jerusalem are ILA-owned. In the early 1980s, believe it or not, the ILA (via Arim Town Planning, Ltd.) sold a quarter acre or one-third acre plot in Mevasseret Jerusalem – 7 miles out of town – for $60,000-$80,000. The ILA also restricts supply – a few dozen plots at the most – to make sure prices do not drop.

This also happens in places far from central Israel. In Omer, a classy neighborhood built on a patch of wasteland east of Beersheba, the ILA was charging $25 per square meter in November, 1988. That's $12,000 for an eighth of an acre, undeveloped. They were charging roughly the same in Meitar, a new settlement in the wilderness about 12 miles northeast of Beersheba. The actual price paid in Meitar was negotiated between a committee of Meitar residents, the Jewish National Fund, and the Minister of Agriculture. (At the very same time, every Bedouin family who so desired could buy a quarter-acre in the town of Rahat, also not far from Beersheba, for $150.[10]) Another example is Carmiel, a new city established with the express intention of boosting the Galilee's Jewish population. Because prospective residents wanted to build unattached houses, the ILA set a price of $11,000 per plot (including development).[11]

In short, land in Israel has no particular price; it depends on who is paying. A tenant being served by the Ministry of Housing pays one price; contractors building for the private market pay a much higher price for the same land. Land for industry has a price, but an "Approved Enterprise" gets it for less. In 1982-83, for example, a quarter-acre in the development town of Sderot went for about $2,800 for ordinary industry and $1,000 for an Approved Enterprise.[12] According to the Attorney-General, "The Israel Lands Administration regularly allocates state lands to public institutions under special conditions and, at times, at symbolic prices not reflecting the land's value."[13] A Hassidic rebbe was once given 1.5 acres in downtown Jerusalem, worth $1.5 million, for a leasing fee of only 2 percent instead of the conventional 91 percent. When the head of the ILA was asked about this, he "explained" that "Sixty other public institutions got cheap land [too]. And the Mayor of Jerusalem and the Minister of Agriculture recommended it."[14] General Meir Zorea, who headed the Authority during the mid-1970s, said that the ILA had to give out land at preferential terms because various government ministries ordered it to do so. "The pressure and permission slip method is still the way that works." *Ha'aretz* reports. "The Minister of Finance can exempt investors from public bidding at his discretion. The Minister of Industry and Trade can do the same for industrialists, and the Minister of Tourism for hoteliers."[15]

The problem is not only the price but the allocation or non-allocation of land. In other words, those without the necessary connections inside government ministries cannot obtain land in sought-after locales. The ILA has an "express lane" to speed up the process of approving deals for contractors who have been specially "recommended" by the Ministry of Housing.[16] The practice in allocating land to contractors for construction is that the government assessor appraises the land and forwards his appraisal to the committee that sets the price – taking into account, of course, who the contractor is and what he intends to build. The local authorities have a procedure by which the ILA allocates land on preferential terms per recommendation of – the local authorities.[17] The land situation follows the usual pattern. The politicians decide who gets it, in what location, and at what price. Discrimination rules the roost: preferential treatment of the well-connected, the well-positioned, and the well-affiliated. The land belongs to the bureaucrats, and they do with it as they please. The idea that the land belongs to the state, meaning that all citizens have equal rights to it, has not yet dawned upon them.

Even when citizens are given a crack at the land, some are not eligible. You might be eligible – depending on the clerks who implement the guidelines. Here are the cumbersome restrictions applying to the ILA's 1981 sale of forty plots in Mevasseret Jerusalem:[18]

> The right to register is limited to families resident in Israel. Families resident abroad who have opened immigration files and will settle in Israel are also permitted to sign up, if the Jewish Agency Immigration Department confirms their immigration intentions in writing. For the purposes of this program, a "family" is a "family unit," including: a) a married couple without children; b) a married couple with children; c) a couple that has opened a marriage file with the Rabbinate (if the Rabbinate confirms this in writing); d) a divorcee, widow, or widower up to age 35, who has at least once child under the age of 18 and who is regularly living with him/her (in this case, only one spouse will be entitled to register); e) a divorcee, widow, or widower over the age of 35; such a person interested in registering should present him/herself in the aforementioned registration office with all requisite registration documents.
>
> Owners of plots zoned for owner construction, including farms, owners of freely standing one-story homes, or those who built within the framework of a program of this type in Israel, or who have submitted winning tenders in response to ILA solicitations for owner-construction plots, for themselves and their families, and did not return the plots to the ILA, are not eligible for this program.

In sum: singles may not register. Divorcees, widows, and widowers need special dispensation if they are over age 35. One applicant couple was turned down because his wife's parents owned a small farm in one of the country's cooperative villages. After all, the bureaucrats reasoned, it could become theirs in another twenty or thirty years – and owning a second residence would be a sin according to socialist dogma. The ILA devised another bit of petty harassment for people who own a flat or house built on ILA land. If such a person wants to sell his dwelling, he has to pay a "consent fee." Consent fees were computed at three mil of the value of the land from the day it was leased until the day it is transferred.[19] Some people, however, do not have to pay. The ILA has put out a fact sheet with 18 categories of persons eligible for discounts. It doesn't tell you how large the discounts are. It is interesting to note that almost every line requires written proof from someone else, and that many items leave room for bargaining. It's a virtual invitation for influence-peddling and bribery:

Guide to the Payment of Consent Fees

For the attention of the applicant (abstract of decisions by the ILA Board on March 6, 1967, arranged for the applicant's convenience)

1. The obligation to pay the consent fee applies to the party transferring rights, irrespective of the terms of the agreement between the latter and the party acquiring the rights.
2. The party transferring the rights, and this party alone, is entitled to a discount on consent fees if he belongs to one of the following categories:
   a) Social cases.
   b) Workers transferred to development areas or rural settlements.
   c) Persons disabled in Israel's defense or in the war against the Nazis.
   d) Persons who have lost a child or a spouse in defense of the country.

e) Children up to age 18 who have lost a parent in defense of the country.
f) Parents transferring their rights to their offspring, or vice versa.
g) Zionist functionaries and Prisoners of Zion within ten years of having settled in the country.
h) Lessors who exchange their dwelling for the dwelling in question with no capital gain.
i) Lessors who relocate to a larger flat because their family has grown during the period of their residence in the flat being transferred, provided that the sum received for the flat does not exceed that required for purchase of the new flat.
j) Lessors who adopt children.
k) Unwell lessors, or lessors with unwell family members, when an authorized medical document confirms that the transfer is essential.
l) Lessors entering an old-age home or making other old-age arrangements, provided that the sum received for the sale serves as the lessor's major source of income in the future.
m) Minors up to age 18, provided that the sum received is earmarked for their support and education.
n) Soldiers and police personnel who must move because of service demands.
o) Lessors recognized as Heroes of Israel.
p) Lessors relocating to new workplaces and not significantly improving their housing conditions, provided that the sum received for their leasing rights does not significantly exceed 20 percent of the sum paid for the new dwelling, up to a ceiling of IL (Israeli Pounds) 7,000.
q) Lessors moving to a new dwelling because of a need to live close to work, i.e., when the move is made to save money and travel expenses, provided that the lessor does not significantly improve his housing conditions, and provided that the sum received for his leasing rights does not significantly exceed 20 percent of the sum paid for the new dwelling, up to a ceiling of IL 7,000.

After the National Water Carrier was completed and water from the Sea of Galilee began to flow to Israel's south, the government took over all the country's water. The Water Law of 1959 put the Minister of Agriculture in charge of it. Subordinate to him is a Water Commissioner, who wields extensive authority and controls water allocation. Prices are set by the Minister after consultation with the Water Board (most of whose members are farmers) and Knesset Water Committee (all of whose members are farmers). His price decisions are presented to the Knesset Finance Committee for approval.[20] Mekorot Water Co. Ltd., a government-Jewish Agency partnership, drills, pumps, and carries two thirds of Israel's water.

Water is the limiting factor in agricultural settlement; when the country was established, Prime Minister Ben-Gurion made it a top priority. Soon Israel became a world leader in water research, desalination, and development of water-saving systems, of which drip irrigation is merely the best known. Israel's Water Planning Company has been commissioned for engineering jobs around the globe. Over the years, however, bureaucracy has stifled development. During an international conference in England in 1986, Prof. Arje Isar of the Desert Research Institute at Ben-Gurion University of the Negev – one of the most gifted and innovative water experts anywhere – jotted the following in his notebook:

> In the 1960s we were 20 years ahead of the British on the subject of water treatment. Today we are ten years behind, although we are still leaders in irrigation. The reason is that the planning of water projects is handled by a government agency, while irrigation remains in the hands of enterprising people –farmers and industrialists. To lure people with vision and unconventional ideas in this field, a new, competitive system should be put together. The existing institutions get their income from the Treasury, and research is attuned to the interests of the establishment and not of the public it should serve. That's a sure way to failure.[21]

The total amount of exploitable water in Israel, from all sources, is 1.7 billion cubic meters annually. Prior to exploitation, the country had groundwater reserves of some 5 billion cubic meters. Theoretically, some of this can be "borrowed" in dry years and replenished in the next rainy season. In fact, 1.9 billion cubic meters or more are pumped annually, that is, an overpumping of 200 million cubic meters! This over-exploitation has led to an cumulative deficit of over 1.5 billion cubic meters. Groundwater levels have fallen, seawater has penetrated wells on the coastal plain, and some wells have been sealed to prevent further contamination of aquifers.[22]

Since the 1960s, experts have been warning about the consequences of groundwater depletion. In 1962, Water Commissioner Menahem Kantor wrote that overpumping had reached dangerous dimensions.[23] Prof. Hillel Shuval of the Hebrew University warned, "If the Ministry of Agriculture does not drastically change its policies, we are headed for disaster."[24] Even after reserves became salinated and wells sealed on the coastal plain, the government continued overpumping, even though it was known that it might take some of the wells generations to recover.[25]

Of the 1.9 billion cubic meters distributed annually, agriculture gets 1.4 billion.[26] Since farmers are the main consumers, all members of the Knesset Water Committee are farmers. That's like leaving the cat in charge of the cream. The Committee and the Minister of Agriculture are concerned not with preserving groundwater but with "favoring" the farmers. The policy is 'Overpump now, replenish later.'[27] At first, "later" meant after completion of the National Water Carrier. Then it meant after completion of sewage treatment projects, then a flood control network, then repair of leaky pipes, and so on. The future was always sacrificed for immediate political gains. As this went on, budgets for the development of new water sources were severely cut. Existing programs to increase the annual quantity of available water by 100-150 million cubic meters have not been implemented.[28] Other programs progress at a snail's pace. An enormous aquifer – 70 billion cubic meters – lies under the

Negev dessert and can be used in dry years; not a drop has been touched.[29] Desalination research has been abandoned; the desalination plant at the power station in Ashdod, funded partly with American money, has stood idle and rusting since its completion.

The price of water is kept artificially low, providing a built-in incentive to waste. Water prices are equal in all parts of the country, but vary according to the users. In 1976, for example, farmers paid 4.5 cents per cubic meter, industry 13 cents, and home users 34 cents.[30] In 1986, when a third consecutive drought year brought overpumping to outrageous dimensions, the Knesset Water Committee actually reduced water prices to farmers from 10 cents to 9.[31] With water for farmers so heavily subsidized, its cost is divorced from its price. According to senior Treasury economist Dr. Ran Mosinson:[32]

> Water is subsidized yearly to the tune of $200 million. This subsidy is what places water allocations under great pressure and threatens to ruin the water sources... During periods of great demand, the marginal cost of one cubic meter of water in the south of the country is 30-40 cents, but the marginal value of irrigated produce is only half of that. In other words, such use of water is a total waste of money... A farmer who grows cotton on 50 acres uses 100,000 cubic meters of water yearly. When the price of water is 20 cents below cost, the farmer is getting a subsidy of $20,000.

The price of water is responsible for the depletion of aquifers. It misleads farmers trying to calculate what is profitable to grow, by making them consider the price of the water and not its cost. An example is cotton, a water-intensive crop. Until 1984, Israeli farmers profited from cotton and prided themselves on the record crops they achieved. None of this would have happened if they had to pay the real cost of water. When in 1986 the cotton growers hit upon hard times despite the subsidies, the Knesset Water Committee reduced the price of water to farmers by 10 percent.[33] All this is most blatant in the Negev. Because farmers everywhere in Israel pay the same subsidized price for water, Negev farmers grow highly water-intensive crops. In Kibbutz Sde Boker, for instance, the real cost of water – piped from far away – is at least four times the price charged. The result may produce lovely photos for Diaspora fundraising, but it is far from economical. The agricultural establishment objects to raising sheep on pastureland, although vast tracts in the Negev are suited to this purpose. Consequently, large parts of the Negev remain desolate monuments to the dream of "making the desert bloom." This dream can be realized only with vast amounts of water, which, unfortunately, are not available. Since water prices are low, farm villages and every farmer in them are assigned "water quotas" in an attempt to prevent overuse. There is no real way of enforcement them, and violators are never punished despite repeated remonstrations. A "black market" in water has developed, proving that administrative controls cannot restrain economic needs. This can be achieved only by market forces. There is a point where price meets demand. This point cannot be theoretically determined.

Reflecting the cheap-water policy, Israel's gardens and parks are poorly adapted to a water-conserving economy.[34] Water consumption for garden irrigation reached 60 million cubic meters by 1980 and continues to rise. No one bothers to grow flowers, plants, and trees that subsist on little water, although research has introduced a variety of them. Municipalities encourage the waste of water by charging reduced rates for garden use. Tel Aviv, Ramat Gan, and many other cities planted expansive lawns in the mid-1980s, disregarding the acute water shortage. A realistic price for the first few cubic meters of home consumption and sharply rising prices for excess use is the only way to make citizens select the right plants. In fact, local authorities have no incentive to encourage water conservation. One cubic meter of water cost a municipality 15 cents in 1986 and was sold to households for 66 cents. With such a markup, there's no point in even repairing leaking pipes.[35] Although the government's shortsighted, exploitative policies are at fault for the water wastage, the public is handed the blame. Government advertisements admonish the public to "SAVE WATER!" As aquifers are depleted, the ads are run even in winter[36] – as if the reserves vanish by themselves or by natural disaster, rather than by direct consequence of government sins of commission and omission.

Theoretically, one may assume that centralized control would ensure proper distribution and economic use of the available water. In fact, Israel's water history provides an example of what happens when politicians control a nation's natural resources. Water is one of the very few natural resources Israel has. Instead of conserving it, the government has fomented disaster by preferring short-term interests. The politicians' behavior is so cynical that the old joke becomes credible: If politicians were to take control of the desert, there would soon be a shortage of sand.

It has been the policy of every Israeli government to keep the number of private automobiles to a minimum. The government and the public have engaged in a drawn-out, obstinate struggle over the right to own a car – which the government wants to reserve for the rich, the politicians, and the bureaucrats. In 1986, Israel had 190 private cars per 1,000 citizens, compared with 600 in the United States and 400 in France and West Germany.[37] Israel, with pretensions of being a land of modern technology, is less motorized than Greece or Spain.

In the 1950s, one needed a permit to import a car. Top priority went to bureaucrats – government, Jewish Agency, Histadrut –while permits for anyone else were extremely hard to obtain. Public pressure forced the government to switch to fiscal maneuvers to achieve the same end. A description of the various anti-car taxes invoked over the years could fill an entire volume.

On February 2, 1985, *Ha'aretz* calculated the cost of a small (1300 cc. engine) European car:

> The calculation of the price of a car for the Israeli consumer is somewhat complex, but its worth noting how layer upon layer of irksome taxes are imposed on the purchaser:

Factory price	$ 2,500
Price in Israeli port, including insurance	3,000
Duty – 25.2% of CIF price + 2% Lebanese War Levy	816
Importer's profit	4,540
Purchase tax (42.7% of consumer price, before VAT)	3,246
Total Price before VAT	7,602
VAT – 15% of price (including all extras)	1,140
Cash deposit* – 60% of price before VAT	4,561
Total	$13,303

Revenues from taxation of vehicles, fuel, and spare parts came to $1.1 billion in 1984.[38] When Moshe Dayan resigned as Minister of Agriculture, he bought a car at his own expense for the first time in his life. Hearing the price, he said, "I had no idea the price of a car was so high." One has to work 1.5-2.5 years to acquire a car in Israel, compared with some 100 days in Canada and Germany.[39] In 1985, an annual levy of 3 percent of the value of the vehicle was added to the registration renewal fee. It was dressed up as a "one-time" levy, of course, and was renewed in 1986 "for only one more year," of course. In a 1985 five-year plan presented by the Minister of Economics to the government, we find: "Various methods of rendering the use of cars more expensive will be examined."[40] These recommendations, written by people who receive generous state support for the maintenance of their cars, were adopted by other people who enjoy free use of chauffeured limousines.

* This "deposit" was returned a year later without interest and indexation. Israel's high rate of inflation drastically reduces the value of the refund. Thus the Israeli consumer ultimately pays five times the factory price.

Automobile maintenance is similarly exorbitant. For a small car, it averaged $2,325 annually in 1985, not including depreciation. In July, 1982, it cost over 50 cents to drive a small private car one mile. Because prices of spare parts are astronomical, half the vehicles in the country are mechanically defective.[41]

Fuel prices are set by the government, which tries to keep the public in the dark as to their components. In 1980, a gallon of regular gas sold for $3.20. Of that amount, 57 percent was tax. Half of the taxes were excise and VAT; the other half was for the "equalization fund." The 'fund' is an extraordinarily inane Israeli invention by which consumers of gasoline subsidize heavy fuel for industry![42] Economist Yitzhak Tisch asks: "Why must the buyers of gasoline, and not the buyers of carpets, subsidize industry's fuel?" In 1987, after fuel prices came down on the world market, industrialists complained that they were paying 30-40 percent more for heavy fuel than their European counterparts, despite the "equalization fund." At the peak of inflation, the government claimed that it was subsidizing gasoline to the tune of $1 million a day. It soon became apparent, however, that far from subsidizing gasoline, the government was actually profiting by it.[43] What happened? The price of gasoline did not cover the entire subsidy for heavy oil; in the minds of the bureaucrats, this meant that gasoline was being sudsidized. Israel has only three oil companies: Paz, Sonol, and Delek. Until very recently, Paz was owned by the government. Many years ago it gave a third of it, practically as a gift, to a Mr. Wolfson of England. Wolfson became a renowned philanthropist by virtue of his income from this company. Subsequently he sold his shares back to the government for tens of millions of dollars, promising to donate the money to causes in Israel. Eventually he took the money abroad.[44] Private investment in the other two companies is also minimal.[45] Most of their shares are owned by the Histadrut's holding company (Hevrat ha-Ovdim) and bank (Hapoalim).[46] The companies operate as a cartel, coordinating their businesses. They not only sell fuel, but also import it. Import proposals are brought before an "Acquisition Committee" comprising the director of the importing company, the managing director of the Israel Oil Refineries (another government-owned monopoly), and the head of the Government Fuel Administration. The rules for this committee are laid down by a higher committee. Between the two is another "policy-setting" committee, comprising representatives of the fuel companies, the Treasury, the Ministry of Energy, the refineries, and the Fuel Administration. Exceptional cases involving price or quality require authorization by the Minister.

Fuel is purchased on a "cost-plus" basis. This means the companies can never lose, no matter how expensively they buy. Thus they have absolutely no incentive to buy cheaply; the very opposite may well be the case. The Director-General of the Ministry of Energy claims that he relies on "buyers' expertise and, especially, close, efficient supervision." That's nonsense. According to a report by the State Comptroller about Paz, as well as statements made by the Treasury, negligence and erroneous fuel acquisition policies have cost the country tens of millions of dollars.[47] Shimshon Erlich writes:

> The State Comptroller exposed a large government corporation (Paz), which exists for one purpose only: to extract money from the Treasury, from the Ministry of Energy, from the public. It succeeds by virtue of funding arrangements, cost-plus and arithmetical exercises... Its financial arrangements appear to be wonderful inventive, even genial... They're authorized by the Accountant-General and the Treasury's Legal Adviser, both of whom are Paz directors.[48]

On top of all this, the government pays the fuel companies 35 cents for each ton of coal imported. That's $2.5 million per year, an especially handsome sum when one considers that it is the government, not the fuel companies, that does the importing. The government took over that job some time ago; the $2.5

million is "compensation" for having infringed upon the fuel companies' "basic rights."[49] No wonder the fuel companies made profits of $30,000,000 in 1986.

The government determines on the number, ownership, and location of gasoline stations. It allocated 45 percent to Paz, 30 percent to Delek, and 25 percent to Sonol. The government also sets profit margins (fuel prices are identical in all gas stations throughout the country).[50] The salaries of Paz executives are very high. They are paid three months in advance. Summer schedules (shorter working hours) are in effect six months of the year. They get a 15 percent bonus for non-absenteeism, this, too, paid three months in advance. About one quarter of the bureau employees receive seven-year interest-free loans to cover the purchase of cars with 1,800 cc engines, which is large by Israeli standards. They enjoy free medical care. Their children's university tuition is covered. When the CEO of Sonol was asked how much Sonol's high-ranking officials earn, he arrogantly retorted that it was nobody's business, because his company was private![51] By pure chance, Paz's chairman of the board was until recently the Treasury's Accountant-General, and Delek's CEO was the Treasury's Director-General.

But there is another side to the coin. While the companies are getting rich at the public's expense and its directors and officials enjoy the good life, gas station attendants are paid starvation wages – less than $200 per month in 1985, with perhaps another 10 percent in tips.[52] This is the result of "governmental supervision" and Histadrut ownership. Since it is neither possible nor desirable to supervise the directors and officials or to inspect profits which accumulate partly as a result of corruption, supervision is applied to the poor, miserable attendants. This is yet another lesson in socialist rule and in the hypocritical use of the term "egalitarianism."

If private cars are so expensive, how can so many people afford to purchase and maintain them? The answer: not everybody pays the full price. In 1971, over 50 percent of the automobiles purchased were tax-exempt, since the purchasers were immigrants, Israelis returning from long stays abroad, invalids, and owners of approved enterprises.[53] Additional details came to light as the result of a parliamentary question submitted by MK Dov Shilansky in 1978. A citizen who chose to remain anonymous reported that "Only 8-15 percent of the purchasers of private cars paid full taxes. The rest are partially or fully exempt. Many others write the cost off as a business expense, which is partially tax exempt."[54] According to Shilansky 85 percent or more of the owners of private cars do not pay all taxes due. After a delay of five months, the Deputy Minister of Treasury replied that only 45 percent were exempt. According to Shilansky, 55 percent of the car owners are given a car maintenance allocation from their employer; the deputy minister's reply – only 31 percent. From experience it is reasonable to assume that the anonymous citizen (probably a high-ranking government official) came closer to the truth than did the deputy minister.

There are people whose cars cost them nothing. For 56,000 "high-ranking" officials of private or public bodies, a car comes with the job – and that includes its taxes, licensing, fuel, repairs, and all other related expenses. These cars enjoy considerable tax reductions[55]. When an Israeli is asked how much he earns, his reply may be incomplete; the car component can double one's salary. The expenses these cars entail, which are unproportionally high because of the taxes, are a further burden on the employer and are ultimately reflected in the prices of Israeli products and services.

Taxes on private vehicles generate vast revenues. In 1975, according to the Minister of Transport, they brought in 12 times as much as the entire public expenditure on highways and similar uses. The gap between government revenues derived from vehicle taxation and the government's direct investment in highway development is steadily increasing.[56] In 1979, Zvi Weiss published a study on relative infrastructure cost for all kinds of vehicles. He found that private vehicle tax revenue was twice the cost of the infrastructure installed for these cars, while trucks and buses, which account for most highway depreciation, were subsidized.[57] In 1985 vehicle tax revenues came to $1.1. billion, while infrastructure investment dropped to $38 million – less than 4 percent.[58] Israeli governments have adamantly refused to accede to legislation pledging a fixed proportion of vehicle tax revenues to roadbuilding and safety installations. The government insists that this revenue is part of its overall income, to be used as it sees fit.

In 1987, the entire country had only two freeways – Tel Aviv - Jerusalem and Tel Aviv - Ashdod. Only half of the 60-mile road from Tel Aviv to Haifa is a freeway. After 40 years of statehood and constant exhortation for population dispersion, the divided highway to Beersheba has not yet been completed, and work on such connections with the Galilee has not begun. The police refer to about 135 miles of highway as "red asphalt" because of the high rate of accidents there. Somehow, there is no budget available to take care of more than a small section at a time. The sums allocated for the construction and maintenance of roads are ridiculously small, and are frozen altogether whenever the government has budget problems elsewhere. Transportation expert Dr. Moshe Becker estimates that the financial damage stemming from the delay in road construction comes to about $800 million per year.[59] The ratio between the road mileage and the number of cars is steadily deteriorating. Between 1977 and 1982, the number of vehicles in the country grew by 35 percent, while the length of roads increased by only 1 percent. Consequently, Israel is presently the Western leader in road density, and is second only to Hong Kong in the entire world. In 1981, Israel had 140 vehicles per kilometer of road. Italy, the next challenger, is far behind at 66 per kilometer.[60]

An example of what goes on is the construction of a freeway within Tel Aviv – the Ayalon River Project, expected to speed up the city's crawling traffic. The project was planned in the

1960s, and the Ayalon River Company was established in 1970 as a partnership between the government and Tel Aviv City Hall. The World Bank put up a loan, and the project was scheduled for completion in 1976. By 1986, less than half of the freeway was open. To compensate for its disastrous neglect, the government periodically presents various land transportation development plans. Since they all remain on paper, they are obviously no more than public relations gimmicks.

Drivers' licenses, annual vehicle tests, transfers of title, and similar affairs are under the jurisdiction of the Ministry of Transport's Licensing Bureau. All over the world, obtaining a driver's license is a simple matter. In Israel, it is a drawn-out trauma fraught with complications.[61] After a detailed test on driving law and theory, the would-be driver takes a half-hour practical test behind the wheel. Because each examiner can test only 10-12 people per day, and because the number of examiners is strictly and deliberately limited, there is a waiting list of three to six months. At one time, 40,000 people were waiting for their driver's test. Tension rides high throughout the whole affair. In one extreme case, two examiners were shot dead by an examinee who failed. Financial and sexual bribery are not uncommon in this unruly, frustrating business. Judge Edna Bakenstein asserted that "The issuance of drivers' licenses has become an arena of baksheesh."[62] No Minister of Transportation was ever perturbed by it, nor has any of them dared to confront the examiners and establish order.

How do Israelis prepare for the exam? Yifat Nevo of *Ha'aretz:*

> The Vehicle Licensing Authority (VLA) in Holon deals with more than 10,000 driving students, who undertake to master this skill with about 200 teachers in private driving schools. Each student has to fill out two VLA registration forms (medical checkup and application for driver's license). The teachers are willing to provide their students with the forms in their offices. Thus 200 instructors would spare the

> licensing clerks the need to deal with some 10,000 students – a savings of 50:1. No way, says Authority! A clerk in Holon, basing himself on an "administrative" guideline, is willing to provide teachers with such forms at the rate *of two forms per teacher per visit*. Thus a teacher may obtain ten copies of the form by waiting in line five times.
>
> After all this, with a little instruction thrown in, the student is finally ready for his long-awaited driving test. Now he waits another three of four months until a tester is available. Those who fail the test must wait another three or four months to try it again.[63]

The annual motor vehicle inspection is no better. At one time it was performed by the government licencing bureaus. It involved a wasted workday, many hours of waiting, violence in line, bureaucratic harassment, etc. The examiners would march off for a mid-morning "breakfast break" while a long line of edgy citizens stretched out for hundreds of yards. Nowadays, private cars can be tested in privately-owned licensing bureaus. That's quite a relief. The licencing bureau still afflicts owners of trucks and other vehicles, however, and everyone still has to go there for various services and permits. Most of these arrangements could be handled by mail, but the bureaucrats will have none of it. Despite the astronomic sums the government collects from car owners, there is "no money" to renovate the bureaus' premises. Some of them bring to mind scenes from Ellis Island – masses of angry people pushing and fighting in an atmosphere unbecoming of a civilized country. For a suitable sum, one can engage the services of middlemen (known in Yiddish as "machers"). They know how to get even a mechanically defective car through the test.

Israel's licensing procedure is an example of how a self-serving and powerful bureaucracy can turn a trivial matter that should take no more than minutes into a via dolorosa for the citizens. The inevitable consequence is rampant protectionism and bribery.

The large number of traffic accidents is not surprising considering road conditions: few divided highways, high vehicular density, inadequate safety and lighting arrangements, a shortage of policemen.[64] Aging cars are kept on the road because of the exorbitant cost of replacing them; they are badly maintained due to the exorbitant cost of fixing them. Thus traffic accidents have become the scourge of the country, reaching truly catastrophic proportions. They have claimed the lives of about 16,500 Israelis, far more than have fallen in all the country's wars. Additional multitudes have been injured and maimed, and uncountable work days have been lost. The financial damage is enormous. In 1982, 150,000 cars – one out of five – were involved in accidents, claiming 370 lives and causing an estimated $400 million in damage.[65]

Experts from Israel and abroad deplore the unbearable traffic conditions. The government blames the "human factor." There is no doubt, however, that a good road network does much to prevent accidents. This was proven when the number of accidents on the road between Haifa and Hadera dropped from 120 per year to 40 after that section of the freeway was completed. The construction of the Ramle bypass on the Tel Aviv - Jerusalem highway lowered the accident rate in that area by 80 percent. In contrast, a Japanese government report recently disclosed that while the number of cars in Japan doubled in a decade, the number of accidents decreased by half as a result of the construction of a good transportation infrastructure. An Australian research study has shown that half the accidents caused by driver error can be prevented by proper road engineering.[66] One of the factors contributing to accidents in Israel is the high percentage of drivers using cars that are not their own, so that the cost of repair does not come out of their pockets. Buses take first prize for involvement in traffic accidents – 3.03 accidents per million kilometers. Egged (the bus monopoly) and some large corporations such as the Israel Electric Company pay the fines incurred by their errant drivers.[67]

In other words, no few Israelis take to the roads without fear of penalty or impending repair costs.

The vast material damage resulting from the accidents does not seem to concern the Treasury, which shows no willingness to allocate even "first aid" for the so-called "red asphalt" roads. The Treasury would have to add a mere $60 million to the budget for two years to overhaul these roads, thus preventing $250 million in accident damage over the next decade. Yet, in 1985, only 1.5 percent of revenues collected from drivers were pledged to roadbuilding.[68] In 1987, this was raised – to 2.5 percent. The head of investigations for the Israel Police sums up the situation: "Since the State was founded, no government has ever devoted serious thought to traffic accidents."[69]

On land, on the high seas and in the air, monopolies rule Israel. Israel Railroads is a government service. The Zim shipping company is a public corporation co-owned by the government and the Histadrut. El-Al Israel Airlines is a government corporation. Egged and Dan, Histadrut bus cooperatives with strong government involvement, dominate public transportation. All are monopolies. Each needs constant government subsidies for its survival; each is plagued by strikes, labor unrest, and power struggles, leading to inefficiency and waste of public funds.

Israel has two giant cooperatives that control bus transportation: Egged throughout the country (about 7,000 members) and Dan in greater Tel Aviv (some 3,000 members). The Histadrut guarantees Egged's monopoly and ensures "the rights of Hevrat Ha-ovdim" (its own holding corporation). During a prolonged Egged strike in the early 1950s, Prime Minister Ben-Gurion summoned his economic affairs ministers – all Labor Party members – and asked them: "Are we with the people against Egged, or with Egged against the people?" Everyone present asserted that Egged belonged to the Histadrut and therefore had to be supported. This approach prevailed, and

Egged was elevated to a special status. It became a strong pressure group with electoral power. Together with their families, Egged members wield more votes than are needed to put a representative in the Knesset. Traditionally, then, Egged has a Labor Knesset member of its own.

Egged's service is poor, but has improved in the last few years with the proliferation of private cars.[70] Many still recall the long waiting lines for interurban buses. When the buses finally pulled up at the head of the line, their front seats were already occupied by privileged passengers. Even those with shorter memory tell of long lines at urban bus stops, of buses arriving in pairs and leapfrogging so as to skip stops, and of filth, broken seats, and rude drivers. After a week-long strike in 1982, Egged members were astounded by the hatred they encountered from the public.[71] The causes for this animus were well expressed in a newspaper caricature showing Egged members exploiting their monopoly to get rich at the public's expense, while showing utter contempt for their passengers.

Egged constantly bickers with the government over the size of the subsidy it receives. In addition to the regular subsidy, the Treasury provides various kinds of support to prevent the cooperative's collapse – covering its deficits, exempting imported buses from customs, providing 47-year loans for members' early retirement, purchase of spare parts, and more.[72] Essential clauses in the agreement between Egged and the government are concealed from the public. Only from the State Comptroller's report did the public learn that in January, 1984, the government undertook to pay Egged's debts of $235,000,000. How the debts has accrued remained secret.

Every Egged member owns one share in the cooperative. Despite the cumulative deficits and danger of collapse from which the government is obliged to save Egged every so often, the value of these shares miraculously soars. A Histadrut commission appointed to study Egged share values found that "Over the past few years, the value of the shares has risen 40 percent per year, discounting inflation." During the 1984 election campaign, Labor Party chairman Shimon Peres sent a personal letter to every Egged and Dan member. He pledged to exempt every member who sells his share from capital gains tax, "Please consider this promise an IOU," he wrote. Each share is worth tens of thousands of dollars, because its value is determined by the cooperative itself. To be on the safe side, Egged extracted an identical pledge from the Likud. As expected, these promises became law in 1987, with the support of both parties. Another 90 cooperatives promptly demanded – unsuccessfully thus far – that the law apply to all cooperatives.[73] This episode demonstrates the extraordinary political clout of Egged and Dan, as well as the discriminatory manner in which the political establishment administers in order to gain votes. Perhaps it is no surprise that Egged – whose power derives from a government-granted monopoly – dared to stage a strike in 1987, defying court orders.

The salaries of Egged members are among the highest in the country. Perks include presents on their birthdays and on the cooperative's anniversary, free education and summer camps for children, unusually generous pension funds, and more.

A word about Egged's subsidiary policy. The cooperative has been ridding itself of assets over the years, transferring them to subsidiaries owned – you guessed it – by the share holders, that is, Egged members. While continuously transferring money from the cooperative to its members pockets, Egged creates the impression of being poverty-stricken and in constant need of support[74] and subsidies, surely because it strives to enrich each of its 7,000 members. The cooperative's board regards this as its main duty, essential for being re-elected. Thus the members make a nice living, while the company perpetually teeters on the brink of bankruptcy.

On the face of it, Egged is hamstrung by supervising bodies: its own supervisory committee; the Histadrut comptroller, the State Comptroller, the Transportation Ministry, the Treasury. Yet all are ineffective. Under the headline "Supervision as a Sad Joke," *Ha'aretz* writes:[75]

> Supervision of schedules is deficient, as is control of Egged's financial affairs. Public supervision is incapable of coping with this giant cooperative... The financial reports, even when Egged submits them, do not include the necessary details... Negotiations between Egged and the government are generally on a niveau of flea market haggling... Egged demand a price hike of 40 percent, the government agrees to a mere 5 percent... and a compromise of 20 percent is reached.

The lesson to be learned is that the government can subsidize economic enterprises but only market forces can control them. The government invests vast sums in Egged. It dictates prices, routes, and types of equipment. But it is kept in the dark as to the true cost of running the buses. This is convenient for the cooperative and its members, as well as for the Histadrut, which will go to any length to preserve Egged's unlimited monopoly. The losers are the public and the Treasury.

Egged claims it needs subsidies to cover losses on unprofitable routes in the Galilee and other remote areas. Therefore the government allows rates on the profitable Tel Aviv - Jerusalem and Tel Aviv - Haifa lines to exceed expenses. Yet the Galilee lines run very few buses, and even those are half empty. In a rare lucid moment, Egged's spokesman once admitted that Egged is incapable of competing with (unsubsidized) vans and taxis. Municipal authorities in the Galilee have repeatedly asked the Ministry of Transportation to dispose of Egged and let them deal with their own transportation problems. Private tourist bus operators have repeatedly offered to take over all of Egged's subsidized routes at the present prices with no government subsidy. They are turned down each time. The conclusion is that both the monopoly and the subsidy are superfluous. The attempt to intimidate the public – "No transport for residents of the Galilee without us!" – is in fact intended to sustain a favored pressure group.

Egged's competition, the obsolete, rundown, government-owned railway, reminds one of Turkish trains at the turn of the century. It employs 2,300 workers but carries a mere 5 percent of freight and a ludicrous 3,000,000 passengers per year.[76] Most of the tracks date from Mandate times. The only truly functioning passenger line is from Tel Aviv to Haifa; the 60-mile stretch, which a fast train could cover in 25 minutes, takes the train 60-90 minutes. Not only are trains consistently late, most are filthy as well. David Guy, spokesman for Israel Railways:

> Cleanliness inside railroad cars, including windows, is a topic to which we devote a great deal of attention and thought. Tom my sorrow, however, conditions in this country make it very difficult. Every passenger car is washed from the outside at least once a week, but because of last week's heat wave, and the combination rain/sandstorm that followed, the windows were covered with a great deal of dirt, as were the windows of private cars. It was hard to overcome this in one day. However, we made efforts, and within several days all the windows were cleaned. We shall continue to try to keep the cars as clean as we can, in hopes that the public and the weather conditions will be on our side.

On the freight line from Dimona (central Negev) to the port of Ashdod, four accidents occurred over a period of six months, causing seven-digit damage. It surprises no one that the railway's budget shows a chronic deficit.[77]

In 1975, Israel Railways appointed a new managing director who took over, looked around, and said: "The railway is in a scandalous, downright criminal state of neglect." Why does the government prefer to invest hundred of millions of dollars in buses? The following story may help us understand why. In 1966, a well known and respected entrepreneur presented the Minister of Transportation with plans for a rapid train from Tel Aviv to Jerusalem. He supplied letters of intent for funding the project from Swedish and English firms. The minister did not even open the file. Instead, he cut the interview short, saying: "Are you trying to get me into trouble with Egged?" This points to one of the major drawbacks of centralized economy: political considerations leading to preferential treatment of certain sectors, irrespective of the damage it causes the economy, irrespective of the inconvenience it causes the public. For the sake of a pressure group which milks the Treasury, the government thwarts development, tolerates chronic deficits, and refuses to sell the railroad to private entrepreneurs. Israelis are reminded that the railroad is a "national asset" and must be government-controlled as a matter of principle! In 1983 the Treasury refused to allocate several hundreds of thousands of dollars to examine a project for a 28-minute train from Tel Aviv to Jerusalem via Ben-Gurion Airport.[78]

As a government corporation, Israel's airline, El Al, was doomed to lose money. Shimshon Erlich writes:

> In a private enterprise, a drop in revenues or a rise in expenses forces management to adjust operations. Not so when the government foots the bill. Workers can strike without having to worry about going down together with the company.[79]

In no other government corporation, however, have workers displayed such limitless hutzpa as in El Al, and nowhere has the government capitulated more abjectly. This went on until a strike several months long so paralyzed the company that it tumbled into receivership. Like most Israeli enterprises, El Al has demonstrated great technical ability from the beginning. It quickly made a name for itself for safety, and achieved several technological firsts. Its deterioration is the result not of lack of technical prowess but of mismanagement and wobbly labor relations – inevitable developments in a company where profits and losses are meaningless. The extent of government support of El Al has always been unbelievable. The government bought El Al a fleet of airplanes at zero interest. It let El Al overcharge as it wished. It let El Al charge Israelis more than foreigners on group flights. It let El Al pay less income tax than required by law (much of the pilots' salaries were paid in pounds sterling, which were treated for tax purposes as equivalent to Israeli pounds, while the real ratio was about 10:1). It forced its employees to fly El Al only. It sold El Al fuel at reduced rates and charged it lower airport fees than it charged other airlines. It forced KAL (the monopolistic carrier of agricultural exports) to lease planes from El Al only, although this raised export expenses. It constrained the activities of charter flight companies, notwithstanding the damage this did to tourism.[80]

What were the consequences of this excessive support? The employees ran amok and the management caved in all along the line – with Ministry of Transportation and Treasury support – until things got out of control. The number of employees swelled to over 5,000. El Al had more employees per plane than any other Western airline: about 400 compared with 200 at Swissair and fewer in American airlines. Each occupational group was represented by its own works committee – eleven altogether. Each imposed its own sanctions, held protest assemblies during working hours, threatened, struck, and disrupted flight schedules. The employees never came off second best in a strike. A special building housed offices for the 45 works committee members, whose sole occupation was "committee affairs" and whose salaries were paid by the company. They were the real managers of El Al; they determined salaries, promotions, and appointments. They rapidly secured work conditions unknown elsewhere. For instance, about 1,000 of El Al's 5,000 employees had to work on the Sabbath. In return, each received 325 percent overtime and a day off. The stewards' labor contract was 200 pages long! It determined that some of them could board flights to Europe or the United States, spend a few days in a good hotel at company expense, and return as passengers. Lest they get "tired" on the flight home, a few back rows were reserved for their slumber and covered with a canopy. Passengers were scolded for "making noise and preventing the tired stewards from sleeping." Employees were given access to free (and tax-free) tickets, subsidized food vouchers, and free air transport of refrigerators, bathtubs, and more. "When I came to El Al, I found a hair-raising, distorted, and corrupt situation," said Buma Shavit, former chairman of the board.[81]

Despite massive government support, waiver of interest, and quashing of competition, the company's deficit grew steadily. In 1984 it came to $330 million. Without government support, it would have been double or more. "Past losses will be covered by the taxpayer," said board chairman Nahman Perl.[82]

Matters eventually became intolerable. Like spoiled children who know no limits, the works committees went too far, and El Al spent more time striking than flying. Finally the government initiated a lock-out and considered permanent shut-down. The employees responded with violence, riots, and threats to burn the planes.[83] El Al went into receivership, where it has remained ever since. It has reorganized, laid off many employees – though not enough – and maintains a regular schedule of flights. No one wants to contemplate what will happen when the receiver hands the company back to a fully-empowered directorate.

Ehud Shilo, former Director-General of the Ministry of Transportation, said that "El Al has no future under government ownership."[84] Typically, he did not make this statement until the day he left his post. Nevertheless, anyone who broaches the idea of privatizing the company is shouted down with the slogan: "It's our national airline." The word "national" is meaningless in this context. It is interpreted, as in the case of a National Theater or somesuch, as justification for government financial support. Israelis should bear in mind that all the American airlines and some of the European ones – including the most profitable, Swissair – are privately owned. But brainwashed citizens are worried about what will happen in times of emergency. It is not generally known that air routes are government property. When assigning them to airlines, governments reserve the right to requisition the aircraft in times of emergency. Hence the cliche "national airline" is just another fig leaf. What harm would be done if Israel had, say, two national airlines, or even three? They would compete with each other, to the benefit of the passengers.

One of Israel's charter airlines petitioned the High Court of Justice because it thought itself discriminated against by the government, which gave preferential treatment to El Al. Rejecting the petition, the Court ruled that "One of the factors the Minister of Transportation is authorized to take into account is the interest of El Al. As Israel's national airline, it is only natural that it be subject to the responsibility of the Minister of Transportation."[85] This alone is reason enough to disqualify the government from involvement in the economy through its own corporations. The government inevitably favors its own company over the interests of other citizens! In a democracy, government must avoid granting preference to anyone. Yet even judges do not operate in a vacuum. They are part of society and rule according to accepted norms. The employees of the Airport Authority (another government corporation) follow in the footsteps of El Al's workers. They do not hesitate to cut Israel off from the world during wage disputes. Ben-Gurion International has the highest use fees of the world's 27 major airports. When asked to send a delegation to Washington to deliberate the allocation of air routes, Israel sent the largest entourage of all.[86]

Few things have aroused Israelis' imagination more than the Zim ships, sailing the seven seas under the Israeli flag, carrying on a tradition dating from the time of King Solomon. Zim was founded in 1945 as a Jewish Agency-Histadrut partnership. Later, the government invested large sums in Zim, mainly from Holocaust reparations, and bought up over 40 percent of the company's shares in 1959. This left the Histadrut with 10 percent, and 50 percent were transferred to the Israel Corporation. From its founding, Zim was considered a "national" company. Zim is one of the ten largest shipping firms in the world. In 1981 it had 53 ships afloat, half owned and half leased. It handled international freight transport and employed 5,000 people – some at sea, others in its 38 branch offices around the world.

A maritime recession in 1976 hit Zim hard, and by 1981 the company was in deep trouble. During the preceding fat years, it had acquired all the characteristics of government corporations: a bloated shore staff of 1,300 in Haifa; wasteful, faulty, and careless management; decision-making hampered by a multilayered bureaucracy; overt and covert benefits to high-ranking officials; ill-advised appointments; dilution of responsibility; discounts to some industries, which benefited Zim in no way; refraining from collecting debts ($40,000.000), and so on. Dr. Naftali Vidra, chairman of the Institute for Shipping Research, summed up the situation: "Obsolete technology, an inflated manpower roster, and exaggerated salaries." Another expert said bluntly: "Nobody's in charge."[87] Zim's 1985 and 1986 balance sheets improved, showing a considerable operational profit. Some of this was due to the layoff of some 600 employees, extensive streamlining, and less waste in offices abroad. The main source of increased revenues, however, was the formation of a "conference" (i.e., cartel) of shippers to and from Israel, which hiked freight prices significantly. In other words, Zim profited by having made all exported and imported goods more expensive.[88]

The salaries of Zim's overseas representatives are 60 percent higher than those paid to Foreign Ministry personnel, which are by no means low. Zim reps have been known to make up to $7,000 a month, in addition to rent for luxury apartments, use of company car, children's education expenses, promotions for hundreds of officials, etc. The consequence of this and other examples of extravagance is a cumulative deficit of $450,000,000.

The company's real situation is even worse, for many of its ships are outdated and their value is less than the number appearing on the balance sheet.

Additional reasons for Zim's red ink are high taxation, featherbedding, and obstinate unions. However fat the salaries may be, employees net much less than they gross – unless they are highranking officials. For example, Zim shells out $7,000 per month for an Israeli captain, who takes home no more than $2,000 or so. A European captain who costs his employers $3,500-$4,000 nets $3,000. For ordinary sailors, the situation is even more absurd. An Israeli sailor costs Zim $2,277 and takes home about $1,000; a foreign sailor costs only $1,350 but swims home with $1,180 – because foreign crewmen are exempt from Israeli income tax. The unions do not allow Zim to adopt efficiency measures because they consider it not a company but an institution, like the Electric Company or City Hall. They believe Zim will survive irrespective of profits and losses. One must assume that management shares this view in order to understand the following news item: "The Zim directorate has adopted austerity measures. Instead of several waitresses serving tea in company offices, an electric cart will be installed on each floor."[89] Thus far, the government has adamantly refused to sell its share in Zim to private investors. In 1980 a large Belgian company offered to buy the company – whereupon the government quickly announced that it was not considering the sale of its shares.[90]

To sum up, Israel's government control and monopolization of transport services have had serious consequences. When service is good – as in air and sea transport – the government firms cannot afford to compete, and have run up debts of $1 billion on top of vast government investments. International cartels of carriers have hiked prices by 30-40 percent, doing serious damage to both the economy and the populace. Egged's land transport monopoly is exorbitantly expensive and results in the transfer of government funds to private pockets. In order to protect Egged's monopoly, the government makes sure the railroad system remains substandard, while other countries run trains at up to 200 kmh. and expect to reach 500 kmh. in the near future.[91] Last but not least is the astronomic price paid by Israelis for inadequate highway construction – in money and in lives.

During the 1950s, only 7,000 telephones were installed annually in Israel. Most of them were allotted to politicians and high-ranking bureaucrats in the government, the Histadrut, the Jewish Agency, municipalities and the like. The political establishment visualized Israel as an Eastern European country of the 1930s, never imagining that telephones should be provided for all. Phone installations increased to 30,000 per year in the 1960s, 50,000 in the 1970s, and about 100,000 in the 1980s. In the meantime, the waiting list grew to over 200,000. Abut 5,000 families had been waiting over 10 years.[92] Delays of two to four years are a regular occurrence – unless you have pull.

Every Member of Knesset receives a free telephone for life. In 1982, although 200,000 people had been waiting years for phones, the Knesset House Committee awarded its members a second telephone with unlimited free calls.[93] At the same time, ordinary folks paid hundreds of dollars for the installation of home phones; businesses paid about 50 percent more.[94] It is difficult to comprehend why payment for the office phone is higher, unless it is a penalty for opening a business. In the Western world, one pays little or nothing to order a phone, and the telephone company stands on its own feet. In reply to a proposal to speed up the rate of telephone installations, the Treasury objected to the idea of wiping out the waiting list in less than seven years. It goes without saying that senior Treasury officials have phones at home and do not pay for them.

In 1974, the Prime Minister was not ashamed to say that "Israel cannot afford to develop a proper telephone system."[95] The Treasury, however, never paid for the installation of a telephone network from its own budgets. The government makes a wopping 67 percent annual profit on the capital invested in the telephone network, including the "security stamp" it imposed "temporarily" in 1956 and somehow forgot to cancel.[96] "Telephones were always among the best business deals in Israel," according to *Ha'aretz*. Not only does the government not invest its own money in these golden geese, but it actually charges more than the cost of installing them."[97] This profit accrues even after a good many citizens pay nothing for the use of the phone: high-ranking officials in government offices, municipalities, government corporations, and so on. Even so, Shimon Peres asserted in 1973 – while he was serving as Minister of Communications – that the waiting list could not be shortened, because it costs the government $1,200 to install a phone.[98] The Minister forgot to mention that the installation charge, payments for calls made, and the monthly use fee cover this amount and leave a nice profit. He also neglected to say that costs could be considerably reduced by streamlining management. This is one of the many instances where the government distorts the facts and deceives the public.

To relieve the pressure of hundreds of thousands of clamoring, phone-less citizens, the Ministry of Communications printed in the telephone directories its list of priorities for "fair distribution." Only a bureaucracy with pretensions of divine insight can assert that bereaved parents are in greater need of a telephone than people aged 71-80, or that both these groups are less deserving than former "Prisoners of Zion." Dividing the population into more than 100 categories and subcategories of greater and lesser right to communicate is more than silly; it leads by necessity to a struggle of everyone against his fellow. Telephones were quickly given to those with "proper connections." People who had spent years on the waiting list once organized a "Telephone Users Association;" the leaders of the group were promptly given telephones. This method of diffusing protest movements is routinely applied in other areas, such as housing. Because of the difficulty of obtaining a telephone, many instances of bribery have come to light. The most notorious was photographed by a "candid camera" and shown on television. The stunned viewers saw a phone company technician demand $2,000 to speed up the installation of a phone.[99] When the telephone company filed against two technicians who were accused of taking bribes and of stealing telephone equipment, a judge let the defendants off lightly because "their offense is a widespread phenomenon."[100] No less astonishing was the phone company's decision to give to every employee a push-button telephone free – so they would stop stealing them.

True to the system, the cost of a phone depends on who you are. Many thousands of Israelis pay nothing at all. Government employees, including teachers, employees of the defense establishment and the police, as well as widows and pensioners of these groups, enjoy a 50 percent discount on installation and use charges. Whether other groups or individuals enjoy similar benefits is anyone's guess. In 1981, the Ministry of Communications revoked the discounts of 35,000 phone owners whose privileged status could not be proven. That left only 126,000 users paying reduced rates.[101]

Some people paid out hefty sums to tie into someone else's telephone illegally. A desperate resident of Herzliya ran an ad offering to buy a phone line from a neighbor for several thousand dollars. (Such deals are prohibited by law.) Anyone who moves, even across the hall, forfeits his/her phone and joins a new waiting list – the "transfer" list. Such transfers are liable to last many months. When people sell their apartments, their phones are disconnected and the new tenant joins the waiting list. To avoid this labyrinth, tens of thousands use telephones listed under names of previous owners, including some who are no longer alive. These are known as "black" telephones; their users are not listed in the telephone directory. In 1981, the Ministry of Communications announced a one-time "telephone cleanup" project, in which subscribers would come forward and identify themselves. Thirty thousand applied, resulting in another waiting list that took the clerks many months to sort out.[102]

After your long-awaited telephone has been installed, you get acquainted with the service. You sit and wait for a dial tone. On interurban calls, you hear, "All lines in the direction you have called are engaged." Lines go dead after dialing. Service numbers – information, repairs, overseas calls – are chronically busy. Forty out of every 100 attempted calls fail.[103] Calls are abruptly cut off. Disturbances, noises, and other conversations on one's line are routine occurrences. Telephones are frequently out of order. "The number of phones out of order is about 5,000 at present, in contrast to 4,000 phones that are usually out of order in the summer," said the Director-General of the Ministry of Communications. But there is a winter season, too: "The Ministry of Communications' technicians hope that once the rain stops it will be possible to fix most of the telephones that broke down over the last few weeks... There are more than 8,000 in the central district alone."[104] Is rain a phenomenon unique to Israel? There's a waiting list for repairs, of course. There it's the same old story: long lines, "pull", running back and forth between clerks, bribery, etc. Sometimes people wait for weeks and even months for a repair that should take a mere couple of minutes. Thus, for example, the story of Iris Dishon, as recounted in the letters column of the daily *Hadashot*:

> When my phone went dead three and a half months ago, I went into a regular regimen of talks with the people on the telephone company's repair service line. I spoke with a number of technicians. "Technichian number twenty-five, good morning" promised to attend to the matter; he sent a technician, who wandered around in the yard and found nothing. "Technician number forty, good morning" took over six weeks later; he could not find my recurrent complaints and slipped me into the work plan as if mine was a new job. The 'control center' told me my problem was still being dealt with, and that I must not forget that it was a matter of an underground cable. I went on

vacation, leaving a note on the door and key with the neighbors. I came back; the phone was still on vacation. The district engineer put me at ease by noting that he was already recording my new complaint. After waiting a few more days, I capitulated once and for all. I would like to be very practical and give you the phone number of my friend with the golden hands, who fixed my phone in no more than six minutes by jiggling some loose wires in the metal box in my yard. But I must not do that, because the rules forbid me to hire a private technician."[105]

Prof. Joan Flanders of the Tel Aviv University Department of Economics stated that the shortage of telephones and the overloaded lines harm the economy in hundreds of thousands of work hours, inefficient allocation of manpower, and impaired productivity.[106] Former MK and Communications Minister Meir Amit said: "Without a modern communication system, there will be neither economic growth nor development." He knew what he was talking about. Optrotech Ltd., a high-tech firm with 175 employees, tried unsuccessfully to order a telephone in 1984.[107] When the hospitals wanted to link their computers for rapid transfer of information, the lines could not be made available. Foreign investors threatened to call off industrial projects because of the telephone shortage. Aryeh Feingold of Ramat Gan, an ex-paratrooper and engineer who established a prosperous computer company in California, told *Maariv* correspondent that he wanted to return to Israel and hoped to find a suitable location for his plant – one with a telephone.[108] With such an infrastructure, how can Israel possibly compete abroad?[109]

Telephone directories proved to be "mission impossible" for the Ministry of Communications. Phone books came out at intervals of three years or more. They were partially obsolete before the ink dried, and contained numerous errors and misprints. In 1982, the job was turned over to a private company. Lo and behold! Now the directories are up-to-date, convenient, and on time.

Negligent planning and amateurish administration are some of the causes of the telephone fiasco. In some cases, telephone centers were built yet remained empty for years, while the equipment rotted in some storeroom. Ministry officials always imagined that the demand for telephones would be less than it actually was. Lack of productivity characterized telephone company workers. In the country's early years, one would see a van or even a truck with six employees going to install a phone. In 1978, a team of two technicians plus driver would install two telephones daily, this feat being rewarded with a 30 percent premium. Absenteeism ran at 20 percent, and a similar percentage of employees showed up late. In the early 1980s the press reported that two telephone technicians escorted by a driver hooked up one and only one phone in a whole day's work. At the end of 1981, the Ministry of Communications and the union signed an agreement whereby phones would be installed by one employee.[110] But how would he get there? He needed a driver, of course. *Ma'ariv* sums up the situation as of 1984:

> According to the "norm," the average Communications Ministry employee finishes work before noon and is free to moonlight. It has to be seen to be believed: a technician who's done fixing phones at 11 a.m. goes to work in a shirt factory. An employee whose job it is to empty tokens from public phones holds a second job at the same time. Even an idiot wouldn't need more than 10 minutes to splice a pair of switchboard wires. The Ministry of Communications gives its employees 30 minutes. So why should anyone make an effort?[111]

Under the weight of mounting public pressure, the Ministry of Communications decided to transfer telephone affairs to – you guessed it – a government corporation. After years of negotiations with the union, Bezek Ltd. (the word signifies blazing speed) came into being. This company is financially autonomous; the only funds it transfers to the Treasury are taxes. As for productivity, no great achievements have been registered to date. "As Bezek's second year of operations draw to a close,"

Aharon Dolav of *Ma'ariv* wrote in 1985, "telephone distress has reached new heights. Israelis have run out of patience, and despairing calls for civil disobedience have been sounded."[112] At first Bezek promised to clear away the waiting list within three years, then four, and finally five.[113] A reporter who followed phone technicians on their way to work saw them stop at a supermarket to do some shopping. When she queried their superior about it, he admitted: "Some go fishing on the job, too."

CHAPTER SIX

STRUCTURE OF THE ECONOMY

"Economic independence is not as far away as the pessimists think.... I draw my faith in the future from the facts of the past." Finance Minister Pinhas Sapir, 1960[1]

Despite Israel's success in numerous domains, and notwithstanding the countless talents and abilities of its citizens, Israel's economy was never healthy and, indeed, has steadily deteriorated over the years. This is reflected in the devaluation of the Israeli currency by a factor of 60,000 (6,000,000 percent) over 40 years: from $4 per Israeli pound to NIS (New Shekel) 1.5 to the dollar; the new shekel is worth 10,000 pounds. The economy has always been centralized, although the means of control have changed. There were periods with differential foreign exchange rates, administrative or fiscal constraints on imports, price and wage control, subsidies including incentives to investors, administrative edicts, and more.

It may come as a surprise to learn that the economic problems today were already there during Israels early days. As early as 1952, the government unveiled a new economic program to fight inflation and raise productivity.[2] The government promised that small industries and workshops would not be harmed.[3] The Manufacturers Association pledged the program its support, on condition that cost-of-living compensation be paid "at a suitable time" and that industry be partially exempted from income tax.[4] A month after the program got underway, inflation soared.[5]

True to the political establishment's tradition, Minister Dov Joseph blamed the public: "The new economic program is imperative because the population lives in luxury and waste, contrary to the basic laws of economics."[6]

In May, 1953, it was reported that production and exports declined since the new program had gone into effect.[7] This program was followed by a "Five-Year Plan" requiring vast investments. In 1961, the government established an Economic Planning Authority.[8] Other "solutions" to Israel's economic problems included repeated devaluations and "absorption" of money from the public (the Hebrew term for this literally means "sponging"). In 1962, Finance Minister Levi Eshkol decreed a compulsory loan as part of a New Economic Policy. In 1964 Minister Pinhas Sapir announced a still newer New Plan to cure the economy of its ills. Since then, Israelis have been blessed with any number of new economic programs: repeated devaluations, compulsory loans, taxation on whatever possible, three-digit inflation, and so on. The National Unity Government's New Economic Program (mid-1985) slashed inflation to 15-20 percent annually by means of price and wage control, but failed to cut the government budget sufficiently to eradicate it completely. The program also helped some industries by allowing them to lay off unnecessary employees. Basically, however, the structure of the economy remained unchanged: centralized, wasteful, unattractive to investors, and not conducive to development of high-tech industry. Israel's GNP and productivity are still the lowest in the Western world. Forty percent of the workers earn less than $450 a month. The balance-of-payments deficit grows steadily. Bureaucracy is bigger than ever. The economy is structured along obsolete lines. Taxes are the highest in the world, as are domestic and foreign debts.[9]

Between 1955 and 1960, Israel spent an average of 8 percent of its GNP, or 6.5 percent of all resources at the government's disposal, on defense.[10] This last figure includes foreign aid, and is about equal to the percentage of GNP devoted to defense in the United States. This alone refutes the establishment's claim that Israel's pre-1967 economic difficulties resulted from the heavy "defense burden." After the Six-Day War the defense budget doubled, reaching about $1 billion in 1972, $300,000,000 provided by the United States government. Defense expenditures increased steeply after the 1973 Yom Kippur War. American support also increased, reaching $3-4 billion per year in the 1980s. This sum is given partly in grant form, mainly for the procurement of equipment in the United States; some is a low-interest loan. As a result of these loans, Israel's external debt swelled by 300 percent between 1973 and 1983.[11] Why was the entire sum not given as a grant? After the Camp David accords (1979), Prime Minister Menachem Begin refused to accept "charity" and insisted that most of the support be given in loan form.[12] Before Camp David, too, the government did not ask that all the support be in grant form. This was a grave mistake. One takes out a loan to build an industry in expectation of repaying it from future profits. A defense loan, however, is a yoke which cannot be borne indefinitely. Washington eventually understood the consequences of this policy and started supporting Israel by way of grants only, adding an "economic grant" to cover debt repayment. Nevertheless, Israel is at a disadvantage compared with NATO countries, which do not pay for the research and development included in the price of arms, and which receive additional discounts not given to Israel.

In the Israel-U.S. military relationship, the U.S. comes off best. Experts believe that the existence of the Israeli Army saves America the cost of maintaining an expeditionary force in the Middle East. It is argued in response that Israel may not always be able or willing to serve as America's surrogate. Even so, America still gets the better of the deal. Israel's major contribution lies in combat-testing American arms, suggesting important improvements, and supplying information about Russian arms and other confidential matters. Affluent countries like

West Germany and Japan survive with minuscule defense budgets because the United States carries their defense burden. Why than does the Israeli government insist on imposing this unnecessary financial burden on its populace?

Economic experts differ over the actual size of Israel's defense budget. Some assess it at 32 percent of GNP; others speak of 5 percent, taking American economic aid into account.[13] The latter approach is basically correct, for the "economic aid" is intended to compensate Israel for repayment of military loans incurred in previous years. The entire defense burden comes to some $5.5 billion annually, the Bank of Israel reports. Net American aid is $3 billion. Diaspora Jewish support brings in another half-billion or so. Subtracting $3.5 billion from $5.5 billion leaves $2 billion, or approximately 8 percent of GNP. Some economists add to this sum the loss of production from compulsory military service, estimated at $1.5 billion, justifying this by noting that military service does not pay a salary. While this approach is right in principle, the financial estimate is highly exaggerated. The Army supports many soldiers' families. Others study during their service, completing high school or acquiring specific skills such as electronics, mechanics, or truck driving, for which they would have to pay in civilian life. The Army also performs many non-military duties, such as teaching in development areas, extricating tourists lost in the countryside, and many other tasks whose expense would normally be considered civilian. In one army formation (Nahal), soldiers spend part of their military service doing farm work on kibbutzim. Irrespective of the merit of this arrangement, it certainly should not be included in the defense budget.

Although it is very hard to quantify the Army's contribution to the development of technology and to furthering military exports, there can be no doubt that it plays a leading role in these domains. Moreover, the Defense Ministry pays duty on every item of imported military equipment, thus "reimbursing" the Treasury for a substantial proportion of the defense budget.

Taking all this into consideration, one should add no more than half-billion to the defense budget, and certainly not $1.5 billion. Summing up, Israel's defense burden costs somewhere between $2-2.5 billion per annum, or 8-10 percent of GNP. This would seem rather high compared with the United States, where the defense budget is only about 7 percent of GNP. Per-capita defense spending, however, is $980 per annum in the U.S. and $480-$600 in Israel. This is because per-capita GNP is approximately $14,000 per year in America, bust just $6,000 in Israel. In other words, the major problem is Israel's low GNP. Were it twice as high as it should be considering the country's potential – Israel's defense burden would be 4-5 percent of GNP, as it is in NATO nations.

The Lavi fighter craft would have cost much less than it did, were it not for the extensive featherbedding that pervades the government-owned aircraft industry. Neither is the government-owned armament industry the epitome of efficiency, to say the least. Colonel (Res.) Shimon Ziv, an economist who served many years in the Army General Staff's Financial Advisory Unit, has detailed the blatant waste of manpower in the IDF, especially among the higher ranks; the overstaffed headquarters; the plethora of unnecessary aides for senior commanding officers (and aides to aides), and so on. "These faults are minor compared with the Ministry of Defense," according to Ziv. It is frighteningly bloated... Instead of this awkward body serving the needs of the Army, the Army serves the Ministry... It's high time to ask if the entire ministry, especially as it functions at present, is not superfluous..."[14] Typically, the Soldiers Welfare Society, originally a volunteer organization, now employs about 700 people.[15]

Some think the army is immune to the problems that plague the civilian society and economy. This is a myth. One cannot expect the prevalent norms of civilian life to fail to penetrate the army to some extent. Were the economy based on sound principles, the defense budget could be much lower.

No country can survive without a defense budget. NATO nations allocate 4-5 percent of GNP, or half Israel's burden. Were Israel to defend itself with a similar level of allocation, between $1 billion and $1.5 billion would be saved every year. Would this make a substantial difference? Doesn't the government waste much more than that? Don't the ministers exceed the annual budget by at least that much? Following the 1983 bank share collapse, the government pledged to "compensate" shareholders to the tune of $7 billion. Hearing this, the Minister of Defense said: "This is three times the development budget of the Lavi fighter... It is a social, economic, and defense disaster."[16] What of the $3 billion dollars' worth of debts run up by farmers, and the $8 billion by the Histadrut's economic empire, which the government is covering one way or another? What about the 25 cabinet ministers? Not only does every ministry cost a fortune to maintain, but each minister strives to enlarge his empire's allocations. What about the presents given to industrialists and hoteliers, the enormous financial support awarded to the political parties, the legions of unnecessary bureaucrats, the political establishment's material benefits and overseas junkets, and so forth?

It is not defense expenditure that keeps Israel in a constant state of economic disaster, but the country's socialist, centralized regime, which has not changed since the 1920s. When Israel's politicians blame defense expenditure for the economic and social woes caused by their policies, they are simply throwing sand in the public's eyes.

Israel's labor legislation is considered among the most "progressive" in the world. It offers maximum protection versus the employer, and makes termination almost impossible. Ironically, this may be the main reason that the minimum wage stood at $320 per month in 1987 (under $300 a year earlier), and that 47 percent of salaried employees earned less than $400 per month.[17] By law, wage earners are organized under a works committee that represents them vis-a-vis their employer. Works committees enjoy legal immunity and cannot be held to account for breach of contract or damage done to employers or third parties in the strikes they organize.[18] Except for a small number of professionals (doctors, journalists, high-school teachers), all Israeli workers belong to the Histadrut, and all works committees are organized under it. A works committee requires Histadrut approval to declare a labor dispute. Since the Histadrut has historically (until 1977, and again since 1984) been controlled by the party heading the government, and because it owns economic enterprises of its own, it actually functions as a mediator between works committees and employers, rather than representing the workers directly.

All salaries are determined in the wage agreement that governs the so-called public services. It embraces all employees of the government (national and local), the Jewish Agency, the universities, and related institutions. It is a comprehensive, national-level agreement between the Treasury, the Histadrut, and workers' representatives. Since it encompasses a very large percentage of employed Israelis, it serves as a model for a second national contract, between the workers and the Coordinating Bureau of Economic Organizations. The latter body represents manufacturing, trade, hostelry, agriculture, services, and the like. The Treasury and the Histadrut participate in these negotiations, too. The moment this accord is signed, the Minister of Labor usually issues an order expanding its application to all employers, that is, those who were not parties to the talks. Finally, local negotiations adapt the national agreement to particular prevailing conditions. Thus the government and the Histadrut actually determine every salary, irrespective of productivity or effort. Since it is virtually impossible to discharge anyone who has tenure (and tenure is acquired automatically after six months on the job), the productivity of the least efficient becomes the norm. The inevitable consequence is low productivity, featherbedding as high as tens of percent, contemptuous attitudes toward work, moonlighting on the job, and more.

Another Israeli practice with ruinous effect on work morale is "linkage," i.e. occupational wage scales attached to each other in a certain order. If workers in a given trade get a raise, there is no way of denying it to everyone. The impact of linkage on true wage equilibrium, which can be achieved only by the law of supply and demand, is disastrous.

The truth is that neither employers nor employees ever really let the comprehensive agreement and linkage regulate wages. The two practices wreak too much havoc on productivity and on labor relations in general. They cause incessant economic unrest and pit everyone at each other's throats. Powerful unions, like those of the Israel Electric Company or El Al (both government corporations), claimed that their jobs required "greater effort" than the jobs of others. The result is a set of special bonuses for persons employed in particular industries. When this epidemic was at its pinnacle, there were some 1,000 "special" salary increments; in 1986, some 200 still existed. The most absurd of these was the "shame bonus" once given to income tax collectors for the embarrassment that allegedly came with their job. In 1977, various groups of microbiologists obtained the following "special" bonuses: academic, special effort, continuous education, hospital duty, "on call," clothing, and "encouragement."[19] Chauffeurs of cabinet ministers received bonuses for serving as "bodyguards" and for bearing arms. When El Al's fourth Boeing 747 went into service, most El Al employees received a "Jumbo" bonus.[20] In certain professions where there is virtually no chance of being summoned after working hours, lump sums are paid for "preparedness" and "superpreparedness," whatever that means. Some members of these trades were awarded no less than 45 days of "preparedness" pay per month.

Another way of circumventing the comprehensive agreement is to disguise raises as "reimbursement of expenses." People who never work at home are reimbursed for use of home phones. People who do not own cars receive car allowances. People who neither travel nor dine away from home are routinely paid per diem. Perks include fictitious working norms and premiums, special terms for loans and retirement, "professional literature" allowances for unskilled laborers, and more. Thus the Treasury assists cheaters and, since it is the country's largest employer, it cheats itself. The sheer volume of the perks and bonuses gave rise to the unique Israeli pay slip, known as the "noodle." This large computer printout records all current payments, retroactive payments, advance payments and deductions against previous advance payments. A representative section of such a sheet appeared in the *Maariv* business supplement in 1984:

SUM*	ITEM	CODE
100560	Combined wage	
13000	Seniority bonus	101
1470	Family bonus	100
56290	Cost-of-living increment	
34410	Exclusivity bonus	102
24950	Travel time	132
7220	Travel	146
2600	Literature	153
8600	Miscellaneous payments	165
5770	Telephone	185
9000	Clothing supplement	187
25200	Vacation supplement	186
7800	Vehicle supplement	105
7100	On-call supplement	131
12500	Royalty supplement	134
10800	Parity supplement	155

* Figures listed are in old shekels, when the rate was $1 = 200 shekels.

SUM	ITEM	CODE
22100	Management supplement	156
11000	Staff supplement	133
5600	Per diem	110

NET	WITHHOLDING
146388	219582

But the noodle does not tell all. Employees' "social benefits" augment pre-tax pay by up to 40 percent. One of the most conspicuous of these is the Supplementary Education Fund, a dollar-indexed tax shelter originally intended to enable academics and researchers to refresh themselves abroad. Similar is the sabbatical year. Full professors receive close to $50,000, tax-free, plus travel expenses for themselves and family members. A professor foolish enough to spend his/her sabbatical year in Israel stays on regular salary – about $12,000 per year net. In other words, Israel's professors are, in effect, expelled from the country every seventh year. By 1984, so many other groups of workers were awarded the supplementary education benefit that some 460,000 people, a third of Israel's work force, were on the wagon. They have the option of taking a trip abroad after three years or taking the money, tax-free, after six. Their Supplementary Education Fund has ballooned into a monstrosity in which $10 million accumulates monthly.[21] A report in *Ha'aretz* entitled "A Joke Called the Supplementary Education Fund" describes this ridiculous product of the obsolete, inadequate, and wasteful wage system in force today:

> 'Join the Navy and See the World' used to be the British Navy's popular motto. This week, the Journal of Academicians in the Social Sciences and the Humanities brought that slogan back to mind, but with a small difference: Join the Supplementary Education Fund and see the world. It appears in a

> full-page ad run by the Organizing Committee for Professional Tours. The 24,000 members were offered two options: 21 days in Southern Africa, or 23 days on an "extensive professional tour of Kenya.
> Looking at the program, I wondered what kind of professional education one can obtain in the nature reserves of Kenya or in Sun-City, Kruegger Park, Swaziland, Zululand, Garden Road, and other exotic places in Southern Africa. Everybody knows, of course, that these "professional tours" are nothing but fiction. This time, however, it seems that the organizational committee did not even attempt to camouflage that fact.[22]

All these additions wrought havoc with the salary structure. In 1963, the wages of civil servants comprised 98 percent base and 2 percent supplement; by 1981, the ratio was 61 and 39 percent, respectively.[23] Yet this is not all. Journalist Shoshana Hen reports:[24]

> Hundreds of thousands of workers in government enterprises receive full-course meals on the job, either free or at a ridiculously low price. The heavily subsidized meals, which cost the taxpayer tens of millions of dollars yearly, permit public employers to circumvent the rigid salary agreements and give their employees an untaxed, covert raise. Private enterprises and Histadrut companies charge employees 10 to 30 percent of the cost. In the (government-owned) Israel Aircraft Industry, employees are allowed to take home rolls, cheese, and canned fish, instead of eating them at the plant.

Although these meals were fully taxable at the time, the authorities overlooked that little fact; in 1986, the meals were officially declared tax-exempt.[25]

Holiday gifts to employees, another tax-exempt component of wages, have become a $60-120 million industry. The value of these presents varies from one employer to the next.[26] Some give several bottles of wine or something to put in the kitchen. Others hand out silverware or gift certificates. A few say "happy holiday" with leather coats, carpets, or even washing machines.[27]

Then there is "overtime," in which one's salary is boosted for doing nothing. One of the Jewish Agency departments, for example, pays some of its employees 165 hours of "overtime" per month throughout the year (that's 1,980 hours, or seven hours a day for each of the 280 work-days in the year!) for "work" performed at home.

Above and beyond all of these are "social conditions," a catch-word for all additional fringe benefits employees have managed to obtain. While these "conditions" are theoretically taxable, it is more than doubtful whether the tax is actually paid. At the Histadrut-owned Vulcan Batteries Ltd. in 1986, employees enjoy assorted social benefits:[28]

1. 4 small towels and 2 large ones
2. 63 bars of soap ("Hawaii" Brand)
3. 45 lbs. of washing machine detergent
4. 2.5 lbs. of instant coffee
5. Vouchers for 20 containers of milk
6. 66 lbs. of sugar
7. 6 packages of tea
8. 6 undershirts
9. 6 pairs of socks
10. 1 hat
11. 1 wool sweater (every two years)
12. Vouchers for women instead of items 8-11
13. Additional vouchers for not missing any work days for a month [29]

Is that all? Hardly. Egged members and their families ride the buses for free. That's a modest perk compared with the unlimited free electricity enjoyed by the Electric Company's 8,000 employees and their families. In many cases their enjoyment reaches twice or three times national average, and cases have been uncovered where such employees sell electricity to their neighbors. Electric Company employees have often been asked to relinquish this bonus, or at least to agree to limitations. They reply: "When everybody else, including cabinet ministers and Members of Knesset, gives up his benefits, we'll give up ours." This, of course, puts an end to the matter.

Children of University employees do not pay tuition fees. When the bank employees caught on, they used the same logic and demanded zero-interest or, at least, low-interest loans. Believe it or not, management acceded. And so on, wherever possible.[30]

Another salary bonus is a special variety of severance pay called "compensation." By law, discharged workers are entitled to severance pay equivalent to one month's salary per year of employment. In reality, terminated employees often get up to three times more. The copper miners of Timna (near Eilat) got 400 instead of 100 percent.[31] "Compensation" is paid not only upon discharge but, at times, when the place of employment changes ownership or moves to another site – even when this does not require the employee to move.

The results are massive featherbedding, wide salary differentials based on ability to exert pressure, higher salaries in the civil service than in industry, and strained labor relations accompanied by strikes, sanctions, and demonstrations. A good example is Chemavir Ltd., which specializes in aerial cropdusting of cotton fields. For some time its pilots received 12 monthly salaries of $6,000 each, although less than half the year is suited to cropdusting. Every summer they spent one week per month with their families in a luxury hotel. Every pilot had a company car, including gas and maintenance at company expense. Nor was this all. As a result, the price of aerial cropdusting rose 500 percent within 5 years, and it became cheaper to spray on the ground. Chemavir's losses mounted; ultimately the company nose-dived toward bankruptcy.[32] This is why manufacturing in Israel is unprofitable. The cost of labor is exorbitant and has nothing to do with output and productivity. Executive salaries, especially in banking and insurance, are notorious. At the Histadrut-owned Tadiran plant in Afula, the average production worker earned about $260 a month while the CEO was paid $8,000 monthly – thirty times more! (1985 figures)[33]. One of Israel's highest salaries is that paid by one of the Histadrut's concerns to its CEO: $36,000 per month.

And so, despite the utterances of Histadrut functionaries about the glories of socialism, simple laborers do not have an easy time of it. Not only does the Histadrut neglect to protect their interests, it is actually an active partner in the negotiations that keep their pay low. In 1985, half of the salaried earned less than the minimal taxable wage of $360 per month.[34] At that time the minimum monthly wage was $187;[35] it was raised to $220 in mid-1986 and to $320 in 1987. While serving as Prime Minister, Shimon Peres noted that 40 percent of the adult population was earning less than $265 a month.[36] In 1985, the secretary of the Beersheba Workers Council said that many Negev employers pay their workers no more than $150 per month, as in underdeveloped countries.[37] The Knesset recently passed an "income maintenance" law, a Social Security supplement to salaries below a certain minimum. All this occurs in a country where most salaries are determined by the government!

Studies have shown that Israeli labor is potentially among the best in the world.[38] Reality, however, differs. Salaries depend neither on effort, nor diligence, nor talent, but on how adept the workers are at milking the government. This leads by necessity to productivity that starts out low and gets worse with time. Overemployment, outdated equipment, indifferent and incompetent management – often hired because of political pressures – all contribute to low productivity. In 1981, Israel's Labor Productivity Institute found that Israeli workers are about half as productive as their Western counterparts.[39] In 1979, product per employee was $14,300 in Israel compared with in $32,000 in Switzerland and $24,000 in the United States.[40] The

President of the Manufacturers Association blamed this on featherbedding, which he estimated at thirty to forty percent.[41] Yosef Lapid of *Ma'ariv* offered an eyewitness account:

> They're fixing a sidewalk. A municipal van is parked alongside. The driver's listening to music. The foreman sits in the shade. Two workers are at work... Had the city hired a private contractor to fix the sidewalk, the driver would be laying the flagstones. One man instead of four.[42]

Between 1974 and 1984, output per worker grew by the negligible increment of $700 – from $16,800 in 1974 to $17,500 in 1984, that is less than half a percent per annum – while the cost of labor soared by about 5.3 percent per year, or 65 percent for the decade! In this respect, Israel is first in the West. Only France came close at 45 percent; all the other countries had rates less than half as large. That means the gap between labor costs and output is on the rise.[43]

What Israel's unskilled workers produce is unprofitable and unfit for export unless heavily subsidized. Their salaries are not much higher than those in Korea or Singapore, but the product is immeasurably inferior. Hence, Israel must pin her hopes on sophisticated, technologically advanced industries: electronics, aircraft construction, and so on. Salaries in these fields consist of three components: net wage or take-home pay; gross wage, that is, take-home pay before tax deductions; and total cost to the employer, which includes additional payments by the employer that do not appear on the pay slip.

In 1985, Prof. Yair Aharoni compared the salaries of American and Israeli engineers. Each grossed about $2,000 per month. The American engineer cost his company $2,500 (after Social Security and income tax withholdings) and took home $1,500. The ratio between employer's cost and net wage was 1.67:1. In Israel, engineers' salaries included cars owned or paid for by the firm. They cost their employers $3,100 per month, $600 more than the American engineer. Yet their net wage was $700, resulting in a 4.5:1 ratio between cost to the firm and takehome pay. Income tax withholding was about $1,000 – twice that in the United States.[44] Since then, Israel introduced a "mini-reform" that lowered tax rates somewhat. Because the U.S. implemented a major tax cut at the same time, the difference is even greater now. Deductions for Social Security and other social benefits are also larger in Israel than in the U.S. Bear in mind that workers' output relates to take-home pay, not to the cost to the company. As the former Director-General of the Finance Ministry, Yaakov Neeman, put it, "Israel is among the most regressive countries in this respect... Nowhere else in the world does a worker cost his employer three times his net wage."[45] Under these circumstances, profitable exports are virtually out of the question. Hence the need for government subsidies, in various forms and amounts chosen by the government for each industry and individual plant. The attendant bureaucratic process wastes time, costs money, and obliges companies to run after the officials, begging for support. Is there a better way to render industry dependent on the regime?

In a free society, strikes or threats of strikes are a valuable means for regulating salaries. If workers feel their employer is taking too big a "cut" and leaving them with too little, they threaten to strike and follow through if the employer does not make sufficient concessions. The usual result is a raise in pay, if the company's profits permit it. If not, management demonstrates that a salary hike would cause the plant to shut down. Then labor may even agree to a pay cut in order to avoid layoffs. This actually happened in the early 1980s in the American automobile industry.

When salaries are directly or indirectly paid by government or other bodies that do not have to show a profit, matters are altogether different. Profit and loss considerations do not apply. When the employees of any such enterprises strike, they do so not against their employer but against the government. The

Labor Productivity Institute found that Israel's "public" sector is one of the world's most prolific strikers.[46] Under the existing system, even private enterprises are completely dependent on the government. It awards them protective customs and duties, tax exemptions, and even direct support. The result is that almost all strikes are directed against the government.

Labor disputes take the form of sanctions, strikes, demonstrations, and sometimes threatened or actual violence. The outcome is usually the same: the economy is severely harmed, the public suffers, and the government comes under pressure. In general, the government gives in – but not before the elderly and ill are hauled out of government-supported geriatric homes and dumped at hospital entrances, public transport is paralyzed, electric current cut off, and more. Needless to say, participants in Histadrut-approved strikes are immune to damage suits from injured third parties. In the end, Israel's occupational wage scale largely reflects the ability of various occupations to cause damage.

Sanctions mean partial cessation of work or what is known as 'non-performance of work while working.' Before national wage contracts are signed, tens of thousands or even hundreds of thousands of workers may be involved in sanctions. In January, 1984, several newspapers ran a daily "sanction directory" indicating which services could not be obtained. Who can count all the strikes aimed at Israelis with the intent to disrupt vital services? Teachers have spent years terrorizing mothers with threats of strikes; it is almost part and parcel of the beginning of each school year. Municipal workers strike every so often, allowing heaps of garbage to block sidewalks. Television employees darken the screens over every little dispute, even between a single technician and producer. Electric Company employees pull the plug because some politician suggested that their perks be re-examined. Civil servants walk out for reasons that are hardly explained. For years, dock workers sabotaged the economy with repeated strikes. Citrus fruit truckers caused growers grievous damage by striking at the height of the season.

The government has taught the workers over many years that by striking, they have nothing to lose but much to gain. In fact, the strikes can be viewed as a constant struggle to break the linkage between the various occupations and to earn a pay raise, usually "under the table." This is the inevitable result of a situation which, at first glance, seems to be the epitome of justice in an enlightened society: salaries are set not by "profit-crazy capitalists" but by the people's elected representatives. In reality, power bases and pressure groups determine who gets what. The most shocking manifestations of this never ending free-for-all came to light in the medical industry. Several years ago, Israel's doctors went on strike for months, treating only emergency cases. Their support professionals – nurses, X-ray technicians, hospital administrators – launched intermittent sanctions and strikes shortly after the doctors' strike. Ambulance drivers employed by the Red Magen David stunned the country by refusing to transport a child hit by a car and lying in the street, because they were on strike.[47] No less shocking was an announcement by striking firemen: "The whole country can go up in flames; we won't budge." They proved their point by allowing a large fire in the Carmel forest to run wild. In the end, they did budge – to prevent volunteers from extinguishing it.[48]

The fact that the government is the final arbiter on salaries lead to another type of labor struggle: public protests and demonstrations. Buses bedecked with slogans drive up to the Knesset in Jerusalem, packed with workers who have come to demonstrate. Some random headlines from the daily press: "500-Truck Convoy to Converge on Jerusalem Tomorrow for Demonstration on Knesset Plaza" (June 11, 1985); "Rishon Lezion Winery Workers Demonstrate Tomorrow in Jerusalem" (May 29, 1983); "Engineers and Academicians on Strike as of Tomorrow – Demonstration Today" (July 2, 1984); "Diamond

Workers in One-Day Strike in Sympathy with Employers" (August 3, 1983); "Public Works Department Workers Block Major Intersection; Traffic Jam Stretches for Miles" (August 1, 1985); "Taxis Converge on Jerusalem in Convoys of Hundreds for Demonstration" (June 5, 1985).

Actual violence by strikers often includes breaking into offices of company executives, the Histadrut Secretary-General,[49] or government ministers; disrupting board meetings; blocking factory gates to prevent shipment of goods; obstruction of tourist sites by tour guides, and more.

In the country's earlier years, the government set up labor-intensive enterprises "to create jobs" irrespective of profitability, knowing that it could always keep them afloat with subsidies of one kind or another. This approach attracted "industrialists" and Histadrut go-getters, who discovered a golden opportunity to get rich. Labor, too, got the point. Salaries may not have been high, but they were practically guaranteed. No large plant was ever allowed to go under; the government always came through at the last moment to ensure survival.

In the spring of 1985, the Ata textile concern went broke despite massive subsidies, and the government decided to let it expire. The workers were flabbergasted. Out of the blue, someone was suggesting that a factory running at a deficit had no right to exist. But why introduce this novelty at Ata? When management pulled the plug, the workers barricaded themselves in the plant, threatening to "horrify the whole country."[50] The next day, word got out that the Ata workers were armed with clubs and iron crowbars. They piled inflammable material around the gates and proclaimed, "This will be our Stalingrad." The chairman of the works committee said, "If police attempt to enter the plant, they'll be risking their lives. Blood will flow."[51] In the end, the workers were given extraordinarily generous severance pay (the "compensation" described above), and the plant was closed.

The Timna copper mines near Eilat went bust some years ago, but a skeleton crew stayed behind for maintenance. In 1985, the government decided to lay off these workers, too. In their struggle for higher severance pay, they locked themselves in the shafts with explosives and threatened to blow themselves up together with the mine.[52] They won 400 percent "compensation."

The workers of government-owned Israel Shipyards – a company characterized by low productivity and large deficits – went even further. After the government decided to close the yard and lay off 450 workers, the head of the works committee said: "I warn the ministers: they're risking their lives. We'll take to the streets, and the struggle will be bitter... We're not going to be another Ata... We'll prove that we know not only to build but also to destroy; we'll destroy missile-boats and submarines." After a court-imposed unpaid vacation, hundreds of workers forced their way into the shipyards and locked themselves in. "They've betrayed us...stabbed us in the back... We have nothing to lose... We'll dig in here and fight for our bread." The government capitulated. Today the shipyards continue to limp on, with heavy financial aid.[53]

The government and the Histadrut have convinced the public that they are duty-bound to provide "jobs." On the face of it, guaranteeing jobs even in money-losing plants is good for the workers. This is an obsolete thesis. To put it into practice requires heavy taxation that paralyzes the economy. Salaries are kept low by necessity. Management is not concerned with efficiency, renewal of equipment, and productivity. Products have to be protected from competing imports. The invariable results are high prices and inability to compete in foreign markets. Last but not least, the very existence of such plants prevents the establishment of profitable ones, because of the monopoly status they usually enjoy and the low productivity norms they have established, scaring off potential investors.

Israeli thinking assumes that the choice is between jobs in non-viable enterprises and no jobs at all. This is ridiculous. A wise taxation policy, coupled with a moratorium on aid to losing plants, would permit some to recover and start paying decent wages. It would also attract investors to establish profitable enterprises. Peter F. Drucker, the American management expert, points out:

> Between 1973 and 1985 manufacturing production in the United States rose by almost 40 percent. Yet manufacturing employment went down steadily. There are now 5 million fewer people in blue collar work in the American manufacturing industry than there were in 1975. Yet in the last 12 years total employment in the United States grew faster than at any time in the peacetime history of any country: from 82 to 112 million between 1973 and 1985, that is, by a full third... A country not increasing its production sharply over the coming years and not cutting down its manufacturing work force significantly at the same time cannot hope to remain competitive – or even to be considered a "developed" nation!... A nation preferring the preservation of places of employment for its blue-collar workers to its ability to compete on the international market – a condition requiring a steady decrease in the number of workers – will quickly find itself with neither production nor places of employment. The attempt to guarantee the places of employment of blue-collar workers is, in reality, a prescription for unemployment.[54]

One often hears Israelis complaining about the poor "work ethic" in the country. This concept is borrowed from the Soviet Union, where workers are awarded medals for high "work ethics." Similar prizes are awarded in Israel. Elsewhere (Switzerland, West Germany, the United States), good workers are rewarded with higher pay. When there is no connection between output and salary, there is no incentive to increase output. As long as Israel's economic structure clings to Soviet concepts, its labor productivity, too, will resemble that of the Soviet Union.

The government spends billions of dollars annually to sustain its deep involvement in the economy. Citizens are taxed mercilessly in order to satisfy the government's appetite. Despite American aid, Diaspora fundraising, domestic and foreign borrowing and all the rest, heavy taxation is still needed to cover government expenses. The nationalized economy, subject to politicians' whims, has turned the Treasury into a bottomless pit.

Even though the top marginal income tax bracket was 87 percent in 1974, taxes claimed only 40 percent of GNP, because many components of income were not taxed. After the 1975 reform, income tax was lowered to a maximum of 60 percent but was broadened to embrace all wage components. The tax burden grew steadily; by 1986 it set a world record: 56 percent of GNP according to the Bank of Israel,[55] and 69 percent according to reliable independent sources.[56] The latter figure includes Social Security remittances, because Social Security surpluses are transferred to the government and because its rates are the highest in the Western world. The marginal tax was reduced to 52.8 percent in 1987 and 48 percent in 1988. For most taxpayers, the difference is between two and four percent.[57] In 1989, Finance Minister Shimon Peres raised it again, this time to 51%.

The government resolves to cut its budget every year, but each minister resists any pruning of his own empire's outlays. Consequently, budget cuts are negligible. Even these are on paper only, because ministers routinely overrun their budgets. Then there is "no choice" but to raise existing taxes or invent new ones. In other words, talk of "budget cuts" usually ends up as a tax increase.[58]

In European countries where the tax burden exceeds 40 percent – Norway, Sweden, and the Netherlands – the take-home pay of wage-earners nevertheless supports a standard of living twice that of Israel's. In Israel, too, the lower income classes are heavily taxed. The lowest decile pays out 32 percent of its income in taxes. Until 1986, anyone earning more than $300 per month had to pay income tax. As of 1988, those earning less than $600 are effectively exempt. Everyone, of course, pays all indirect taxes.[59] The result is low productivity, lack of investment, flight of capital overseas, and rampant tax evasion. No wonder that Industrialist Stef Wertheimer has blamed taxation for "destroying" industry.[60]

The inevitable result of a hike in taxes is demand for wage raises with which to pay them. Then, of course, come new and higher prices. Since it is the government that sets wages, a never-ending round of threats, sanctions, and strikes develops -- leading sooner or later to the government's capitulation and, shortly thereafter, to another tax increase to cover the additional expenditure caused by the wage hike. So it goes, around and around like a dog with its tail on fire.

Although income tax brings in no more than 25 percent of the state's revenue, it severely damages the economy and public morale.[61] It interferes with citizens' lives, and makes labor so expensive that even though Israeli electronics engineers take home less than half an American engineer's salary, they cost their employers more. Israel's income tax hounds small businesses and the self-employed. It brought into existence a huge industry of consultants and accountants. It spawned an underground economy. It set prices on an unrealistically high level. It makes Israeli products non-competitive on world markets, unless subsidized. It stifles labor productivity and throttles investment.

It is a myth that income tax is "progressive" — that it takes from the rich and gives to the poor. The top 1 percent garner 11 percent of all income and the top decile close to 40 percent, while the bottom three deciles, taken together, live on 3 percent.[62] If the Israeli way is "progressive," why do salary embellishments and other giveaways accrue so blatantly to those of high rank? Anyone familiar with the mechanism of political pressure in a centralized economy knows that it cannot be otherwise. The lower strata are thrown a bone before elections.

As for tax deductions: Industrialists may travel abroad at least twice a year on "recognized" business trips. "Recognized" means tax-deductible and charged to the company. The same applies to company cars and other perks. In addition, companies hire lawyers and accountants, whose high salaries are at least partly deductible, for the purpose of reducing the taxes their clients have to pay. The underpaid income tax officials lack the professional know-how to contend with them. The fact that Israel taxes low incomes while showering the wealthy with a stable of tax breaks refutes the claim that this tax is meant to narrow economic or social disparities.

Next in importance is Value Added Tax (VAT), presently set at 15 percent. Import taxes reach absurd levels – from 160 to 300 percent on private cars, depending on engine displacement. There is also an annual property tax of 2-3 percent of the car's value. This tax does not affect the 56,000 "senior executives" who enjoy the use of company cars, nor the tens of thousands who are reimbursed for car expenses.[63] This is a deliberate and selective way to hurt "simple people" as well as academicians and small merchants.

Electric appliances such as TVs, refrigerators, ovens, and vacuum cleaners are considered "luxuries" and taxed from 75 percent (washing machines) to 130 percent (air conditioners). Again, the main burden is on the weaker social strata; after all, who can maintain even the most modest household without a refrigerator? A fixed tax of $440 was imposed on VCRs. An automatic answering machine costs six times as much in Israel as in the U.S. After continuous pressure, taxes on automobile air conditioners were cut in order to make driving safer. A week later, air conditioners of all kinds were hit with new taxes, sending the prices of auto air conditioners up again.[64]

Payroll tax, levied since 1975, presently stands at 4 percent; manufacturing, hotels, construction, and agriculture are exempt. It punishes those who create jobs in any other sector.[65]

Travel tax is somewhere between $100 and $200, depending on officials' thinking at any given time. For some time they added a 20 percent levy on airplane tickets. That was an act of desperation. About half the travelers had somebody buy the tickets abroad, repaying him illegally at some later time. In addition, a high percentage of travellers are either civil servants whose expenses are covered by the state, or businessmen whose travel expenses are deductible.[66] Travel taxes bring in little net revenue, but they make life difficult for the average citizen. Again, they put the main burden on the lower income classes, who are reimbursed by no one and have no business expenses against which to claim a deduction.

To finance the war in Lebanon, a "Peace for Galilee levy" was imposed; the self-employed had to pay three times the amount charged to wage-earners with identical incomes.[67]

Though the architects of Israel's economy are rarely noted for innovative thinking, they seem to outdo themselves in the field of taxation. Taxes recently proposed[68] or imposed include a tax on withdrawals from bank accounts; a 2 percent levy on selling shares on the stock market; a tax on acquisition of foreign currency; an apartment purchase tax; a levy for medical services; a cash flow tax; a tax on all self-employed whose prices are not controlled; a platform tax on air cargoes; a tax on entry into Israel; taxation of supplementary education funds; a capital gains tax; a net capital tax (for those who have no gains); and a "luxury apartment" tax.

To this, one must add municipal taxes, which weigh heavily on residents and even more heavily on businesses.[69]

Preferential treatment of the rich is evident from the taxation of yachts. In 1980, the Finance Minister was asked why commercial vehicles were taxed at 100 percent of their value, while yachts were taxed at only 16 percent of theirs. He explained that yachts "generally serve commercially, in tourism." In 1982, taxation of yachts was raised – to 28 percent. The preferential treatment of the wealthy and the difficulties imposed on the less privileged are also obvious in many other areas of taxation. "Executives Insurance" (a form of comprehensive pension plan) is not taxed. The Labor-Likud "national unity" government slashed taxes on the cars of "senior executives". Journalist Yehoshua Meiri's comment: "The Treasury asked the Knesset Finance Committee to reduce taxes on the company cars of 56,000 high-ranking employees and increase the tax burden of the elderly and the infirm at the very same time." Low salaries are still subject to income tax, as we have seen, and rates for middle-decile salaries are very high. Again, the weight of the tax burden rests on the lower income strata. Other Treasury proposal include taxes on retired couples who earn more than $400 per month, and an education levy on all schoolchildren from first grade up.[70]

In 1980, wage-earners remitted to Social Security almost as much (80 percent) as they did to income tax. Economists noted that Social Security had evolved into a second income tax, and began to call it "Social Taxation."[71] Why does Israel's Social Security apparatus (called the National Insurance Institute) need so much money? First, surpluses are forwarded to the Treasury. Second, its own expenses are high because of the other taxes. In 1985, for example, Social Security paid NIS 48.07 (about $30) for every medical opinion it solicited. After deducting 15 percent VAT and 50 percent income tax, the doctor came away with NIS 16.72. In other words, for every shekel Social Security paid the doctor for an expert opinion, he/she kept 35 percent and handed over the rest in taxes.

The indirect taxes imposed on construction include: land property tax; construction property tax; municipal construction and development fee; customs and purchase tax on construction materials; value added tax; purchase tax paid by the buyer; and land registration fee. Together they account for 33 percent of the price of an apartment.[72] In addition, large sums are paid out for electricity and phone hookups – payments which are absent or insignificant in other Western countries. These two payments are nothing but taxes.

On top of all these is income tax. The labor component of construction is about 50 percent of the total cost. The income tax authorities estimate contractors' profit margins at about 30 percent, and tax them commensurately. Thus, the assumption that income tax accounts for an additional 20 percent of an apartment's cost is clearly not exaggerated. It follows that over half of the price of an apartment comprises taxes. This fails to take account of the excessive prices of cement and iron, which result from both being (Histadrut) monopolies.

For decades, the government has declared itself in favor of "encouraging" the construction of apartments for rental. This is clearly the proper solution for new immigrants, young couples, and many others. A rental building has to make good on its investment in 10-12 years. At the present cost of construction and the average Israeli salary, it takes twice as long. This is why no contractor can undertake such an enterprise. Thus young Israelis leave the country when they realize they will never be able to acquire an apartment. This is particularly true for those who leave kibbutzim, and helps explain the high rate of emigration among kibbutz youth. Others struggle for years under the yoke of a high-interest, fully-indexed (interest and principal!) mortgage. Potential immigrants are repelled for the same reason. Many Jews in South Africa claim they cannot take more than, say, $100,000 out of the country. In Australia or Canada, that suffices to buy a shop or some other source of income. In Israel, it barely puts a roof over one's head. Finally, the high price of apartments — caused mainly by the abnormal taxation -- is one of the reasons for the overall high cost of living.

The income tax authorities employ about 4,000 clerks. Their work pace and motivation, however, adhere to the civil service standard: empty offices, arriving late, absenteeism, and reading newspapers on the job. That is what they do. What they do *not* do is coordinate and exchange information with the other revenue-collecting bodies. It often happens that one roving tax bureaucrat, another from Social Security, still another from Value Added Tax, and a fourth in charge of "deductions" will all visit a single business within a short period of time. When the property tax was abolished in early 1981, hundreds of employees who had been handling it refused to move over to the income tax apparatus, and wandered around doing nothing, drawing their salaries, for nearly two years. Tax return audits are hopelessly in arrears, and countless households are not audited at all. Because they must show results, the clerks hit well-known taxpayers with huge assessments and send them scrambling to prove their "innocence." Consequently, it is the honest taxpayer who is increasingly pinched. The Bureau of Certified Public Accountants has noted in alarm that half of the tax clerks' assessments against the self-employed and corporations are erroneous and result in harassment of the public. Quality people in the tax system who master the rules leave the service and become private consultants. Former Income Tax Commissioner Dov Neiger once claimed that if he had 300 additional inspectors, he could give Ronald Reagan a loan. The current Commissioner recently asserted that thousands of delinquents are not taken to court, and millions of dollars in revenue not collected, due to lack of manpower in the prosecution and legal attachment bureaus. Summing up, Israel's tax collection apparatus has thousands of employees, and is typified by an absence of professionals, numerous errors, unchecked harassment, damage to the public, and failure to cooperate with other revenue-collecting agencies. That makes it an expensive, inefficient, and obviously unjust business.[73] Therefore, the Income Tax Commission has to flex its muscles. In 1985, for that very purpose, it set up a "tax commando" unit to launch raids on the public. Tax commandos set up roadblocks, stopped cars, and confiscated the vehicles of anyone appearing on their blacklist unless he paid up on the spot. Maybe they were wrong, but there was no one to complain to. The legality of this operation was called into question, but it went on anyway. Other operations include attempts to ambush drivers in parking lots, frisking of businessmen by VAT clerks, forcing storekeepers to disclose the identities of anyone making purchases of more than $250, and other similar measures.[74]

How has the government responded? By granting exemptions to select groups. Thus, the marginal tax rate set for the "Israel Company" for 30 years was 28 percent! In 1976 tax relief was extended to recipients of compensation and wage differentials, and to homeowners, landlords, and farmers. Next in line were industrial workers. The kibbutzim were awarded their very own tax computation system. Then came newly demobilized army veterans with jobs in agriculture, construction, and manufacturing, and people renting flats to soldiers. Married college students were granted a credit for rental housing, and all students an exemption for "study equipment." Then came relief for butchers and a refund of the Peace for Galilee levy paid to exporters and to businesspeople who spend 181 days per year abroad. Additional benefits were given to new immigrants, shift workers, ex-soldiers, frontier settlements, imported goods for hotels, Eilat and Mitzpe Ramon, VAT for hotels, exporters' dock fees, and executives' pension plans. The latter is in fact a tax shelter for the uppermost income decile.[75] The list is hardly complete, but it shows where things are headed.

Exemptions can be terribly humiliating. Because work clothing is tax-exempt, employees of Tel Aviv University have been issued coupons for buying clothes with labels reading "Tel Aviv University" in the envelope; they are asked to attach the labels to the clothes they buy.

The tax breaks and exemptions add up to a set of camouflaged subsidies. There is no difference between handing money to people or organizations and awarding tax relief, except that the latter method is less conspicuous, less infuriating, and often less verifiable as to its magnitude.[76] Things have reached the point that the volume of exemptions was estimated in 1986 at some $1.8 billion, or about 30 percent of tax revenues.[77] It is self-evident that a more logical way to handle the matter would be to lighten the entire public's tax burden by 30 percent and do away with the relief and exemptions. That, we may reasonably assume, would result in higher total revenues. The political establishment, however, prefers to disregard this possibility. Anything by which it can retain power, keep the public dependent, and decide who pays a lot, who a little, and who nothing at all, is better.

As if the official exemptions with their implications were not bad enough, the system's unofficial exemptions are comparably repulsive. Income tax hardly hits some parts of the ultra-Orthodox community. The Tax Commissioner says: "When we go into an ultra-Orthodox quarter at one end, they've already shut down the stores at the other end. They have a highly developed intelligence network. We haven't yet found the right tactic for dealing with this sector." In other cases involving the ultra-Orthodox, tax inspectors were physically assaulted and political pressure was applied to close files.[78] In short, the T-men are frightened off, leaving a cross-section of the public untaxed.

The problem is more serious among Israel's Arabs, who comprise almost 20% of the national population. Arabs on the payroll of large enterprises remit withholding tax, but self-employed Arabs and Arab farmers pay virtually nothing. Several Knesset committees have studied the matter and found that even as the Arabs' standard of living has soared, the Arabs pay only about 2 percent of income tax.[79] But attempts to collect taxes from the Arabs are regularly met by mob violence. The authorities usually prefer to turn a blind eye rather than make waves.

In this context, it is interesting to note that since 1967 the standard of living of the Arabs in Judea and Samaria has risen by 200-300 percent. Enterprises in these areas compete with Israeli ones (at least with respect to simple industrial goods). In construction and almost every other skilled trade, Arab contractors underprice their Israeli competition. They are able to do so because they pay negligible income tax and value added tax. As the Israeli economy stagnates and deteriorates before our very eyes, Judea and Samaria are the scene of a kind of controlled laboratory experiment on how well a virtually untaxed economy can perform.

When the tax burden crosses a certain threshold, all income earners become lawbreakers. Basic economics texts mention this truth as self-evident. Indeed, a tax burden such as ours makes evasion a virtual imperative for anyone who can engage in it. When more than half the price of an apartment is tax, when people in business and services are little more than tax collectors, the incentive and temptation to cheat on taxes becomes almost irresistible. Furthermore, both sides to a transaction come out ahead by paying under the table. Anyone offering a service answers queries about prices with another question: "With or without a receipt?" All the underground repairmen combined are still small potatoes, of course. The large-scale evasion is committed by big companies, including some that are respectable and well-known.

How much money is involved? Estimates vary. A study by Dr. Y. Kondor assessed income tax and VAT evasion at $3 billion per year, mainly in construction, transportation, and diamonds. Uriel Lynn, the former Supervisor of State Revenues, estimates the volume of the "black" economy at 30 percent of GNP, and most appraisals in the mid-1980s approach the higher figure.[80] Some of this wealth, converted into foreign currency or gold, is stashed in people's homes in what Israelis call "floor-tile accounts." Some is simply spent on consumer goods. Much of it is smuggled abroad and invested there. According to World Bank estimates, Israelis hold $2.6 billion in overseas bank accounts. Others believe the sum to be much higher. All in all, the "black" or underground capital accumulated over the years is estimated at somewhere between $15 billion and $30 billion.[81] All levels of the country's economy deal in underground capital, either sneaking it in and out or handling it in some other way. Banks set up straw companies. Travel agents are suspected of smuggling tickets. Importers present inflated bills so as to leave dollars abroad. Exporters falsify their added value figures for the same reason. Much of the economic power of Israeli firms is abroad.

For years, proposals on laundering underground capital have been bandied about; anyone with such capital would be given a chance to declare it, pay a little fine, and come away clean. The proposals are turned down every time. Economists and Treasury bureaucrats admit that as long as the tax burden is not reduced, the underground economy can never be eliminated.[82] Not that Israel is the only country with an underground economy. Similar shenanigans have been the salvation of the Soviet and Italian economies, to cite two examples. Other Western countries, too, have their under-the-table dealings. Almost all Western countries, however, have seen the light and brought their tax rates down. Israel is left with the highest burden in the Western world. The volume of the underground economy stands in direct proportion to the level of taxation.

A veteran businessman who has toiled all his life to establish an export industry contends:

> The difference between a free country and a nationalized one is like the difference between prosperity and economic collapse. Even countries rich in natural resources collapse when they nationalize the economy. Israel, which has absolutely no natural resources apart from the added value produced by skilled labor, is already approaching the last stage of nationalization. We see the results in the field... Government tax collection has reached 80-90 percent: now as income tax, then as Social Security, then again as National Insurance, and finally as city rates... And they're still at work devising more... My basic premise is that almost as many people are engaged in tax dealings – collecting taxes for the government or seeking ways to evade them for every system and factory – as in the export industries. It's only a matter of time until every-

> one understands that it doesn't pay to work and produce, especially when unemployment compensation is very close to workers' take-home pay...[83]

All told, it's a sad picture: a stagnant, shrinking economy that cannot keep itself afloat even though it abounds in the most important resources of our time: resourcefulness and education. It has wallowed in chronic crisis for decades, and survived only because of support from abroad. Productivity and standards of living are low. Capital taken out of productive use ("black" capital) reaches a magnitude of $20 billion and perhaps more. With such a sum one could rebuild the economy and make it prosper, but that's out of the question as long as taxation reaches or exceeds 60 percent of GNP and socialist-minded politicians hold the reins of the economy. The first and most important step toward a solution is to set the total tax burden at 30 percent of GNP. This measure would catalyze investment, boost productivity, and bring prices down. It might even save the government more money than it would lose by slashing taxes.

As might have been expected, the government has adopted measures that rapidly led to full takeover of the capital market. After studying the development of the financial market, Professor Ben-Shahar and his colleagues concluded:

> Instead of seizing the public's savings and allocating them to investors by itself, the government has transferred the technical execution of these transactions to the financial institutions, reserving to itself the right to make decisions. Thus Israel has something that looks like a financial system but has no content of its own.[84]

Israel's three large banks handle about 85 percent of all banking activity in the country. One of them (Hapoalim) belongs to the Histadrut, another (Leumi) is controlled by the World Zionist Organization, and the third (Discount) is owned and controlled by the Recanati family. A fourth bank (United Mizrahi) is owned by the National Religious Party. Other parties, too, set their eyes on having their own banks but have been turned down thus far – at least for now.[85] Even so, the banks – acting as a cartel – have been nationalized *de facto* by the instruments of monetary policy.[86] According to the managing director of Bank Hapoalim, "The government has in fact nationalized most financial resources and presently has full control of everything done in the money markets."[87]

It is the government that determines the types of savings schemes, the profits that banks may make, and to whom. Fifty percent of loans are issued to the government, and another forty percent are "directed" loans, that is, given to borrowers to whom the government has instructed the banks to lend. Less than ten percent of bank credit is used for loans to the public. "True, the government does not interfere in the operational management of the banks," says Dr. M. Heth, former Examiner of Banks and Chairman of the Board at Bank Leumi.[88] "But its massive involvement in determining how money is raised and credit allocated denies the banks their own judgment in a large proportion of their transactions." The same is true for special-purpose banks, such as those that provide mortgages, promote industrial development, or finance agriculture and pisciculture. Some of them are governmental *de jure*; the others are governmental *de facto*. The activities of the Industrial Development Banks, for example, may be considered virtually part of the government budget.[89]

Much of Israel's capital market is tied up in pension funds. Until 1957, these funds had nearly total discretion with respect to investments. Then the government decided to take over. At first, sixty-five percent of their money had to be put into "recognized investments" – government securities or bonds – with thirty-five percent left over for investments at their own discretion, including loans to members, insurance, and so forth. Since then the "recognized investment" proportion grew and grew, reaching some 92% by 1984. With regard to the social benefit funds and their money, another typical attribute of the Israeli regime surfaces: discrimination among citizens. By agreement between the Treasury and the Histadrut, the latter was allowed to channel half of the "recognized investment" to Histadrut company institutions – with government guarantee, of course.[90] Not until 1981 was this accord nullified. Insurance companies, too, have to keep much of their holdings in government bonds. Because Israeli banks could not profit by banking as their counterparts everywhere else do, two phenomena emerged. The Treasury and the Governor of the Bank of Israel compensated them by letting them rake in easy profits at the public's expense; and the banks looked for other areas of activity, leading them to embark on activities on – and past – the threshold of legality, and to play the stock exchange.

The State Comptroller's Report, No. 30, mentions various gifts and benefits to the banks. For one, large sums were granted to Bank Hapoalim as a result of faulty considerations and miscalculations by the Treasury with respect to indexation insurance arrangements. For another, banks were debited for indexation differentials on loans that had already been repaid. In other cases, fictitious indexation differentials were paid. Commission rates were set at unwarranted levels. Banks were allowed to profit on the taxes remitted through them. Excessive profits on savings schemes were approved.[91] The banks set up straw companies overseas to carry out fictitious transactions in order to whitewash infractions of foreign currency laws. They issued statements that presented fake profits, and used mutual fund and social benefit fund money not for the customers' benefit – thereby embezzling from their own customers.[92] It is hard to imagine that the Bank of Israel and the Treasury knew nothing of all this.

The "regulation" of bank shares on the Stock Exchange led to pernicious results. First, the background: to cover its expenses, the government always needs much more money than it can gather from overseas and by the taxes it collects. The solution, of course, is to borrow from the public. By the end of 1985, then, Israel's domestic debt had reached $42 billion.[93] To tempt citizens to keep their money in the country, the government had to come up with ever-growing incentives. The inevitable result was that credit in Israel became exorbitant – except for those who qualified for government handouts in the form of cheap credit. Here the bank shares came into the picture. As early as 1972 Bank Hapoalim began to regulate its shares: whenever their prices would fall, the bank would buy up the excess and thereby stave off any further downslide. Other banks joined in. By the late 1970s the bank shares became the "smash hits" of the Stock Exchange, guaranteeing a hefty profit. Indeed, between 1978 and October, 1983, their yield after adjustment for inflation, was 20-50 percent per year.[94] To pay out sums such as these, the banks always had to make sure to keep their turnover – that is, the sums their customers were willing to invest – on the upswing. Thus, beginning in 1981, they prevented even the slightest dip in share values. They also pressured their customers to buy shares and issued cheap loans at a loss. Consequently the public snapped up bank shares to the tune of nearly $8 billion.[95] At first everything looked fine. A miracle was unfolding in the land of miracles: in an economy that had stagnated for ten years, since 1973, a tremendous bank boom was underway and financial assets proliferated. The banking system also began to grow as it never had: the labor force of the five largest banks reached 35,000 in October, 1983. The number of branch offices reached 1,175 – an extremely high rate, if not a world record, relative to population.[96] Thus nearly three percent of the labor force was employed by the five largest banks, and every 3,500 persons had their own branch office! Wages, too, rose steadily. The devices used included "thirteenth" and "fourteenth" monthly salaries, a variety of perks, and, at the managerial echelon, absurdities that are hard to describe. And then it all came tumbling down. On October 6,

1983, the government announced that the bank shares had been "frozen," and that it had undertaken to redeem them five years hence at a rate of $104 per $100. The arrangement covered shares worth $7.8 billion. This was clearly a burden the public could not bear. The government argued that it had acted thus out of concern for the "little investor." That was an incredible thing to say in view of the facts: the government had never asked the banks to categorize its investors by size of investment so it might find out whether the percent of small investors was significant and find a way to help them. Instead, the government handed the bill to the entire Israeli public, most of whom owned no bank shares and were not of the "small investor" type. And it took this step at a time when much of the government budget went for repaying internal debt.[97]

This was the outcome, not of the common fraud, but governmental control, bank operation as a cartel, and government approval for the regulation of bank shares. If Israel had a Western-style, free capital market, and had the banks been competing with one another and known that they would have to face up to the results of their entanglements, such a thing could never have happened. It was government policy that led directly to a burden of nearly $8 billion thrust upon the Israeli populace.

A government commission of inquiry was set up in the wake of media pressure. Its conclusions were grave: the banks had harmed the public, broken the law, and introduced distortions in client relations. The committee recommended that the Governor of the Bank of Israel and the CEOs of the four banks involved be forced to step down. Two ministers of finance were involved in the matter, knew of the share manipulation, but did not prevent it; nothing was done to them.[98] There were also recommendations for modifying the capital market's structure and procedures.

Some of the CEOs dug in their heels. Ernst Japhet's resignation was purchased at tremendous cost. Rafael Recanati of

Israel Discount Bank simply refused to quit. The matter was taken up by the cabinet and dragged on for quite some time. Nehamia Stroessler of *Ha'aretz*:

> Rafael Recanati is one of Shimon Peres' closest friends. In the unholy conspiracy of money and politics, the Recanati family helped Shimon Peres finance various projects, including personal and general election campaigns and the promotion of relations with moneymen in the United States. The two would meet regularly in Recanati's apartment or in Peres' home. Now the debt has fallen due.[99]

This matter, verging on if not crossing into illegality, has not been investigated – nor, we may assume, will it be in the future. The fact, however, is that Peres abstained when the cabinet ministers put the issue to a vote. Perplexing facts have come to the surface in the meantime. The salaries of Bank Leumi's senior executives had been pegged at up to $23,000 per month. Furthermore, there were more such executives than necessary: some do nothing, and most could be dispensed with by all accounts. Ernst Japhet's resignation was bought with a $5 million early-retirement grant and a $30,000 monthly pension; his previous salary, including perks, was about one million dollars a year. Retirement benefits for another two senior executives ran into seven figures (in dollars).

Something like this could happen only in a country with a centralized economy, where profit and loss don't matter to a soul – and where everyone feeds at the government trough. What would befall the board chairman of a bank who ran up nearly two billion dollars in debt if his country had a market economy? If the board had not stopped him beforehand, he would have been fired the day after the crash. That's not how Israel does business. Three directors sat on the committee that approved the executives' retirement payments. One, a kibbutznik with a senior position in the Histadrut's agriculture center, made a fool of himself: "I did not know. They told me that

that's how things are done in banking." Another was an industrialist who had been generously helped by the bank. The agreement was approved by the bank's new chairman of the board, who remarked, "It's all legal and I had no other choice" – although it later proved to be illegal, and there certainly were other choices. The bank's chairman ex officio, the Chairman of the Jewish Agency Executive, first claimed that it was none of his business and then argued that he was "less than a rubber stamp."[100] Every country has its scandals. But wasting the public's money without batting an eye, evading responsibility, wiggling out of punishment, and lording it over the public – these are the trademarks of the Israeli economy. After all, the captains of Israel's economy all deal with money that is not theirs, and know that whatever happens, the government will hand the bill to the public.

The bank shares mess was only the tip of the iceberg. Bank Leumi's senior officials might have gone a bit overboard in any setting, but surely would not have dared to behave as they did if this behavior was not more or less within the range of "accepted norms" in the world of Israeli high finance. After all, senior bank officials routinely enjoy a variety of perks, including travel abroad, sometimes for business purposes; payment of salary three months in advance; recognition of business expenses; easy-term loans, especially for housing needs; company cars; participation in education expenses – kindergarten, summer camp, high school, higher education; private medical coverage; comprehensive pension plan; advanced study fund, commensurate with rank; and a professional literature bonus.[101]

In the meantime, the public is told that Israel is an equitable country where the salary disparities that occur in capitalist economies do not exist! Here, however, is the true face of Israel's economy: although government sets salaries, prices, and all its other attributes, the government cannot control its senior bureaucrats. It succumbs to their demands, papers things over with lies, and, after the scandal breaks, stonewalls with everything it has. But there's something else we should learn from this scandal and its aftermath. In free-market countries, able people earn a lot of money. People who succeed in producing a profit for their employers are rewarded with fat salaries and generous bonuses. If you fail, you're out. This arrangement keeps the economy moving forward. A centralized economy works differently. Here appointments are determined by factors that have nothing to do with talent. A person can be so incompetent as to run up $2 billion in losses, and still head for the pasture with $5 million in early retirement payments (even though he's reached ordinary retirement age anyway) and a pension of $30,000 per month! In this affair, yet another attribute of the regime, present in almost every domain, stands out. In all the Western democracies, the government ensures that the banking laws are obeyed, that the banks have a reasonable liquidity ratio, and that the banks have enough cash around to cover the deposits of their clients. The Israeli government, however, is so heavily involved as to be an interested party; thus it is not strong enough to supervise. In the case at hand, two ministers of finance, the examiner of banks, and the governor of the Bank of Israel – together with their underlings – knew what was going on; for about ten years, none of them lifted a finger. The governor of the Bank of Israel expressed this attitude magnificently: "It did not begin during my tenure, and it wasn't my duty to stop it."

Foreign currency restrictions were introduced by Israel's very first government and have been left in place to this day. As of 1948, the maximum amount of foreign currency a citizen could buy – after applying to the controller of foreign currency – was ten dollars. From 1956 onward, overseas travelers were allowed to take out $100. The ceiling was later raised to $400 and the list of eligibles was broadened. Not all citizens, however, were equal in the eyes of the law: the Treasury let different kinds of people take out different amounts of dollars. If you brought foreign currency into the country you could buy foreign securities worth one-third that amount. Exporters were allowed to keep ten percent of the proceeds of overseas sales abroad for "sales promotion." One exchange rate was set for the import of basic commodities, another for overseas travellers abroad. After a 1977 liberalization, every citizen was allowed to hold up to $3,000. Later on they could do so only if they produced an airplane ticket, and after that the sum per foreign traveler was knocked down to $800.

The foreign currency restrictions are integral to the state's takeover of the capital market and the entire economy. Under the present circumstances, every transaction by an Israeli involving import or export, and any investment of money from abroad, needs government approval. This obviously created distortions from day one, and special regulations were promulgated for different types of people and transactions. These limitations were shot through with innumerable loopholes, of course, and the papers were full of hair-raising stories about how the banks exploited them;[102] about how importers fraudulently – and successfully – demanded more dollars than they needed for the purchase of merchandise; about how exporters who doctored their price ledgers,[103] and more.

The foreign currency restrictions – together with price and wage control, inflation, compulsory loans, and high taxes – were the tools by which socialist politicians built their apparatus of control mechanism over the economy. These, like other devices, have caused serious damage. Economists of stature sounded the alarm as far back as the 1970s. Professor Assaf Razin called foreign currency control an "economic distortion" and a "social blight."[104] Professor Ben-Shahar called it "an anachronism resulting in waste and a black market."[105]

Under the laws of economics, a black market develops wherever trade in foreign currency and gold is restrained. There's nothing astonishing about that. Neither should one be surprised that until 1977, and in certain subsequent periods, Israelis had to pay much more than the official rate for foreign currency – at differentials that changed from time to time. But something about the government's attitude does seem to be a bit surprising. The black market dealers do their business in public, in places known to everyone. The law calls for heavy penalties, including prison, for foreign currency offenses. Policemen go up and down writing out parking tickets – but they don't lay a hand on the money dealers.[106]

Even when foreign currency violations involving large sums are discovered, legal action is rarely taken – although the law spells out prison terms of three to five years in these cases. The ledger of a money runner to Swiss banks was found in the early 1980s. Sixty people were listed there, including some of fame and repute. Each had used this man's good services to spirit between $50,000 and $1,000,000 or more out of the country. None of them was brought to court. A Bank of Israel bailout committee was put on the case, with members representing the Bank, the Attorney-General, and the police. The committee is authorized to set a fine that, once remitted to the Treasury, would free an offender from having to stand trial. The committee's decisions have not been made public. Neither has it revealed the criteria under which it works, and one might doubt that it has criteria at all.[107] That is quite a procedure for a democratic country: a committee acting in contravention of the law, without defined criteria, far from the public eye, virtually "underground." And who was co-opted into it? The Attorney-General and the police! In late 1983, when the government again outlawed the possession of foreign currency, the police quickly announced that they did not have the manpower to enforce the prohibition and had no intention of frisking erstwhile foreign travelers.[108] Here, in fact, is a law that in effect makes everyone an outlaw. But then, those in charge of enforcing it treat it with total disregard.

Now, however, another factor enters the picture: the government was a partner in the "black" money market for many years. The Treasury, it transpires, was using its own dollars to attempt to regulate the price of black-market dollars – and was doing good business in the process. So while it would not permit its citizens to buy "official" foreign currency, it sold them dollars at a much higher price on the Tel Aviv black market.[109]

Another matter of grave social consequence is the preferential treatment of foreign citizens. Because everyone knows that foreign residents cannot be hobbled with foreign currency restrictions as locals can, special regulations were introduced permitting foreign citizens to make foreign currency deposits and to take foreign currency out of the country. The result is that Israeli citizens feel inferior to foreign citizens.

In early 1987, the government's domestic debt stood at $47 billion, and its foreign debt was some $16 billion out of the country's total foreign debt of $24 billion.[110] The total, $63 billion, is roughly two and one-half year's GNP. The domestic debt comprises compulsory loans, bonds issued by the Bank of Israel, and the social benefit sector including social benefit funds, pension funds, life insurance, and advanced training funds. On top of these are loans from the Social Security Institute, local resident deposits in the equivalent of foreign currency, foreign resident deposits, and German reparations. The government has swallowed and spent all of these to meet its routine needs,[111] and has undertaken to redeem the collapsed bank shares – after their value was raised artificially with its approval. How did the government get together such a sum of money? First of all, it is illegal to take money out of the country or to invest in foreign currency or gold. Second, the law requires the banks, savings schemes, social benefit funds, pension funds, insurance companies and the like to invest in government securities. Although quite a few citizens salt their money away in gold or foreign currency in their homes, or succeed in spiriting it out of the country, all official bodies, as well as private companies and institutions. (whose accounts are subject to review) have no choice but to use the official savings channels. On the stock exchange, too, the government, in the guise of various firms, has in fact taken over many financial assets.

Then there's the compulsory loan, used several times since the establishment of Israel. These are tantamount to taxes. Furthermore, the government has taken over the financial reserves of the Social Security Institute, which, on paper at least, is an independent institution. These reserves – meant to cover old age and survivor's benefits, child allowances, reserve duty payments, disability allowances and maternity benefits – have been expropriated by the government in return for a commitment to repay with interest and indexation differentials. To maximize the benefits from this arrangement, the government has set the highest social security rates in the Western world – 22.5%! – which is why many Israelis refer to their social security premiums a second income tax.

Alongside the incentives, the government reduces taxes on deposits in social benefit schemes, and exempts the interest and indexation-differential incomes on the profits. Savings are indexed – about two-thirds to the CPI and the rest to the dollar -- and bear real interest on top of indexation. Bonds issued in recent years bear real (that is, above inflation) interest of six or seven percent.[112] Indexed loans alone cost the government $2 billion per year! The chairman of the Knesset Finance Committee once asserted that the interest on these debts costs more than all of Israel's exports bring in.[113] On the other hand, because the government lends to many actors, including industrialists, at subsidized rates that amount at times to negative interest, the recipients of these loans often invest not in their designated activities but in government securities for a handsome, easy profit. This cheap "directed credit," manifested mainly in (subsidized) "development" loans, is one of the reasons Israel's domestic debt is ballooning as it is. After all, it costs the government to issue loans at lower interest than it had paid for the money in the first place.[114] Israelis refer to this process as "Israel's gold mines." In other words, to be a "gold digger" and to secure one's financial future, one has only to nuzzle up to the government trough for "development" loans.

The Treasury's capital market commissioner asserts that rolling over the country's domestic debt has become quite difficult, and will cost $4.5 billion in 1987.[115] The reason is that the public has to be persuaded to leave its savings in the government's hands by buying new securities in place of those that have expired. The government therefore has to entice the public, in other words, keep the yield on investment high. So it does. Hence the burden to be borne by the State Exchequer will only burgeon as time passes. As for foreign debt, more than two-thirds – about $10.5 billion – is owed to the United States; almost all of this represents defense aid.[116] Unless a way is found to reschedule the debt or reduce the interest, foreign debt repayment is going to cost us more than the entire American grant.[117] It is clear that the debt repayment burden is more than the Israeli economy can bear, and that it throttles any possibility of recovery.[118] As a proportion of the government budget, debt repayment rose from 15 percent in 1970 to 24 percent in 1983.[119] Professor Assaf Razin then computed the ratio of government debt repayment to GNP: 8 percent in 1971, 21 percent in 1983, and 36 percent in 1984.[120] No wonder Israel's total debt per capita is approximately $15,000.[121] That's more than a world record; it's several times greater than the per-capita liabilities of major debtor countries such as Algeria, Brazil, and Mexico.[122]

The Minister of Economics and Planning, Gad Ya'acobi, estimated that as of 1985 Israel had received a total of $64 billion from the United States. Roughly half of this sum – $29 billion from the U.S. government and $3.5 billion from American Jews – is in the form of grants.[123] Adding transfers from other countries, including Holocaust reparations from West

Germany and remittances from world Jewry, we arrive at $40-45 billion in gift form, some of this in dollars of the 1950s and 1960s. That, in addition to the domestic and foreign debt, brings us to something like $110 billion. On top of this, of course, is the onerous tax bill the government hands out.

One cannot but ask how, and on what, they succeeded in spending these enormous sums. The government claims time and again that most of the money goes for defense and "building the country." But the sum we're talking about exceeds all defense expenditures. In late January, 1987, the Minister of Defense said that the defense budget, not including American aid, consumes only 7 percent of GNP.[124] What, then, about building the country? They've told us for years that they "produced a country ex nihilo." No bluff can be more egregious than this. Not only does Israel not reflect an ex nihilo state of affairs, but everything here costs lots of money – much more than it should cost and more than it usually costs elsewhere. In the end we are left with many industrial plants that are obsolete and rickety, and with debts that consume all our labors.

This is what happens when politicians take over the economy: exploitation, wasteful and irresponsible use of assets and resources; finally, saddling the public with a burden that leaves it struggling to make ends meet.

CHAPTER SEVEN

THE BILKERS

Subsidization means governmental support of various interests, mainly economic ones, extended in order to reduce the price of a certain service or product. It is not like government support for the weak and poor on a personal basis. Subsidies have a great impact on the structure of the economy, because they facilitate the introduction of decisive changes in its sectoral structure; they are also a very important tool in governmental control of the marketplace. Israel's subsidies have also caused various disruptions. One is the support of industrial sectors whose *raison d'etre* is dubious. Another is their exploitation as a way of reducing rises in the price index. Because wage agreements stipulate that cost-of-living increments be paid when the index crosses a certain threshold, the government has sometimes found it cheaper to raise subsidies and postpone the increment for a month or two. Israel's governments have clung to subsidies even though all finance ministers have favored trimming them, and the amount actually expended has often been several times greater than that budgeted.[1]

Bread has been subsidized for many years, at a rate that sometimes reaches 100 percent or even 200 percent.[2] This means that the consumer has at times paid only one-third the real cost. In those periods bread was used as chicken feed because it was cheaper than seed. Bread also became an important component in individuals' and public institutions' garbage cans. Subsidized flour, for example, is supposed to be used for standard bread and hallah alone. If, however, bakeries bake less than reported of these products and more of the non-subsidized, more expensive types, who is to know?[3]

The milk subsidy gave rise to similar results. When the subsidy rose, so did consumption,[4] until a milk shortage came about and farmers increased their dairy herds. When some time later it was decided to reduce the subsidy, demand fell, dairy herds were liquidated, and both the farmer and the state that supported him came out at a loss. The situation is much the same for the other types of subsidies for food commodities, whose number and type fluctuate from four to eighteen as decided upon by the judgment and caprice of the sitting finance minister and his advisers.

No one disputes the fact that subsidies are bad for the economy. They undoubtedly foster waste and artificially promote the use of products that are not necessarily the least expensive or most desired. Furthermore, some of the subsidies are paid out according to fictitious reports, and encourage forging of receipts and smuggling.[5] Subsidized products such as flour, cooking oil, and sugar are exported over the Jordan River bridges into Israel's neighbor, Jordan. A number of people have become rich this way. Moreover, it has been found that those who benefit from the subsidies are not necessarily the indigent. Many subsidized commodities are consumed in greater quantities by the affluent than by the poor.[6] There are more efficient and less costly ways of supporting the needy.

The case of turkeys provides an excellent example of the distortions created by the food commodity subsidies. In 1969, the government began to set the country's turkey industry on its feet by massively subsidizing it, and new turkey growers emerged all over the place to partake of the handouts. When the subsidies were slashed in the autumn of 1983, the industry was thrown into crisis – whereupon the government had to bail out the turkey growers directly, to the tune of $26 million. Then the chicken subsidy was increased, demand for turkey fell, and lots of turkey runs were liquidated at heavy losses.[7] This is one example of many of how subsidies and other kinds of price manipulation send the farmers distorted signals, resulting in a crisis for the industry and steep losses for the growers. As we shall see, food subsidies often reach not the farmers but rather various agricultural establishment echelons such as "purchase and credit associations" or production boards.

Most of the public associates the concept of "subsidy" almost exclusively with consumer commodities such as food and public transportation. But these are only a small proportion of the total subsidies. The Treasury established what it called a "committee for the study of the depth of subsidies in the economy." In its report, issued in February, 1986, it ruled that subsidies reached a total of $4.9-5.5 billion in fiscal 1985/86! That includes about $2 billion in subsidies of public services such as education, health, immigrant absorption, religion, and rural settlement, of which some should probably not be considered subsidies. The health services subsidy of an estimated $200-700 million comes on top of sick fund premiums. There is no doubt that by restructuring the health system and eliminating waste it would be possible to maintain the system without subsidies, and, it would seem, at a lower cost. In this case the subsidy is meant to keep the existing system going, resting as it does today on a set of political-party sick funds, their affiliated institutions, and government-run hospitals.

Treasury economists estimate that subsidies consume about 20 percent of GNP. Even if we subtract the public service subsidy, we will be left with a sum of $3.4 billion, about 14 percent of GNP.

Nor does this figure include state-owned land earmarked for construction and industry at subsidized (below market) prices, sometimes by hundreds of percent. Finally, if we take note of the subsidy committee's admission (repeated several times in the report) that its data are incomplete and conservatively biased, we come up with a sad picture.

In plain English, a "tax expenditure" is an instance in which government forgoes taxes that are due it. That is a very convenient way of awarding a subsidy. When government gives money to a person or a company, it is a high-profile transaction that appears in the newspaper and sparks opposition. Waiving taxes is much less conspicuous. The public does not know how much money is involved; everyone understands that in order to "encourage" exports (or to "help" Eilat or the farmers) it is good to reduce their taxes – as it is in general.

Finally, and most serious of all, most of Israel's subsidies are actually expended on production and not on support of the indigent. Farmers receive water, capital, and tax breaks; industrialists clean up on all sides. A short time after Eli Hurwitz resigned as chairman of the Manufacturers'Association, he said that aid to industry amounted to $1.5 billion per year![8] That is more or less equal to the added value of Israel's industrial exports, since their average added value runs at 30 percent. Even so, Mr. Hurwitz apparently flinched from describing the state of affairs in its full gravity, because his figures do not include the voluminous loans given to "approved enterprises," direct support at times of crisis, fuel and water subsidies, and more.

The data cited herein demonstrates that the main function of the subsidies is to strengthen government control of the economy. We are also witness to struggles between and within sectors for pieces of the pie. The result, of course, is politicization, inefficiency, waste, misreporting, and fraud. The visible sums spent on support for the purpose of lowering the prices of food, housing, and transportation are only a small proportion of the total subsidy, and it hardly seems to be the best way to help the needy. However, the subsidies do conveniently permit the government to lead the economy by the nose. By their use the government can determine which sector or factory will become "profitable" and survive, and which will collapse. The turkey farmer episode cited above is a classic example, but similar cases are daily fare in industry, agriculture, and other sectors of the economy. In sum, the larger the volume of subsidies is – and in our case it claims 14-20 percent of GNP – the more government-dependent the economy becomes.

When Israel was established it had a number of sizeable industrial enterprises, and a large number of small and mid-sized plants. This was the result of private initiative, and they were profitable because they had to be in order to survive. The Mandatory Government, after all, did not hand out subsidies, and the Jewish Agency put its money to other uses. In the early 1950s, waves of mass immigration overwhelmed the capacity of the country's existing industry, and additional sources of livelihood had to be found urgently.

In this sense, Israel's situation was much like that of West Germany and Japan at the end of World War II. There, too, one found a yawning chasm between the few means of production remaining after the war and the throngs of people in need of work. The governments of West Germany and Japan solved the problem by minimizing their own involvement, reducing taxes to near-zero level, and letting their citizens operate freely, without bureaucratic constraints. Just before the West German Finance Minister announced this policy, American officials warned him that his scheme was dangerous. The West Germans stood fast, and the result is well-known:the so-called "economic miracle." The truth is that it was no miracle at all, but the simple consequence of adopting a wise policy. America's Marshall Plan did provide considerable aid for postwar Europe. But in absolute terms, and certainly by per capita computation, it was a drop in the bucket compared with the tremendous sums given to Israel by its foreign allies.

In Japan, General Douglas MacArthur had the sense to introduce a minimum- taxation regime and the possibility of unlimited private enterprise. That set the stage for Japan's premier industrial position in the world today. The Israeli government did not choose this course. Although many Israelis had money to invest, although Jews all over the world wanted to invest, although many of the immigrants had production expertise – the government did not want to follow the road that had led to dizzying success in West Germany and Japan. To create as many jobs as possible, yes. This, however, was not its only goal. An aim it considered no less important, and which has guided its actions from the outset to this very day, was to secure the socialist political establishment's control over industry, as it has previously controlled agriculture.

The first major source of jobs, on a scale of many thousands, was the civil service. A massive bureaucracy came into being, and its maintenance required high taxes. For private investors, both of these are disincentives of the highest order. Worse still was what those regiments of clerks were given as their marching orders: to build massive obstacles against all freedom of economic action by means of regulations, prohibitions, and "procedures." At the same time, the government secured its domination of land, air, and sea transportation and energy. Then it took over the country's communications. Some of these activities were co-opted by government ministries, and others were entrusted to "government companies." The next stage was to tell the public that private capital shunned the more remote parts of the country. Using this slogan, the government attached the riches of the Dead Sea and the mineral deposits of the Negev – ignoring the fact that a profitable private enterprise had existed at the Dead Sea during the British Mandate. Meanwhile, the various government companies began to dabble in all areas of economic activity – a theater in Tel Aviv, arms production, supermarkets, mass marketing.[9] Potential investors from overseas were referred to the Histadrut's enterprises. They were given the opportunity to put up 49 percent of the investment – in other words, to leave control in the hands of the Histadrut. As one might expect, most investors found these terms less than enchanting. Using German Holocaust reparations funds and other sources, the government began to flood Hevrat Ha-ovdim (the Histadrut holding company) with massive subsidies and to let it do what it let no one else do:

to use the social benefit funds of Histadrut members to establish economic enterprises. At the same time, the political establishment took over the country's pre-independence industrial base. Nesher Cement, Shemen (edible oils) and other plants were bought up by the Histadrut. Others were closed. A 1957 strike at the Ata apparel concern was a sign of things to come. Hans Moller, Ata's owner, believed that profits were the whole point of industry. To keep his firm profitable, he set out to fire a few workers and rejected demands for a small wage hike. "The man who squared off against him was Yosef Almogi," journalist Roman Prister reported.[10] "He was a typical product of Israel's 'take-care-of-me-and-I'll-take-care-of-you' reality, based on grants for inept enterprises and party interests..." The strike lasted 103 days. When Moller finally caved in, it was the beginning of the end for any hope of making profit in Israeli industry. These machinations combined to form the basis for today's socialist political control (government ministries, Histadrut companies, alone or in partnership) of nearly two thirds of Israel's industry. Some economists predict that the share of private industry will continue to diminish in the years to come.

A law to "encourage capital investments" was passed in the late 1950s, lending de jure support to what had developed in any case as de facto reality. The law effectively rules out the establishment of economic enterprises without government approval, even if it does not say this in so many words. Approval of a project under the law's auspices confers far-reaching benefits, officially gauged at up to 70 percent of investment but in fact frequently reaching or exceeding 100 percent. It also guarantees the enterprise's survival by means of long-term subsidies, tax breaks, and the like. The effects of this law were disastrous, as we shall see.

Thus the fate of industry was sealed, notwithstanding the efforts of many industrialists such as Moller, who wanted and still want to have profitable industry. They've been brought to their knees. Israeli industry provides work for no more than 300,000 people, or 26 percent of the labor force. That includes a healthy measure of featherbedding. Industry is characterized by low productivity, miserable wages for unskilled workers, unprofitability, a burden on the economy, a constant need for fiscal protection and government support, and – by contrast – easy riches, gross manipulation, and even fraud. The basic guidelines for industrial development, formulated in the early 1950s and unchanged to this day, ensure total government control of industry and sentence industry to deterioration and inability to contribute to the country's existence and well-being.

A 1985 report on government companies[11] records 209 such entities, of which 100 have commercial purposes. The preface reports: "The government's major holdings in companies were concentrated in economic infrastructure and other areas of activity meant to help attain governmental objectives that are unattainable by other efficient means." Reality does not bear this out. As will be seen, efficiency has nothing to do with it, and one who reads the list is increasingly puzzled. What "governmental objectives" justify government ownership of companies such as a wedding hall in Tel Aviv, shops in the Jerusalem "House of Quality," Habimah Theater, the Israel Consumer Council, the Israel Wine Institute, Laromme Hotels or the Shalom Tower in Tel Aviv? Another question is whether oil refineries, El Al, a fertilizer manufacturer, Israel Chemicals, the Dead Sea Works, Israel Cables, Beit Shemesh Engines, Zim (shipping) and many of their like, really have to be government-owned. What "governmental objective" is being served? Professor Yair Aharoni:

> The range of government operations might astound the reader who expects to find the government engaging in infrastructure services only, or operating only in fields where no one objectively expects profit-based private firms to go. In fact, not only does the government engage in business activity throughout the economy, but its operations have proliferated precisely in those sectors conventionally considered the most profitable,

> such as commercial banking, mortgage banking, or construction during that industry's boom years.... The government's proportional share in the national economy is growing, and, it should be re-emphasized, precisely in those fields into which, according to the official spokesman, it is not at all interested in entering.[12]

The government companies employ about 65,000 workers, or nearly 5 percent of the labor force. In 1984 their turnover was $6.18 billion.[13] Of this sum, $28 million, or 0.4 percent, was transferred to the Treasury. That is a negligible amount, and it attests to the inefficiency of these companies. The cumbersome system is "supervised" by a government "Companies Authority" that impedes the operation of the companies, dictates procedures, wages, and standards. Even as it thereby ties their hands, it also forces them at times to "outsmart" it and withhold information.[14] The companies are also subordinate to the government ministries in their respective fields of business, and it is clear that both the minister and the senior officials in these ministries intervene in company affairs. In an instructive if amusing one-liner, the Minister of Energy once staged a symposium for the directors of the government companies under his ministry – "to strengthen their attachment to the Ministry of Energy."[15] Furthermore, a government company is a convenient tool with which ministries can circumvent the Knesset's budget review. In the 1960s, for example, the Ministry of Housing used its construction company as a device for lining up financing help for contractors and housing companies – outside the budget.[16]

The matter of appointing directors to the boards of government companies is of greater concern to the politicians than perhaps anything else. Most of the 1,200 directors are appointed by the ministers. Apart from having to obtain the Finance Minister's signature, each minister handles the companies affiliated with his ministry. This results in relentless give-and-take among the partners to the government coalition. This had an important role to play in the Labor-Likud national unity coalition agreement of October 28, 1984, inaugurating the national unity government.[17] Journalist Gabi Kessler:

> ... The government companies serve inter alia as a highly powerful political tool for those who hold the reins of power... The election of public figures to boards of the government companies has long since become one of the ministers' prerogatives and a tool that they use to hand out goodies and honoraria for their party cronies... [Some board chairmen also receive] a handsome salary, company car, various perks, trips abroad, and reimbursement of travel expenses.[18]

All this can lead only to inefficiency and losses. And so it does: to the tune of hundreds of millions of dollars. The Finance Minister at the time, Pinhas Sapir, explained away a $50 million loss in 1972/73 as "the price of development."[19] For years a newspaper has hardly hit the street without reports of disgrace, failures, losses, and chronic incompetence at the government companies. In a chemical conglomerate in Arad (one of the Negev development towns), it was decided to invest $100 million or more of public money in an untested process. They kept at it until the plant physically caved in.[20] Little is known about what goes on in the armaments industry, but some reports have claimed that waste reaches extremely serious magnitudes.[21] The refineries have twice as many workers as their overseas counterparts, and their prices are twice as high.[22]

The Dead Sea potash works have earned the sobriquet "the jewel in the crown." That is because they have made a little money in recent years. In 1985, for example, they earned $63 million on sales of nearly 2 million tons of potash – in addition to exports of salt and bromine. The company was founded in 1953. The factory established at that time, and an additional factory, have since turned into piles of junk.The government wrote off $300 million in debt. The company's electricity, other energy inputs, and water are subsidized. Those millions of tons of potash, too, are hauled to the port at subsidized rates. All this notwithstanding, the enterprise would not have come as far as it has had it not been headed by Arie Shahar, a highly competent Managing Director who has attained a degree of autonomy. Already years ago, he asserted that the government ought to get its hands off of the potash works so they could embark on rapid development and make a real profit.

Despite everything invested in the government companies—tremendous sums of money, tax breaks, subsidies of various kinds, diverse support payments and grants – they either lose, or, at least fail to show a profit. Their trademarks are cumbersome management, bureaucracy, waste, featherbedding, profligate perks for executives and unnecessary overseas travel. There can be no doubt that under conditions of a normal, competitive economy, all of them would be much better off. Whoever needs proof that government should not be running economic enterprises can find it by comparing the potential of the Israeli government companies to their achievements.

The significance of the so-called "Encouragement of Capital Investments Law" (ECIL) is explained in the Dictionary of Economics and Business Administration Terms put out by the kibbutz management services company:

> In Israel, an industrial enterprise that meets various criteria defined in the ECIL is eligible for "Approved Enterprise Status." Approved enterprise terms are usually awarded only to enterprises that do not appear on the "negative list" (a list of manufacturing sectors or products for which the State is not interested in encouraging investment), but even when a certain entity appears on the negative list, Approved Enterprise Status is still attainable if most of the enterprise's output is meant for export from which the national economy profits. In settlements in A+ Development Areas, a firm may also be given approved enterprise status if its activities expand employment in the settlement, on condition that the enterprise is good for the national economy and the additional production capacity is of interest. Approved enterprises receive financial benefits at the

> investment stage (standard grant, credit reimbursement grant, development loans), and tax benefits upon implementation (accelerated depreciation, special income tax rates for the first five years of taxable income). The benefits are ranked in keeping with the enterprise's location in terms of development area (A, B) or elsewhere in the country.[23]

This law showers so many benefits on "approved enterprises" that no one stands a practical chance of setting up a firm of large or even intermediate magnitude without invoking it. Hence it gives the government control in determining what factory will come into being, where, and by whom. An enterprise in a development area, or one that produces for export elsewhere, may have some 70 percent of its cost covered by the government – part in grant form and part via loans whose terms have been called "Israel's gold mine." That's the law. Actually, however, an entrepreneur can receive much more if he knows how to present the plan. The State Comptroller's Report, No. 34, describes two electronics plants in Jerusalem that cost $160 million to establish. Government handouts covered 85 percent of that sum, with "additional exceptional benefits" which come to more than 100 percent. One of these companies was Intel Inc. of the United States, which had already begun losing during this period. Many observers thought the government could have taken the money it had handed Intel (for nothing) and bought up enough shares to exert influence the policies of the American company. Intel's Managing Director was asked why he set up shop in Israel; "We were given an offer we couldn't refuse," he replied. Is anyone astonished? In his book on investment law, Attorney A. Berlinsky shows that the government puts up more than 100 percent of investment in some approved enterprises, and throws in another wallop of unindexed loans from other sources.[24] As far back as 1974 the State Revenue Administration ruled that rather than promoting investment, overly generous assistance for approved enterprises puts public funds at risk.[25]

An executive of the kibbutz industrial organization told the daily *Al Hamishmar*: "... Money was waiting to be snatched up in those years, and we were swept away. Kibbutzim that set up industrial projects in development areas received development loans on preferential terms: seventy percent from the government, and thirty percent from the suppliers of the equipment and structures. So every industrial venture led to overfunding of tens of percent. There's nothing to hide: the surplus went for consumption..."[26] Isn't there something odd here? Since seventy and thirty are one hundred, how were these projects overcapitalized by "tens of percent"? There are only three possibilities: the government was handed an inflated computation, and the amount received was "tens of percent" higher than necessary; or, instead of investing the subsidized loans and the grant in the factory, they lent them to the government or to the "grey" money market; or, both of the above.

The bureaucratic runaround for obtaining the approval, as reported in 1976,[27] went through 51 stops – and was quite time-consuming, as one might expect. Obviously, however, the personally or politically well-placed, such as Koor, breezed through. Others had to hire expensive lawyers who acquired expertise in this special brand of intermediation. Professor Y. Gross of Tel Aviv University charges, "There are no clearly defined criteria governing the award of the benefits and Approved Enterprise status. Moreover, there are plenty of exceptions, including preferential treatment for 'our boys.'"[28] An American investor, for example, insisted on terms normally awarded for Class A Development Areas even though the site he had in mind was near Haifa. At stake was a grant of more than $1 million. With the Prime Minister's intervention, the request was approved. *Ha'aretz* commented, "That set the norm: a few threats, a little pressure, and you get anything you demand – and to hell with the rules of sound administration."[29] In another instance, the ministers disregarded Investment Center objections and approved a request by billionaire Shaul Eisenberg for approved enterprise status for Asia House in Tel Aviv, which was turned into an office building.[30] The results of this law were exactly as one might have expected at first glance – disastrous. The government handouts – far too extensive to be called generous – attracted lots of outright con-men and inexperienced but well-connected people looking for a fast buck. Instead of modern equipment, they brought in old or obsolete machinery and recorded it at the price of new or modern goods. In other cases they brought in expensive equipment that was used sporadically, on one shift at the most. They often failed to carry out their promises to engage in export, or produced export merchandise of negligible added value. Their factories, based on obsolete, weak technology, nursed forever at the government fount and drained the public till without letup. For the development towns, their effect was frequently adverse[31] because they hired unskilled labor at miserable wages. The process set in motion was bad for the population, and it was powered by lifeless enterprises established in development areas by force of government grant. Only in one respect did the law hit home: it throttled the establishment of any enterprise that lacked the approval of the socialist political establishment. In all other respects it was a stinging failure. It established floundering, tottering industries, some primitive and obsolete. Many of them, especially those in the development towns, have stagnated and lagged behind the technical developments of the late twentieth century.

When obsolete enterprises are kept alive by artificial means, it becomes impossible to set up technologically modern ones. There is almost no doubt that had the politicians refrained from raping industry with this ill-conceived law, instead building an infrastructure worthy of the name, reducing taxes, and facilitating the supply of credit (as recommended in profitability studies conducted by experts), Israeli industry would have taken up the position it deserves among the world's industrial sectors – the position warranted by technological capabilities of its experts, the labor capacity of its workers and the resourcefulness and international connections of its financiers and exporters.

The policy articulated in the ECIL promoted feather-bedding, a phenomenon that abounds in Israeli manufacturing plants. Because so many enterprises are sustained by the umbilical cord of government grants, the government does not permit layoffs. Because the managerial echelon is clogged with people who got there by request of this or that ministry, there is no incentive to streamline. Adding to this the rampart of protective tariffs that throttles competing imports, it is not hard to understand why Israeli-made goods are expensive and frequently poor in quality, and why Israeli manufacturers prefer to market their wares at home rather than venture into the stormy waters of competitive foreign markets.

As far back as 1974, the Managing Director of the Bank of Israel, Dr. E. Sheffer, said that "They are increasing the subsidies to thousands upon thousands of loan recipients, while the public is asked to pay more for bread.... The State pays 35 percent per year for capital and it lends it to industrialists at 9 percent.... No other country in the world gives out presents like these.... "[32]

In a 1981 study on "The Imputed Subsidy in Export Credit and How It Is Allocated,"[33] M. Atia and A. Liff of the Bank of Israel found that the export funds alone granted subsidies equal to 20 percent of the country's exports. They also found sharp differences in levels of support – not only among different sectors but between different exporters within one sector. Furthermore, the greater their added value, the smaller their subsidy! The volume of cheap credit is equal to one-third of revenues generated by income tax, "which is regarded as a tax meant to redistribute incomes on the principle of progressivity," according to Prof. Haime Barkai.[34] The State Comptroller's Report, No. 34, asserts that while spending billions of shekels each year in support of exporters, the Treasury does not take the trouble to verify the added value of each export. Indeed, some exporters were overstating their added value.[35] The methods of administering these subsidies change at times, but the volume of support does not drop. And there is quite a proliferation of methods: export protection fund, import-for-export fund, shipment finance fund, government-guaranteed trade risk insurance, market development fund, factory reconversion for export fund, transport fund, exchange rate insurance, and more. In 1984, government-directed export credit was allocated at 110 percent interest while inflation ran at 400 percent.[36] The State Revenues Administration computed the value of "encouragement" at 46 percent of GNP in 1981/82. While the industrialists lodged multiple objections against this finding, they evidently failed to undermine it.[37] The story does not end here. Under threats of strike, the industrialists and the government constantly haggle over export profitability, with the former demanding far-reaching benefits.[38] The American-Israeli Paper Mills in Hadera imports pulp from Sweden at a price which, including shipping expenses, does not fall far short of the price of the paper.[39] The State Comptroller ruled that the government broke all the rules when bestowing benefits on the Mills.[40] As a result, paper costs much more in Israel than it should. What mattered about the Mills, however, was the 1,900 jobs they provided (in 1982). When exporters wanted to import an expensive brand of paper not produced in Israel, the American-Israeli Mills brandished the axe of layoffs. Were this to become necessary, company officials threatened, the victims would be bused to Jerusalem in order to demonstrate in front of the Prime Minister's office. They would probably bring their wives and children and, hand in hand, embark on a hunger strike.[41]

Again, the familiar pattern: the chairman of the Export Institute suggests that industrialists be made exempt from the tax on overseas travel; relentless pressure is applied to raise import duties and customs;[42] the government caves in.

Here, then, is the sorry picture: tremendous investment of public funds, bumbling industry incorrigibly addicted to public support, protective customs and tax breaks, obsolete technology, the lowest wages in the Western world, limping productivity, featherbedding, expensive and low-quality production for the local market, absence of real domestic and foreign investments, innumerable regulations and red tape,[43] industrialists tempted into cheating, preferential treatment for "our boys," bureaucracy, and exploitation of industry for political purposes. What does the State gain from all this?

Eli Hurwitz, former president of the Manufacturers' Association computed[44] that government support is equivalent to 26 percent of the value of Israel's exports. The average added value of these exports is about 30 percent – not including indirect goodies such as subsidized water and fuel (there is a "fuel price equalization fund" under which the drivers of private cars subsidize fuel for industry), special subsidies in times of "distress," "emergency" benefits to prevent firms' collapse," land at cut-rate prices, and all the rest. The question is whether industry costs more than it's worth!

The economies of Western Europe and the United States are based on industry. It is the source of their wealth. Relative to several European countries, Israel enjoys a comparative and even an absolute advantage in scientific and technological manpower, experienced and resourceful experts in international trade, and workers whose attributes ought to put them on a par with anyone in the world. Why can't Israeli industry turn a profit? Because of the stranglehold of socialist governmental interference. To really appreciate what the Israeli government has done, compare Israel to Taiwan. The two countries have much in common. Both are new countries, established at roughly the same time. Both were founded by immigrants who put ashore at a small, resource-poor new home. Both have to bear onerous defense burdens. Taiwan, however, has not received nearly as much financial support from abroad as Israel. Today Israel has the world's highest per-capita foreign and domestic debt and an annual trade deficit of $2.4 billion. In Taiwan, by contrast, exports exceed imports by far, and foreign currency reserves stand at $45 billion.[45] Those who would attribute the astounding difference to low wages in Taiwan should know that industrial workers in Isreal do not earn much more. What, then, is the answer? Just as Taiwan and Israel exist under similar physical and other conditions, so are their economic systems different. Taiwan practices economic freedom built on competition, low taxes, and a fit return on ambition and effort.

"Monopoly" is when one economic entity has the market in a certain field all to itself. This by its very nature prevents competition. Monopolists earn more than they possibly could under ordinary conditions of an open and free market. Ever since Absolutist princes and kings vanished from the Western world, the right to award a monopoly has been reserved to government. Although in theory it exercises this right only when necessary to guard the public interest, in practice it often does quite the opposite.

A "cartel" is formed when several companies dominating a certain field agree to set and abide by a uniform price. This, too, requires government approval, with all it entails. In Israel, participants in both monopolies and cartels are subject to full price control and have to announce in advance any planned price increase. The law also lets the government restrain their operations with respect to quality, contracts with clients, and the like. Every year – and more frequently in times of inflation – Israeli monopolists and carteliers have to reveal their computations to officials in the Ministry of Industry and Trade. The officials argue with the manufacturers, decide what to approve and what to reject, with whom to be stringent and with whom lenient. Once the costs of manufacturers are clarified, they toss in a profit margin – and there's the price. This method is called "cost-plus," and it provides an intrinsic incentive to hike prices. The higher the price, the greater the manufacturer's profit. In this process, the manufaçturer is directly dependent on "his" clerk in the

Ministry of Industry and, through him, the government. This is a convivial atmosphere for various dealings that would be better left unmade. Moreover, such manufacturers are less inclined than others to irritate the government with criticism and the like. Shimshon Erlich of *Ha'aretz* describes what goes on in the aviation, maritime transport, and insurance industries:

> For several decades El Al succeeded in arm-twisting Israel's skies and inhabitants in accepting the cartel of the airlines. El Al alone dictated fares that constantly put residents of this country at a disadvantage, splitting up the booty with all the other foreign companies... Only after El Al collapsed – following the nullification of cartel tariffs that were tens if not hundreds of percent higher than competitors' – were Israelis, too, able to benefit from the general tumble of world air travel prices. That remained true until the Minister of Transport saw fit to restore the principle of the airline cartel by issuing regulations that threatened sanctions against anyone who tried to provide cheaper service. That move, travel agents attest, has already forced air fares up by twenty to forty percent... The Freight Transporters' Conference, dominated without challenge by Zim, is a carbon copy of the El Al cartel. Zim is not the only company that charges higher shipping prices; all members of the Conference add the premium...
>
> The Finance Ministry's Supervisor of Insurance sets the premiums. They are uniform and compulsory, and anyone who deviates from them faces jail. Period. The government will act like a street cop, busting anyone who thinks prices are high enough to permit broad discounts without tumbling him into bankruptcy.
>
> All these arrangements have two things in common: they spit in the face of the free market system, and they disregard the consumers and their representatives on the Consumer Board. Insurace rates in Israel are several times higher than those in the United States, Great Britain, India, and other countries, even considering the prices of cars and the terms of insurance... The result: exorbitant prices, waste of foreign currency, artificial inflation and profits, and, in the main, a feeling that the government sometimes acts not on behalf of the citizen but for whomever has the most pull and money, by which they attain its backing one way or another.[46]

As defined by the Restraint of Trade Law (1960), Israel has 171 entities using restrictive practices: 142 monopolies and 29 cartels. They account for about 20 percent of all industrial output.[47] MK Eliahu Speiser, chairman of the Knesset Finance Committee, notes that this is a world record, and adds: "There are several economic reasons for the Israeli economy's great centralization. But there is no denying that the government here has always tended to prefer large enterprises, and the political echelon has always been sympathetic to the high and mighty. Thus there is a lack of political will to grapple with the problem."[48]

The share of the monopolies in Israel's industrial output is steadily rising:

Proportion of Industry Controlled by Monopolies (%)

Industry	1960-1970	1982
Tires	60	100
Cement	70	100
Paint	60	90
Asbestos Products	60	100
Paper	70	95
Chocolate	60	90
Edible oils and oil cake	30	60
Margarine	70	95
Canned food	60	100
Instant coffee	75	95
Dairy products	80	90
Beer	60	100
Metal pipes	60	100

Pasta	60	95
Glass tubing	60	100
Starch and glucose	60	100
Water meters	70	100
Cigarettes	60	100
Aluminum pipes	60	100
Pesticides	70	90
Light bulbs	60	100
Oxygen (two firms)	–	100
Pharmaceuticals	40	70

However, only a few of Israel's monopolies affect manufacture. Electricity, telephone and communications, water, public transportation, and other activities are called "natural monopolies" because some bureaucrat assumed that they have to be monopolies by the "nature of things." This may have been true in the past, when obsolete technology was used. Today there is no reason why all electricity generating stations should be owned by one company, or that every alternative energy venture – wind, sun, and atomic – be owned by the electric company. With modern technologies, the fields of telephone, telex, and so on, not to mention public transportation and all the rest, can surely be opened to competition. In countries that have permitted this to come about, user prices have fallen. In addition to these industries, energy– ncluding the purchase, refining, and sale of fuel – is in the hands of a cartel, as are aviation, maritime and land transport, insurance, and more. When several drugstores tried to sell some of their merchandise at prices below the official list, they were throttled on the grounds that health should not be made into a business.

The transactions of Nesher's cement monopoly (owned by the Histadrut) are typical. Nesher cement went for $72 per ton in 1985, compared with $40, including transport, for imported cement. Those are ordinary imports, not market flooding. The fuel needed to produce cement in Israel costs roughly as much as the cement itself costs abroad. The major reason for this is that Nesher produces in outdated plants where efficiency is low and fuel consumption high.[49] For that, of course, monopoly is directly to blame. Had competition been permitted, Israel would have modern plants and much cheaper cement. Furthermore, in years when local production did not meet demand, 90 percent of the import licenses went to one company – Nesher, of course. In other words, domestic cement costs almost twice the price of imports because of the monopoly.

Nesher also gives preferential terms – an illegal practice – to members of the Contractors Center, according to an updated list that the Center provides. This is how the Center succeeds in collecting dues from its members, the contractors.[50] Moreover, Nesher punishes anyone who buys cement from importers (this accounts for about 2 percent or less of all cement used in Israel) by footdragging on delivery deadlines and using other forms of discrimination. Nesher's monopoly extends to transport, too. Nesher closes its plants to private truckers, reserving this business for Tuval, Ltd. which, like Nesher, just happens to be owned by the Histadrut. Tuval is not a trucker; it contracts with private firms and adds a 4 percent commission, thus making transport more expensive. Incidentally, anyone who thinks Nesher does this for a profit is dead wrong. It's a favor to customers, who thus have "an address for complaints."[51]

As for structural steel, things are much worse. This is a monopoly entrusted to Koor, the Histadrut industrial concern by virtue – so they say – of the several hundred jobs at stake. Koor's use of an obsolete and inefficient factory raises the cost of structural steel by 40 percent and prevents the profitable export of scrap. The Federation of Chambers of Commerce has estimated the government's subsidy to this operation to be $26 million per year.[52] When the Minister of Industry and Trade issued import licenses for small quantities of steel, he was accused of issuing them to insiders – as if government ministries had ever awarded such licenses to outsiders – and the Knesset Finance Committee called for their nullification.[53]

Is it any wonder that prices in Israel are unbearable? Meat costs several times more in Israel than abroad because a handful of local cattle growers are the excuse for the government's monopsony. The price of domestic instant coffee rose as world market prices plummeted. Then there is the effect of Israel's monopolies and cartels on the quality of production for the local market. It is quite poor in most cases, just as one would expect when the government prohibits competition. As economists Yaakov Amihud and Manuel Trachtenberg point out: "Because of its cartelization and monopolization, the Israeli economy is uncompetitive in many of its sectors.... "[54]

As usual, the process comes with demagogy and deceit. Officially, the Restraint of Trade Law is meant "To ensure free competition as a means of attaining business-sector efficiency and protecting the public from exploitation by the economically powerful... Organization under a binding arrangement is illegal without approval by the Restraint of Trade Board. Such approval is given only when the arrangement proves to be to the economy's benefit in terms of balance of payments, efficiency, professional specialization, and more."[55] That's chutzpa for you.

Government is the exclusive importer of many basic commodities, including $500 million in grain and soybeans (from which edible oils, oil cake, and animal fodder are made).[56] For beef, tenders are solicited, and the cost-plus method is used.[57] The government determines what, where, how much, and at what price fuel is bought. It is self-evident that purchasing is more expensive by many millions of dollars, when done monopolistically by bureaucrats rather than competitively by merchants.[58] Although this is well known, the government has no intention of relinquishing its purchase monopolies. The reasons are clear: it keeps the bureaucrats busy[59] and facilitates price manipulation. The companies that supply animal fodder are a case in point. In the distant past, they did the importing. When the "Government Trade Administration" took over this function, it compensated the companies – by making farmers give them a 2.5 percent remittance even though they no longer even set eyes on this commodity. A subsidiary of the Histadrut Consumption Cooperative ("Hamashbir Hamercazi") raked in 72 percent of this sum.[60]

An example of the use of imports for price manipulation is the beef industry. The government buys imported frozen beef at, say, $1,900 per ton and sells it to wholesalers at $3,700 per ton. This is meant to prevent any slump in the price of domestic meat, especially poultry. In fact, the profits are used to subsidize the poultry industry. If the government forfeited the right to set beef prices, it would forego a tool with which it can control Israel's beef market.[61] But by wholesaling beef at a markup of nearly 100 percent to ensure the profits of the poultry growers, they raise the cost of living, triggering subsidies that cost the public dearly and push production and exporting costs to intolerable levels.

There are a number of commodities that the government does not import. For many of these, however, it requires import licenses. This is prime hunting grounds for bureaucrats. Here preference can be shown for various people with pull, either cronies of ministers and directors-general or people with party or other ties. Journalist Shimshon Erlich:

> Every time an imported product, however prosaic, threatens to outprice a local enterprise, the Ministers of Industry invoke customs or other taxes to prevent price wars. Thus producers and importers have the same interests. The importer contents himself with bringing in a relatively small quantity of merchandise and selling it at exorbitant prices, while the producer continues charging outlandish prices, sometimes even hiking them under the protective umbrella of expensive imports.[62]

Import licenses – their issue, renewal, limitation, denial – give the clerks most of their power and force applicants to plead like beggars at the door. Needless to say, political pressure is the name of this game; applicants line up partners who have clout in the Knesset and the political parties. Since the fate of individuals and companies rides on the decision of a clerk, every possible method is used to secure these licenses, including attempted bribery. It is also clear that when the minister or the senior bureaucratic echelon responsible for a given field is replaced, different people start receiving import licenses.

A painful and expensive way of hiking import prices is to tack on customs levies, purchase taxes, and miscellaneous imposts. This sends prices to wholly unreasonable levels. According to Labor MK Haim Ramon, the company best insulated from competing imports, at 230 percent, is Carmel Carpets, owned by MK Avraham Shapira. Protective tariffs vary between industries and between different products within one industry. It is often impossible to understand why one product is better protected than another – unless its manufacturer turns out to be an Approved Enterprise, whose founder agreed to invest the money given him by the government in an industrial venture, on condition that it be effectively protected from imports. Many kibbutz industries play this game, too. The result is a large set of de facto monopolies, since an enterprise that succeeds in obtaining "protection" by administrative restraint of imports or imposition of prohibitive taxes indeed becomes a monopoly or something very similar.

The selective issuing of import licenses discriminates among citizens. The fate of individuals, for better or worse, may depend on their good connections – personal, partisan, business, or financial – with the political establishment and the bureaucracy. The major question, however, is why almost everything is cheaper to import than to produce in Israel. That includes even soft drinks and cleaning materials. This is so even though that Israel is high on technological skills and low on take-home pay. Here, then, is evidence that something quite basic is wrong with the structure of Israel's economy.

CHAPTER EIGHT

THE FARMERS: VASSALS OF BUREAUCRACY

*"There are more people employed in the agricultural establishment than there are Jewish farmers in Israel." **Professor S. Pohoryles**, Head of the Economic Planning Authority at the Ministry of Agriculture*

"Moshav and Kibbutz Debt Burden – $3 billion" **Maariv, February 27, 1987**

"About One-Third of Moshavim – Beyond Rehabilitation" ***Professor S. Pohoryles***, **Maariv, March 2, 1987**

The history of agriculture in Israel is a sad tale Once again, the government establishment has unfurled a human and social disaster – and a stinging economic failure. Agriculture was the purest expression of the Zionist dream: Jews once again working the soil of their ancient homeland. By establishing cooperative agricultural villages, the Zionist movement appeared to have built an authentic socialist enterprise. The success of Israeli agriculture won international acclaim. Naturally, tremendous sums were invested in agriculture, and along with them came benefits, excessive privileges, and so forth – all of which made its failure many times more painful.

During the British Mandate period, agricultural rural settlement – mainly the kibbutzim – spearheaded the expansion of Jewish control in strategic regions of the country. Many settlements fulfilled a crucial military role in addition to their agricultural activity. Even then, however, there was no reason not to make sure the farms stayed in the black. During Israel's first six years of independence, the Labor government established 350 villages. The conspicuous difference between the pre- and post-independence years was that almost twice as many kibbutzim as moshavim* were set up in the earlier period. Because of the nature of the post-1948 mass immigration, more than three of four rural settlements founded in the new State of Israel were moshavim.

The tradition of settlement by party key originated during the Mandate years. Most immigrants of that era were members of Diaspora Zionist pioneering movements that received land and means of production from the Jewish Agency – through the Histadrut's agricultural organization, of course. Then settlement movements were established, each affiliated with a political party. The parties decided who would settle where. They held the purse strings, too, because some of the Jewish Agency support was channeled through the settlement movements, which in turn gained strength. When the State was established, this practice was continued. To this day, an official committee apportions parcels of land among the settlement movements according to their relative strength and party affiliations. In other words, it divides up the parcels designated for rural settlement by party key. The settlement movement, together with the first group of settlers, decides who will be allowed to settle. In our modern era, experts are consulted: psychologists (who administer psychotechnical tests), graphologists (handwriting analysis), and the like.

* A kibbutz is a collective farming community in which members own no private property and work the land cooperatively. The moshav is a cooperative village based on family farms; each family lives and works separately. Land, water, production quotas and the like are in the hands of an omnipotent "cooperative association", which also handles supplies and sales.

Whenever an apolitical group expresses interest in rural settlement, the Jewish Agency demands that it join one of the settlement movements.

The planning of a new settlement is entrusted to the Jewish Agency's Rural Settlement Department. All decisions are made there: the settlement's physical layout, the size and shape of the houses, the size of each family's farmstead, water allocations, and the kinds of agriculture to be pursued, down to the last heifer. The RSD decides exactly what the settlement will grow with what tools, and what materials. During the mass immigration period, they would bring in the settlers first, put them up in temporary housing, and build their real houses later. Things have changed with time. Now, the Jewish Agency first completes the houses and plants nice, green lawns out front by trucking in topsoil. Settlers are ushered to a finished product. What this means is they had no part in planning their homes or farms. Jewish Agency people do not like having settlers in their hair. They find it more convenient to do everything in advance; after all, they are the ones who "truly understand" the settlers needs, up to and including the size of their lawns.

At first, the settlers are in the "care" of the Jewish Agency. That means they don't pay a cent for anything they are given. Believe it or not, some 80 moshavim, including some founded 30 years ago, are still under Jewish Agency "care". Some of them are affluent moshav-suburbs near the major cities, where the "peasants" live in villas and work in town. As they see it, the Jewish Agency still owes them something. It may have been necessary to have Jewish Agency experts do the planning for the early settlers who lacked experience in agriculture. Within a decade or two, however, the settlers were either veteran immigrants or Israel-born. Today such treatment is not only unnecessary but genuinely harmful and costly, because the settlers demand additional budgets to rectify the planners' mistakes. Needless to say, the RSD is a large, fossilized, cumbersome, and wholly redundant entity relying on outdated methods.

If fledgling settlements need advice, any number of consulting firms would meet the challenge quickly, cheaply, and far more effectively than the RSD. But who would allow such anarchy to rule in Israel?

The concept of the moshav was originally based on four principles: family farming, settler labor, mutual assistance, and cooperative marketing. The first moshav, Nahalal, was established in 1921. Today there are 450 moshavim, of which about 280 belong to the Histadrut moshav movement. Nothing remains of the four-point ethos. The political establishment twisted it beyond recognition in its eagerness to control the moshavim, thus spawning a social, economic, and demographic monster that cannot exist without a ceaseless flow of money. Today the moshavim are in economic and social distress, and many are on the threshold of collapse.

The first step towards disaster was taken in the mid-1950s, when the Knesset merged the moshav's cooperative association of farmers with the municipal authority. This legislation had a devastating impact. The cooperative association is responsible for the farmers only. Farmless settlers (teachers, artisans and others) do not belong to this association. Once the association was unified with the municipal authority, the fear immediately arose that the non-farmers would form a majority and act against the farmers interests. Hence the law was amended to require an 80 percent majority of farmers on any moshav. The immediate result was that the moshav children, excluding each family's sole successor, had to leave the moshav. The rule against splitting farmsteads had a certain logic, although many farms could sustain two families because land and water allocations had not changed since the early 1950s, while technology advanced greatly. Had the moshav offspring continued to live on the farm and work elsewhere, they could have pitched in at harvest time as is customary in villages all over the world – including Israel's Arab villages, of course. This, however, would have rapidly resulted in a non-farmer majority, and the establishment made up its mind to prevent this at any price. The virtual expulsion of sons and daughters from their home villages makes a mockery of the Zionist dream of "sinking roots in the soil." The political establishment, however, figured this was a small price to pay for securing its control. As a necessary consequence, the moshavim -- all the moshavim – began to take on wage laborers, thus jettisoning the principle of settler labor. Nearly all of these laborers are Arabs, who are sometimes put up barns or warehouses. Furthermore, the land involved was national property, entrusted to the settlers to be worked by themselves, as they indeed undertook by contract. The outcome is a breach of contract on the one hand, and use of State-derived means of production to exploit wage laborers on the other hand.[1]

Problems arose when it came time to evict the moshav children. Most of them wanted to stay on; some wished to remain as farmers and demanded land for this purpose. Old houses in Galilee moshavim were razed "so they would not serve as targets for invasion by offspring of veteran settlers who have moved into new dwellings."[2] *Ha'aretz* notes that "Because of outmoded regulations, thousands of frustrated young adults on moshavim in the Galilee have to move out of the villages where they were born."[3] This went on at a time when the government was investing millions of dollars to attract Jewish settlers to the Galilee! Even in 1974, youth from Moshav Emka in the Galilee demonstrated to be allowed to settle alongside their parents.[4] None of it helped. A joint government-Jewish Agency committee tackled the problem in 1982. All of its various proposals were based on driving the boys off the farm.[5]

While evicting the children, the cooperative also spared no effort to reduce the number of public employees living on the moshav; it was better to bring them in from the outside. This was the background for scenes that should never have occurred in a civilized country. Children of public employees who had lived on the farm for decades were either evicted or pressured to leave.[6] Thirty-five families of service employees in Nahalal complained of discrimination and of being treated as second-class citizens. Although they had bought their houses fair and square, they were not allowed to bequeath them to their children.[7]

Legally, the moshav belongs to the cooperative and the farmers are licensed. The Ministry of Agricultures land, water, and production quotas, and, of course, the subsidies, all belong to the cooperative. This obviously makes its managing committee a very powerful body. Although the association committee and its chair are elected democratically, in many moshavim one group -- aligned by economic or clan affiliation – takes control of the committee and never lets go. So powerful is the committee that anyone who clashes with it or tries to bring it down does so at his own peril. Once installed, the first thing the committee does is set up a bureaucratic apparatus including a secretary, accountant, water meter reader, an so on. The committees of no few moshavim (usually there are 60-100 families per moshav) have five, seven, or even more salaried employees – at the farmers' expense, of course. All the farmers' accounts go through the committee: procurements, sales, orders of feed, everything. In fact, the committee rarely has anything to do with these operations, which are transacted through the purchase and credit association. Still, it processes the accounts and bills the members.[8] On post-1948 moshavim, established without any ideological underpinnings, the situation is worse. Clans take over, allow their members to overdraw their water quotas, punish opponents by turning off the spigot, and lay claim to uncultivated farms and unused quotas. Some become millionaires.[9] The committee decides who gets loans and who does not. It can decide to participate in building, say, a slaughterhouse. In that case they send the bill to all the farmers, including those not involved in poultry. If the slaughterhouse goes bankrupt, all the farmers again share the expense. Members who want to sell their farms must obtain the approval of the committee. Sometimes it disqualifies all prospective purchasers and lets the offspring or cronies of committee members buy the farmsteads cheaply.[10] The committee also controls the system of mutual guarantees. Anyone who wants a loan has to underwrite the loans of all the members! This can lead to one kind of behavior only: settlers take out loans, build mansions, market their produce "illegally", and pocket the cash. Underlying this way of life is an assumption that the government will pay the moshavs "debts" come hell or high water. So far this assumption has proven true.

The committee is only the first layer of the mighty establishment that smothers the farmer. Above it is the purchase and credit association. Every settlement movement (all are politically affiliated) has regional organizations of this type, and all moshavim in the area must belong to them. They were established in order to centralize and economize on commodity purchase prices, and to improve marketing profits. These organizations gained strength as time passed, and rather than serving the moshavim, they came to dominate them. They decide what will be bought and through whom to market – because under law they can market only through "approved contractors." They establish bureaucratic empires including company cars, entertainment in hotels and meals in luxury restaurants. They establish enterprises (many inept), including a plethora of packing houses, many of them unnecessary and doomed to fail. As all these decisions are made, the farmers are never consulted, only billed, whenever an enterprise collapses. The loans and subsidy moneys to the farmers are channeled through these associations. The history of the purchase and credit associations is a classic example of how bureaucracy swells and cultivates its own interests at the expense of the public which it is supposed to serve.[11] Management, too, is incompetent and negligent, since, after all, managers are frequently appointed by the settlement movements for no logical reason.[12] Should anyone be surprised to find them facing the serious accusations of having provoked the present moshav crisis, engaging in rife cronyism, and thus producing seven or eight digit (dollar) deficits.[13] It was proposed, for example, that the executives of the Northern Moshavim Purchase and Credit Association allocate $10,000 for consulting the Association members themselves on a bond issue![14]

Hovering over the purchase and credit association are the settlement movements. They are the legally mandated conduit by which the Ministry of Agriculture forwards production quotas. Production quotas determine how much a moshav can produce in an activity whose produce the government will buy at a fixed price (usually subsidized, as in eggs and milk). The movement presents the quotas to the cooperative committee, which allocates them among the members. The quotas are of vital importance for the very existence of many moshavim. The settlement movements also serve as the government's middlemen in processing moshav subsidies. When one Minister of Agriculture tried to forward the money directly to the moshavim, the settlement movement fought the heresy with full vigor.[15] Who gets the money is a question the moshav movement leaders wanted to decide for themselves. This arrangement made them so powerful that they are virtually unchallenged; no one is willing to rise up against them. The settlement movement appoints the managers of the purchase and credit associations, names most members of production boards, and has representatives on the boards of the marketing companies and other institutions.

Many products can be marketed – by law! – only by means of production boards. These councils, too, are monopolies that operate directly or via "authorized marketers." This is another way of twisting farmers' arms, unnecessarily raising produce prices en route to the consumer and seriously constricting the farmers' profit margin. This being the case, the production boards posit an army of inspectors on the roads to catch "smuggled" merchandise. Atop them all is the Ministry of Agriculture, which plans overall production and doles out quotas to the settlement movements. Its "planning" produces alternating surpluses and shortages. The Ministry's planning is another way of twisting the arms of the moshavniks. Then there are growers associations, appointed by the settlement movement to fix prices for various items. The association in charge of domestic marketing is Tnuva, owned by the Histadrut; overseas marketing must go through Agrexco, owned jointly by Tnuva and the government.

In addition to all these, the moshavniks have their own quasi-judicial system. Any dispute between a farmer and the cooperative association is brought before an internal Histadrut court. The cooperative association committee may apply to the Registrar of Cooperative Societies or sue in the courts; the farmer has no such right. Is it any wonder that after all this, the agricultural establishment's employees outnumber Jewish farmers in Israel? Is it any wonder that moshav members consider themselves the establishment's vassals, and, deep in their hearts, feel that control of their farms has in fact been wrested from them?

Things have reached such a state that private marketing has become the norm on many moshavim.[16] Many farms have been abandoned and many others leased out, mostly to Arabs.[17] Still others have been sold to people who have no intention of farming; they simply enjoy living in the country. These "settlers" get all the tax breaks, free schooling, and sundry goodies with which the establishment provides the farmers. Professor Pohoryles describes the resulting "desocialization": "Twenty-six percent of the farmsteaders control sixty percent of land and water quotas, and 75 percent of the sectors added value."[18] On some moshavim, a handful of members are millionaires while others are day laborers.[19] Despite the fortune invested by the government and the Jewish Agency in the moshavim, a growing number of them are in stages of collapse and liquidation.

It is hard to avoid the impression that the political establishment does not care about what's happening on the moshavim. Nine-digit subsidies have been (and will be) awarded for no other reason than to strengthen the agricultural establishment and reap political gains. The comments of Shimon Peres (in June, 1983) are typical: "If we [Labor] return to power, we will give the moshavim a hundred million dollars the first week."[20] Our suspicion finds further support in the moshav movement's stubborn opposition to the establishment of industry on moshavim. This is obviously the way to enable stagnating villages to grow and prosper. But industrialization, the movement says, will polarize moshav society into "rich" and "poor"[21] – as if these people do not know that many moshavim are in exactly this state right now, and as if kibbutzim had not easily solved this problem. Better to let the moshavim collapse than to loosen their coercive grip on the moshavnik!

The one sector of Israeli agriculture that does not suffer from socialist governmental strangulation is the Arab community. Arab villages are neither subsidized nor supported by the government. No one sets production quotas. Nobody breathes down the necks. And they prosper. Comprehensive research has shown that Arab agriculture has developed at a dizzying pace since the early 1960s.[22] Although 75 percent of the villagers do not engage in farming, most of them stay in the village and pitch in when needed. The villages are growing. Large, modern houses are being built. Technology is developing. Marketing is direct to consumer whenever possible, and is done in cash.[23] What does the director of Agrexco's vegetable division say about this? "The hegemony of Jewish agriculture in vegetables is being threatened. The Arab farmers are outperforming the Jewish farmers in developing modern greenhouses."[24] Is there any better evidence that the free market is superior to the coercive establishment and its "planning"?

The kibbutzim are much better off than the moshavim. Although they, too, depend on the establishment for land quotas, water allocations, and so on, and although they "obviously" need occasional government support "to prevent collapse," they have greater freedom in using their means of production. Many observers believe that the kibbutzim received more resources per capita than the moshavim. In any event, they were allowed to establish industries, which, in many cases, were granted hefty fiscal protection. More than half of all kibbutz members who generate income are employed in industry, whose labor productivity has proved itself. Outwardly, the kibbutz acts as capitalistic as any other economic concern, and holds its own in a market economy.

While the kibbutz remains egalitarian toward its members, we find that these cooperative socialist collectives cannot refrain from using wage labor and even exploiting cheap labor. Many kibbutzim have hired employees, although others have outlawed the practice because their social structure would not tolerate it. Many kibbutzim also benefit from cheap labor by taking in overseas "volunteers." These people are virtually unpaid, and handle much of the "dirty" work and service functions.

The kibbutz sector faces difficult problems. During the 1980s, 50 percent or more of kibbutz offspring leave the farm, if not the country. In percentage terms, kibbutz offspring are more inclined than anyone else to emigrate.[25] One reason for this is that young kibbutzniks who come to town with nothing but the clothing on their backs cannot figure out how they will ever succeed in obtaining an apartment and a car.

Many of the new kibbutzim hold on for ten years or more with a minimum number of members – fewer than ten or twenty families. Some fledgling kibbutzim have fallen apart; others have issued appeals for help. One example is Kibbutz Tefen, with six members at present (its buildings, meant for a much larger population, were erected by the Jewish Agency). Even so, the kibbutz movements continue to demand and receive land for new settlements. This is how they build their strength, increase their assets, receive Jewish Agency and government allocations, and cultivate their bureaucratic establishment.

Despite the difficulties of the moshavim and the kibbutzim, despite the vast sums of public money, and despite the many failures – the Jewish Agency and the government are not willing to change their ways and provide land and loans to people who want to settle on their own, outside the frameworks of kibbutz or moshav.

Needless to say, almost all the villages established in post-independence Israel are moshavim or kibbutzim. Attempts by individuals to settle the land have been stymied. In the Galilee, where Arab villages regularly encroach on State land, any Jew who tries to settle without permission is forcibly prevented from doing so. A few individuals have succeeded. The Avrutzi family – stubborn, veteran farmers – once applied for fifty acres of arid, rocky land in the Galilee. They had to go through 37 committees! After toiling for a year and a half and driving 80,000 miles, Avrutzi pulled it off. He recalls:

> To this very day young people come to me in the Galilee with dreams in their eyes. They ask me enviously, "Tell me, how did you get the land?" I tell it just like it was, I show them the papers, and in my heart I think: look at all the hardship, the harassment, the running around you've got to put up with! They wont come away in one piece. It will break them. The bureaucracy in this country shatters dreams. I'm afraid that they'll end up in Los Angeles instead of the Galilee.[26]

The results of this planning are exactly what one might expect: a market alternately swamped with surpluses and throttled with shortages. That's under ordinary conditions. Sometimes, however, ministers of agriculture exploit their positions for political gain. A classic example concerns flowers. A new Minister of Agriculture allocated development budgets on terms that turned such investment into "an offer that could not be refused." Greenhouses were erected, flowers were grown – and the surpluses drove many of the farmers into heavy debt, if not collapse.

Eggs are heavily subsidized. Farmers get about thirteen cents per unit. Quotas are not honored, of course, but the Poultry Board buys up the surpluses which farmers produce above their quotas. Newspaper headlines reflect the tragic results: "Cumulative Surpluses: 9,000 Tons of Broilers and 100,000,000 Eggs." "Twelve Million Eggs to be Destroyed." "Poultry Board Loses Millions in Long-Term Egg Exports." "Million Eggs a Day – Into the Trash." In 1987, Israel was exporting eggs to Turkey at 1.5-2 cents apiece. That hardly covers packing and shipping. The Turks were re-exporting the eggs to Iran. Israel exports to Italy and Lebanon under similar terms.[27]

Typical of the situation is how the poultry meat industry is "planned." A few years ago the government invested tens of millions of dollars in establishing a turkey industry; speculators jumped in to benefit from the massive subsidies. Then, in the autumn of 1983, the broiler subsidy was raised. The turkey industry crumbled, and the government compensated the growers to the tune of $26 million.[28]

The milk situation is even worse. When the subsidies go up, so does demand for dairy products; new dairy operations are launched and production swells. Then the subsidies are slashed and dairy farmers collapse. Finally, when Israel has to import powdered milk, the cycle begins anew.[29]

Oranges, as is known, are one of Israel's major success stories; Jaffa oranges are famous throughout Europe. The industry dates from the turn of the century, and much experience has been gained. Excluding the World War II years, citrus fruit was always in high demand in Europe. According to the Citrus Inspection Law, fruit may be sold only through the Citrus Marketing Board. This makes the board – appointed by the Minister of Agriculture – a monopoly. The Board has interests of its own, which are not always consistent with those of the growers. In the 1950s the growers fought with the Board over packing materials; it took them years to convince the Board to change from large wooden crates to cardboard boxes. It had been the Board's practice to send a yearly delegation abroad, usually to Romania, to buy the wood for the crates. The Board refused to change its ways until the differences in price and labor became so big that it had to surrender.

This is typical of what happens when an industry is forced to kowtow to a monopoly. A majority of the Board's members represent several large growers – including the Histadrut's Tnuva Exports, which controls 45 percent of all fruit grown, mostly in moshavim and kibbutzim – and private growers associations. With no competition to threaten them, they have inflated their positions by building a massive bureaucracy and voting themselves hefty salaries. They also built some 64 packing houses at the grower's expense; eventually excess capacity and pressure from growers forced them to close down some of the packing houses in the early 1980s.[30] Overseas marketing has been inept, and the Israeli consumer pays more for fruit unfit for export than the European consumer pays for the export quality he gets.[31] Dr. Yakir Plessner, an expert on agricultural economics and former Deputy-Governor of the Bank of Israel, assesses the situation:

> The organizational and economic system of citrus marketing is inefficient. It lacks incentives; it is based on the principle of giving the grower whatever is left over after all expenses are deducted. From the moment the orange leaves the orchard until it reaches the marketing chains in foreign countries, the system doesn't offer a single efficiency incentive.[32]

This, of course, is diplomatic language. The system does offer a clear incentive – to build bureaucratic empires and to be inefficient. Plessner adds:

> They take what they're paid for a box of fruit, cover the Citrus Marketing Boards expenses first, and then pay off the packing contractor. The grower gets what's left: fifteen cents on the dollar.[33]

Meanwhile, the Board damages the reputation of Israeli fruit,[34] causes ripe fruit to be destroyed, and presides over errors of omission and commission in marketing and shipping. For example, it contracted with a shipping company without obtaining collateral, resulting in an $11 million loss.[35] The Board also drags its feet in paying the growers.[36] Inevitably such behavior has affected the growers. Their profits have shrunk. They no longer keep up with technology and have uprooted thousands of acres.[37] It is no wonder that they began selling fruit directly from the orchard to the consumer, so as to circumvent the middleman – the Board – and his enormous fees. The Board responded by mounting a counteroffensive. Inspectors fanned out on the highways and set up ambushes in the groves. Anyone caught carrying more than 72 oranges without an official shipping invoice is now hauled in on criminal charges of what the Board called "smuggling."[38] The Board also placed a series of ads threatening to undo the livelihood of any grower caught "smuggling."

In 1988 the citrus industry wanted more oranges, and was willing to pay farmers more than they could get from exporting. The Citrus Board forbade the transaction.

In short, inept policies, government intervention, and coercive, monopolistic agencies can wreak havoc with anything, even an industry blessed with natural advantages, such as citrus growing in Israel.

The United States and the European Common Market countries have farm supports, too. This is the result of the tremendous demographic change that occurred during the 20th century, from an agrarian majority to only a few percent of the population on the farm today. The European market also faced the question of several countries with more efficient agriculture, against which the other countries sought to protect their farmers. Nevertheless, most economists in these countries, too, believe that farm supports benefit neither the economy nor agriculture itself. Israel's circumstances are different. It's agriculture is modern; it is only about thirty years old. The number of people previously working the land for a living was not substantially larger. Professionally, Israel's farmers have earned worldwide repute for their accomplishments. The major concern here, however, is not the fact of support – although it is reasonable to assume that without it farmers would do a better job of developing sectors better suited to the country's conditions. Of special interest here is the superstructure imposed on the farmers, the agricultural establishment, which has assumed the dimensions of a bureaucratic monster that treats the farmers like unlanded vassals and consumes the fruits of their labor. It is this establishment that designed the moshav as a structure that cannot grow, forsakes its principles, drives away its offspring, and approaches a state of collapse. All of this is happening in a country where agriculture has every reason to succeed.

CHAPTER NINE

MAKING ISRAEL WORK

In many respects, Israel appears to be trapped in the quicksand of socialist stagnation. Israeli agriculture, perhaps the world's most advanced in the professional sense, is bound and gagged by an agricultural establishment whose "functionaries" outnumber the farmers and deny them the ability to turn a profit. A law meant to "encourage" capital investments chases investors away, thrusts the bulk of investment on the government's shoulders, and causes the establishment of obsolete and unprofitable enterprises. Israeli industry is subsidized at a level that exceeds the total added value of exports. Israel has the world's highest taxes, which, together with a set of exemptions for preferred citizens, incites to tax evasion and spawns a black-market economy that accounts for an estimated one-fourth of all economic activity. About one-third of Israel's labor force earns the lowest salaries in the Western world, while those at the top come away with huge pay packages including a wide variety of perks. An omnipotent bureaucracy waylays and harasses citizens, harms the weak, stifles initiative, favors its own cronies, and is characterized by widespread use of influence, promotion of "our boys," and growing use of bribery. The scale of featherbedding in Israel's economy can hardly be grasped. "Egalitarian" medicine forces some patients to wait up to two years for care, and moves those who can wield influence or bribes to the front of the queue. The political establishment runs roughshod over all fields of life. Its elected officials enjoy a degree of immunity unmatched elsewhere in the West, not to mention lifelong preferential treatment and benefits. To prolong their careers, they bribe the voters with "election economics." No one comes and goes in the political leadership, because functionaries are appointed in an undemocratic manner and the wishes of party members are neutralized. The Cabinet has 25 ministers and six deputy ministers, who devote much of their time to party maneuverings. Political parties exercise direct or indirect control of tremendous economic assets. Party loyalty – rather than competence and or industriousness – is the key to economic advancement. Israel boasts the world's highest per-capita expenditure on general elections. The Histadrut, which pretends to represent "the workers," controls vast assets, and, marshalling tremendous economic might, functions as a state within a state, using medical services and other coercive means to secure its status. Inept land policies make housing more expensive, prevent population dispersion, and encourage illegal takeover of land. Construction is taxed at 50 percent. A hundred thousand flats stand empty, while immigrants and the indigent have trouble finding decent housing. Government control of water has brought Israel to the brink of catastrophe as its water reserves face destruction. The public sector employs about one-third of the labor force. Monopolies and cartels steadily grow in number and extend their grip on most of the economy. Incompetent government companies serve as shelters for cabinet ministers' cronies. Violence in labor relations is treated with benign neglect and spreads into other areas of Israeli life. A capital market under total government control exploits citizens by "stabilizing" bank shares and plundering the nation to the tune of $7 billion, even as senior bank officials and executives draw astronomical salaries. Immigrant absorption arrangements are better suited to the early 1950s than the late 1980s. Roads are deficient; traffic accidents proliferate. Fifty-six thousand executives drive tax-reduced company cars, while ordinary folk pay prohibitive taxes on their jalopies. Emigration has increased at a frightening pace: one Israeli in nine has left the country.

Israel outperforms Western Europe and the United States in the least desirable areas: Per capita debt – the highest. Labor productivity – the lowest. Taxes – the highest. Emigration as percent of population – the highest. Immunity for legislators – the most sweeping. Price and wage control – the longest-lived. Percentage of economic activity handled by cartels and monopolies – the highest. Percentage of GNP claimed by the government budget – the highest. Percentage of wage earners taking home about $350 per month – the highest. Cars per capita – the lowest, except for Greece and Portugal. Proportion of labor force in the civil service – the highest. Foreign currency control – the farthest reaching and most protracted. Number of overseas trips by ministers – the highest. Passenger car prices -- the highest. Per capita expenditure on elections – the highest.

One might well ask if Israel has done anything right. The answer, actually, is quite a bit. Consider how it struggled immediately preceding and during its war of independence, how it absorbed multitudes of immigrants and developed rapidly in the 1950s and, above all, how Israelis identified with their society and state. These are achievements worthy of respect and admiration. Even today, Israel has its achievements: the world's largest number of scientific publications relative to population; the highest proportion of scientists and persons with advanced technological education; agrotechnical capabilities and developments in the fields of instrumentation and irrigation, which experts from all over the world visit Israel to study; the world's highest rate of theater attendance; world records in per-capita new titles and book sales; respectable attainments in literature and the arts; a vigorous press; an army with superb fighters, an advanced weapons development and production system, and some of the world's most sophisticated weaponry. Yet all of these achievements are dwarfed by the yawning chasm between the awesome potential and the feeble reality of modern Israel.

Perhaps the most striking feature of Israel's assorted woes is the fact that, upon careful examination, they all stem from the same source – governmental interference:

- ***Backwardness or stagnation as a result of inability to adjust to changing conditions.***
- ***Disparity between high professional ability and its realization.***
- ***Politicization – preference of party or group interests over the public's welfare (and on the personal level, a connection between advancement and party affiliations).***
- ***Bureaucratic systems which, as they grow in size and strength, increasingly manifest preferences, influence, and bribery.***
- ***Waste of public resources, and mortgaging of the future for immediate gain.***
- ***Greater citizen dependency on government than the Western norm, with the attendant damage to personal liberties.***
- ***Inability to control the tremendous volume of government activity.***
- ***Contempt for law as a result of rules and regulations that provoke public resistance, and as a result of discriminatory application of many laws.***
- ***Concealing facts and the truth from the public, and pulling the wool over its eyes with slogans and programs devoid of content.***
- ***Constant threats to the public's standard of living and its savings, as the public is handed the bill for the government's blunders (compulsory loans, bank share "stabilization," inflationary erosion of loan repayments, currency devaluations, inflation, use of taxation to raise commodity prices).***
- ***Forsaking of profit, along with creation of an economy and society wholly dependent on government support.***

Their common denominator: socialism.

The Israeli government does not merely use laws to guide economic behavior, but exercises direct, real control – of land; water; maritime, air, and land transport; mail and telephone service; energy, health care, education, immigrant absorption, the capital market, public housing, rural settlement, agriculture, mining and quarries, most of industry, wages and prices, and more. The government directly employs about one-third of the labor force, not including the army. Adding the Histadrut holding company and various partners (Klal, the Jewish Agency), we find that about two-thirds of Israel's wage-earners, if not more, are employed directly or indirectly by the government or the Histadrut, entities dominated by the political party echelon. Government control finds expression in the ratio of government budget to GNP. In Israel's case, the government budget is roughly equal to GNP, a phenomenon typical of Soviet bloc countries, in contrast to Western democracies, where the proportion is between one-third and one-half. The Israeli system is unique combining of democracy, including freedom of speech and suffrage, and total government control of the economy. Thiel de Sola Pool,[1] professor of political science at the Massachusetts Institute of Technology, contends that four types of societies could theoretically exist in the contemporary world: a market economy with democracy; a market economy with autocratic government; and a centralized economy with democracy; a centralized economy with autocratic government.

The third type, de Sola Pool remarks, does not exist. Evidently he is not familiar with the world's only democratically ruled centralized economy – Israel's!

"It is the aim of Socialism," writes Ludwig von Mises, "to transfer the means of production from private ownership to the ownership of organized society, to the state." As for private enterprises:

> Limitation of the rights of owners as well as formal transference is a means of socialization. If the State takes the power of disposal from the owner piecemeal, by extending its influence over production; if its power to determine what direction production shall take and what kind of production there shall be, is increased, then the owner is left at last with

nothing except the empty name of ownership, and property has passed into the hands of the State.[2]

The implementation of socialist policies in Israel was the result of a unique process. In other countries, socialism took control through violent revolution (Russia, China, Cuba) or, in its milder variety, through the ballot box (Western Europe). In Israel, socialist hegemony was established years before the state even existed. Then, when Israel was created, the Labor Party leaders and their Histadrut allies moved quickly to place virtually all means of production, excluding retail trade and small workshop industries, under government control. Labor remained in power throughout Israel's first twenty-nine years, during which it made every effort to insure the Histadrut's domination of Israeli life. Although the opposition Likud bloc was, in theory, committed to a free market economy, when it finally rose to power in 1977 the Likud hesitated to undertake the unpleasant but necessary task of freeing Israel from the shackles of Histadrut control. Sacrificing Israel's permanent economic interests for the sake of temporary domestic tranquility, the Likud leadership spurned the advice of U.S. economic experts who warned that socialism would be Israel's undoing; the Histadrut's state-within-a-state was left untouched. Labor leader Yitzhak Rabin was correct when he said that there was precious little difference, on socioeconomic issues, between Labor and Likud.[3] The Likud's own Yitzhak Berman was less polite but no less accurate when he charged that the Likud government was, in practice, socialist.[4] Ultimately a government must be judged according to what it does, not what it says; the Likud has done virtually nothing to liberate the economy from the clammy grip of socialism. During its tenure, in fact, the proportion of GNP consumed by the government budget rose to some 102%. Even the decision by Likud Finance Minister Simcha Ehrlich to allow Israelis to own up to $3,000 was just the culmination of a policy that had been evolving for more than two decades. Such half-measures and gestures can never substitute for what is really required to take a country that is falling apart and put it back together: a complete overhaul.

"Profit" is a dirty word in the socialist lexicon. Socialism explicitly asserts that production is for use, not for gain. Marx, who developed his doctrine in the 19th century – not long after the Industrial Revolution began – failed to foresee the momentous technological and scientific developments and the dramatic rise in standard of living that workers and farmers enjoyed in the years that followed. Marx believed that since labor generated added value, employers who pocketed a profit did so from their employees' sweat. Marx and the 19th-century Western European socialists believed the pie should be divided up equally. What agent was better fit for this task than government, which would apportion the spoils equitably and decide how much of any commodity should be provided to the citizens at any given time?

By eliminating the profit motive, however, Israel's leaders opened the door to a whole host of related social problems. The natural human desire to seek gain is channeled into activities that are illegal and immoral. Ethics are shunted aside as Israelis battle with one another to reap advantages in this field or that. In a totalitarian socialist country, profit is prohibited, and deviant behavior motivated by the profit-instinct is simply suppressed. But in a socialist country like Israel, where citizens enjoy political freedom and a comparatively mild penal code, there is little hope of eliminating the societal evils that socialism produces.

In the competitive world where the principle of profit reigns, the owners of every business enterprise have to be sure they have the right equipment, the latest technology, the right number of skilled employees, and a competent and efficient management. They must keep productivity high by paying proper wages – but not too high, because then they cannot compete. The result is an objective criterion for wage levels – although employees and employers can still debate the exact specifications of this criterion

– and a clear link between productivity and wages. Thus, owners cannot afford featherbedding, failure to use production capacity, or other inefficiencies – again, because of the competition. For the same reason, they cannot keep unprofessional managers on the job. This is how Western Europe and North America developed in the 20th century. This is how they marshalled the profits by which they achieved a standard of living and education unprecedented in history. People's aspirations for economic advancement catalyzed tremendous economic development as well: the electronics revolution, the "green revolution," and the communications revolution, with all these imply. It has been shown, contrary to socialist theory, that there is no contradiction between an economy based on free competition and concern for the weak and the ill. On the contrary: in countries where free economies flourish, such as Switzerland or Japan, few citizens languish on welfare, and concern for them is greater than elsewhere.

The Israeli government's hammerlock on all areas of the economy, and its goal of subordinating the economy to party interests, have produced the inevitable – an economy that cannot do what it is meant to do: sustain the people. It is hard to believe that a people with the potential of Israel's had to tumble into the economic abyss that typifies the country today. MK Uriel Lynn estimates the price of the economic debacles between 1984 and 1986 at some $10 billion – and much of this was (or will be) covered by the state exchequer.[5] They refrained from installing an infrastructure worthy of the name, because their ideology told them that while anyone can use roads, subsidies should accrue only to the chosen few. That is why Israel is peppered with failing factories which pay miserable wages. As a result, the labor force is fleeing from industry into the services. Public-sector employees outnumber production workers. To finance the bumbling economy, the government has to inject money to "save and rehabilitate" manufacturing, agriculture, and construction enterprises. To marshall the necessary sums, they have to burden the population with high taxes that chase investors away, drive Israeli capital out of the country, and create a black market.

Israel's economic and ethical downslide was caused by the nature of its regime – all other factors are of marginal influence at best. What matters today is not whether a country has raw materials or not. For proof, consider Japan and Switzerland on the one hand, and the Soviet Union on the other. The factors that count in our time are modern technology, ability to apply know-how, resourcefulness, speed of reaction to change, and commercial experience. In all of these, Israel has an advantage over most countries in the world. Its anachronistic regime, however, throttles all initiative and, consequently, the development of the country's economic prowess. Hence Israel remains in the throes of economic distress.

In a centralized regime where everything depends on government, preferential treatment for certain individuals is inevitable – especially when the system exists for the express purpose of insuring this kind of treatment, including transfer of government funds to political cronies and parties. The Histadrut factions acted deliberately and almost overtly to anchor the existence of their subsidiaries with government money. Naturally the other political parties have learned the ropes and now play the game with great skill.

Theoretically, the government has to display equal concern for everyone, and give each group and individual an equal portion of the "national pie". For this reason, a great many citizens consider themselves the victims of discrimination. Dr. G. Wolfsfeld of the Hebrew University has found that citizen dissatisfaction with the political leadership's ability to run the country is steadily growing, and that many citizens believe that street demonstrations are the only means left to be heard. The public thinks that politicians respond only to pressure.[6] Development town residents complain about discrimination in services, education, and job opportunities. Teachers feel cheated.

Artisans and merchants regard themselves as the Income Tax Commission's golden geese, while industrialists and others are showered with tax reductions and exemptions. Young couples fume over the meager mortgages available to them. University students rebel every time someone at the top attempts to increase their tuition. Moshavim fare badly compared with kibbutzim, as do new moshavim compared with old moshavim. (Kibbutz Ramat Yishai received greater support than similar communities because it was well-connected with the Minister of Finance.) Doctors, engineers, X-ray technicians, agricultural instructors, social workers – all believe they deserve a bigger slice of that miserable pie.

In fact, every one of them is correct. If incomes are not anchored in economic reality, if it is the government that decides who gets what, then everyone is entitled to think that the accounts were improperly drawn and that he or she deserves more. The result is a free-for-all. Nurses abandon their patients. Doctors sell beds. Teachers exact revenge on mothers. Young couples burn tires. The Public Works Department blocks traffic. Taxi owners demonstrate and burn their cars. Electric company employees shut off the country's lights. TV technicians turn off the screens. Industrialists demand additional benefits. Local councils sputter in rage. A day does not pass without press reports about threats, grievances, and demands levelled at the government by one sector or another, one group of employees or another. This mood of suspicion and covetousness permeates daily behavior. If some Israelis seem to believe that "I've got it coming" or angrily ask "Why did they give to him and not to me?," no wonder: their government prattles incessantly about the need for an "egalitarian society" and "egalitarian medicine." If some Israelis are rude, if they seem unable to behave in line, no wonder: the average citizen thinks to himself, "If I'm not on my guard, someone with connections will step in front of me." Slowly but surely, the individual feels alienated from society, feels that society is not his, not hers, but "theirs." This alienation is a grave phenomenon that jeopardizes a society's very ability to function.[7]

How can all this be reversed?

The system that permits the political establishment almost unlimited power must simply be swept away. The branches of government – legislative, executive, and judicial – have to be separated. Israel must have a constitution that will give the public decisive influence by direct election of its representatives and exercise of referenda on appropriate issues, especially fiscal ones. Switzerland uses this system with great success; in the United States, too, citizens in a number of states have used referenda to reduce bureaucratic control, slash taxes, and revitalize local economies.[8]

Israeli society must treat everyone as equal before the law, and it needs an independent judicial system that will guarantee it.

Israel needs an unfettered, modern economic system similar to that found in the enlightened Western countries. Private enterprise means the ability to develop, create jobs, and adapt to changing conditions and situations.

"Private enterprise" means Switzerland and Japan. Israel needs nothing better. All Israel needs is an economic system liberated from the control of bureaucrats. Government-owned companies have to be sold off. Control of economic enterprises by political parties or affiliated entities should be prohibited. Private owners should promote their ventures, make them profitable – and raise wages. Israel ought to do away with the thousands of laws and regulations that hamstring the economy and turn citizens into perpetrators of victimless crimes. The country needs to enact a new land and water policy and strip the establishment of its control of capital. Agriculture, too, must be freed of the establishment's stranglehold. Israel's farmers are the most competent anywhere; in a free market economy, their successes would translate into profits and prosperity. Israel's taxes keep prices high, hurt the weak, promote emigration, and cause unemployment. These taxes should be slashed drastically.

In short, what Israelis must do is tell their government to get off their backs. Then, and only then, will Israel function as it should, as it can, and as it must.

CHAPTER NOTES

Chapter 1 **The Past**

1 Yonathan Shapiro, The Historic Ahdut Ha-'Avoda (The Formative Years of the Israeli Labor Party), Am Oved, 1975, pp. 10-11 and 200-202. (References are to the Hebrew text and not to the abbreviated English edition).
2 Yona Nutkin, Traders in Civil Rights, Reshafim, 1985, pp. 119-120; Protocol of the meeting of the Ahdut ha-'Avoda Council, September 23, 1925 (cited by Y. shapira, p. 109).
3 Y. Shapiro, ibid, pp. 206-207, including quotation from M. Djilas, The New Class, New York, Praeger.
4 Yonathan Shapiro, Elite without Successors, Sifriat Poalim, 1984, pp. 67-71.
5 Y. Shapiro, the Historic Ahdut Ha-'Avoda, p. 9.
6 Maurice Duverger, Political Partis, Wiley & Sons, New York, 1954, pp. 308-309.
7 Y. Shapiro, The Historic Ahdut Ha'Avoda, p. 9.
8 Davar, August 7, 1928.

Chapter 2 **The Political Establishment**

1 Haaretz, Feburary 2, 1982.
2 Haaretz, December 29, 1985.
3 Haaretz, September 4, 1982, October 26, 1982, August 10, 1985.
4 Maariv, December 18, 1985; Haaretz, October 26, 1982.
5 Haaretz, July 15, 1985.
6 Haaretz, December 29, 1985.
7 Haaretz, April 8, 1982, October 26, 1982.
8 Haaretz, March 3, 1983, February 6, 1987; Maariv, July 14, 1986.
9 Haaretz, December 23, 1985, August 21, 1985.
10 Haaretz, April, 8 1986.
11 Haaretz, January 2, 1984, December 12, 1985.
12 Haaretz, December 27, 1985.
13 Kol Ha'Ir, March 6, 1983.
14 Yediot Ahronot, April 25, 1980.
15 Harretz, January 11, 1983, July 18, 1986.
16 Harretz, December 2, 1986.

[17] Harretz, May 5, 1985; Yediot Ahronot, March 31, 1985.
[18] Harretz, November 19, 1985.
[19] Haaretz, September 14, 1982, October 31, 1983, October 3, 1984.
[20] Yediot Ahronot, May 10, 1985.
[21] Haaretz, August 3, 1983, Feruary 6, 1987, May 29, 1987; Maariv, July 14, 1986.
[22] Ibid.
[23] Haaretz, December 29, 1982; Maariv, December 5, 1986, January 26, 1987.
[24] Ibid.
[25] Haaretz, May 31, 1983.
[26] Haaretz June 19, 1983.
[27] Maariv, June 3, 1983; Haaretz, December 9, 1985.
[28] Haaretz, August 21, 1984.
[29] Maariv, April 11, 1982.
[30] Haaretz, Harretz, October 6, 1975, June 24, 1976; Maariv, March 23, 1979, August 3, 1983, February 27, 1984.
[31] Ibid.
[32] Haaretz, August 11, 1982.
[33] Haaretz, November 24, 1983.
[34] Maariv, October 26, 1982, April 1983; Haaretz, October 17, 1984.
[35] Haaretz, June 21, 1982.
[36] Maariv, March 8, 1984.
[37] Haaretz, June 5, 1982, December 18, 1985; Maariv, March 8, 1984.
[38] Ha-'Ir, March 16, 1984; Maariv, November 20, 1985, November 25, 1985; Haaretz, November 26, 1985 (3 items).
[39] Haaretz, April, 24, 1981, May 5, 1981, March 25, 1984, August 13, 1984, January 14, 1985.
[40] Harretz, July 7, 1983; Kol Ha-'Ir, November 1, 1985; Maariv, February 6, 1985.
[41] Haaretz, November 12, 1984.
[42] Haaretz, March 17, 1973.
[43] Haaretz, Feburary 14, 1986.
[44] Asher Yaldin, Edut (Testimony), Idanim, 1980, pp. 102-103
[45] Ibid., p. 1970.
[46] Harretz, December 30, 1985.
[47] Haaretz, October 4, 1981.
[48] Haaretz, October 26, 1982.

[49] Haaretz, May 16, 1986.
[50] Haraetz, August 22, 1976.
[51] Kol Ha'Ir May 9, 1986.
[52] The University (Tel Aviv), August 1985.
[53] Haaretz, December 12, 1986; Maariv, March 13, 1984.
[54] Maariv, August 31, 1984.
[55] David Ben-Gurion, War Diaries 1984-1949.
[56] Proc. of Sociological Soc. Israel, Jerusalem, Februray 2, 1985.
[57] Haaretz, June 25, 1985.
[58] Harretz, October 1, 1986.
[59] Ibid.
[60] Haaretz, November 14, 1981.
[61] Haaretz, September 19, 1985.
[62] Haaretz, February 2, 1985.
[63] Maariv, November 8, 1985.
[64] Yediot Ahronot, August 11, 1980.
[65] Haaretz, April 6, 1982.
[66] Ibid.
[67] Maariv, November 7, 1986.
[68] Hindenheimer, A.J., J. Politics, 25:790-811, 1963.
[69] Haaretz, March 1982.
[70] Maariv, April 12, 1984.
[71] Haaretz, June 20, 1976.
[72] Yediot Ahronot, June 5, 1981; Haaretz, July 10, 1986.
[73] Haaretz, January 31, 1985.
[74] Yadlin, A. Edut (Testimony), Idanim, 1980 pp. 140-141.
[75] Ibid., p. 147.
[76] Ibid., pp. 149-150.
[77] Ibid., p. 148.
[78] Ibid., p. 148.
[79] Maariv, Asakim, July 1984.

Chapter 3 **The Tentacles Of The Octopus**

[1] Haartez, January 30, 1986.
[2] Haartez, September 10, 1974.
[3] Haartez, September 22, 1983.
[4] Haartez, November 29, 1984.
[5] Maariv, March 6, 1986, September 22, 1985.
[6] Haaretz, November 18, 1984.

[7] Harretz, February 27, 1975.
[8] Harretz, October 29, 1982.
[9] Harretz, August 17, 1982.
[10] Harretz, July 7, 1983.
[11] Maariv, September 17, 1982.
[12] Maariv, February 2, 1980.
[13] Haartez, July 27, 1982.
[14] Haartez, May 28, 1981.
[15] Haartez, December 28, 1981.
[16] Haartez, July 7, 1976.
[17] Haartez, July 7, 1976.
[18] Maariv, November 22, 1981; Haaretez, December 24, 1982.
[19] Haartez, Novemberm 26, 1982.
[20] Kol Ha'ir, November 5, 1982.
[21] Maariv, February 9, 1984.
[22] Maariv, September 18, 1985.
[23] Haartez, October 10, 1984, Novmber 8, 1981.
[24] Haartez, November 8, 1981.
[25] Haartez, June 2, 1987; Maariv, June 8, 1987.
[26] Maariv, June 10, 1986.
[27] Maariv, January 24, 1984.
[28] Maariv, March 3, 1985.
[29] Haartez, December 22, 1985, January 10, 1986, November 3, 1986.
[30] Haartez, May 5, 1985, Ha'Ir April 4, 1982; Kol Ha'Ir, December 11, 1987.
[31] Haartez, September 14, 1982, January 1, 1984.
[32] Ibid.
[33] Maaric, September 31, 1984.
[34] Haartez, 3, September 7, 1982.
[35] Haartez, September 14, 1982, January 23, 1984.
[36] Haartez, January 20, 1984.
[37] Haartez, January 24, 1984.
[38] Haartez, October 12, 1983.
[39] Haartez, October 15, 1975.
[40] Ha'Ir, June 14, 1985.
[41] Maariv, February 16, 1979, September 26, 1975.
[42] Haartez, November 8, 1974.
[43] Haartez, 19, 22, September 26, 1975.

[44] Maariv, February 13, 1984.
[45] Kol Ha'Ir, January 10, 1982, Haartez, November 17, 1983, April 2, 1986.
[46] Globes, May 28, 1984, Haartez, June 9, 1985, October 8, 1985.
[47] Yediot Ahronot, April 13, 1989, Haartz December 15, 1981.
[48] Haartez, September 24, 1975, December 15, 1981, Rehov Rashi, June 24, 1983.
[49] Ibid.
[50] Haartez, November 5, 1981.
[51] Haartez, January 6, 1985.
[52] Kol Ha'Ir, June 1, 1982, Haartez, July 3, 1978, June 15, 1985.
[53] Maariv, December 24, 1982.

Chapter 4 The Histradut -- Guarantor of Labor Hegemony

[1] Maariv, July 8, 1986.
[2] July 20, 1928.
[3] Shapira, Y., The Historic Ahdut Ha-'Avoda, Am Oved, 1975, p. 104.
[4] Bartal, G., The Histradut, Structure and Function, Histradut Pub. 1982.
[5] Idem, p. 156.
[6] Idem, p. 30.
[7] Haartez, June 21, 1976, June 10, 1987.
[8] Haartez, June 22, 1976.
[9] Haartez, July 23, 1976.
[10] Haartez, October 25, 1985.
[11] Haartez, November 20, 1972.
[12] Haartez, October 17, 1985.
[13] Haartez, December 13, 1985, Report of the Sohar Committee for Reform of Health Services, January 1978.
[14] Ibid.
[15] Haartez, June 24, 1976.
[16] Haartez, June 24, 1976, March 14, 1986.
[17] Maariv, October 17, 1985, Haartez, July 2, 1976.
[18] Haartez, November 20, 1972.
[19] Haartez, March 15, 1974.
[20] Haartez, July 3, 1986.

[21] Haartez, August 2, 1983.
[22] Haartez, May 11, 1987.
[23] Haartez, July 11, 1985.
[24] Haartez, April 20, 1971, July 9, 1975, September 1, 1984, Maariv, July 20, 1983.
[25] Ibid.
[26] Haartez, November 12, 1985.
[27] Yediot Ahronot, November 29, 1985, Maariv, November 7, 1985.
[28] Haartez, August 27, 1986.
[29] I. Greenberg, From Hevrat ha-'Ovdim to Workers Economy, Ph.D. Dissertation, Tel Aviv University, 1986.
[30] Maariv, March 20, 1984, March 14, 1986.
[31] Maariv, June 24, 1986.
[32] Ibid.
[33] Maariv, March 16, 1984.
[34] Maariv, May 27, 1976.
[35] Haartez, March 28, 1986.
[36] Haartez, December 4, 1985, February 20, 1986.
[37] Haartez, November 19, 1985, December 13, 1985. Maariv, December 25, 1985.
[38] Haartez, April 14, 1986.
[39] Haartez, March 4, 1986.
[40] Haartez, July 11, 1986.
[41] Yediot Ahronot, January 16, 1976, Maariv, June 12, 1983.
[42] Maariv, March 20, 1984, March 14, 1986.
[43] Yediot Ahronot, April 10, 1987, Maariv, April 15, 1987, April 17, 1987, Haartez, March 25, 1987.

Chapter 5 — The Infrastructure

[1] Haartez, August 27, 1952, Ezra Sohar, The Pincers of the Regime, Shikmons, 1974, p. 80.
[2] Haartez, April 16, 1982.
[3] Maariv, August 24, 1979, June 26, 1980, April 20, 1981, October 24, 1984.
[4] Ezra Sohar, In the Pincers of the Regime, 1974, p.16.
[5] Haartez, July 12, 1981.
[6] Haartez, September 15, 1981.
[7] Haartez, February 7, 1986, September 19, 1986.

[8] Maariv, January 10, 1984.
[9] David Margaliot, Karka ("Land"), December 1983, pp 34-37.
[10] Maariv, November 13, 1980.
[11] Maariv, March 18, 1981.
[12] Karka, December 1983, p. 38.
[13] Haartez, December 27, 1984, Maariv, December 28, 1984.
[14] Haartez, July 11, 1984.
[15] Haartez, April 20, 1973, May 5, 1974.
[16] Haartez, November 15, 1981.
[17] Haartez, July 18, 1977.
[18] "Build it Yourself," Israel Land Authority and Arim Co., Sept. 1981.
[19] Haartez, December 6, 1981, Maariv, July 8, 1982.
[20] Maariv, February 5, 1976, May 6, 1980.
[21] Maariv, May 28, 1986.
[22] Haartez, March 12, 1984, Maariv, July 29, 1973, June 5, 1986.
[23] Haartez, August 24, 1962.
[24] Haartez, March 1, 1974, May 29, 1986, June 3, 1983, Maariv, June 2, 1986, Kol Ha'am, January 21, 1974.
[25] Haaretz, December 17, 1986; Haaretz, March 12, 1984; Maariv, July 29, 1973; Maariv, June 5, 1986.
[26] Maariv, June 2, 1986, June 17, 1986; Haaretz, March 1, 1974, May 29, 1986, June 3, 1983, Kol Ha'am, January 21, 1974.
[27] Haaretz, December 17, 1986.
[28] Maariv, June 17, 1986.
[29] Maariv, July 20, 1986.
[30] Haaretz, June 23, 1986.
[31] Haaretz, July 28, 1986.
[32] Ibid.
[33] Ibid.
[34] Haaretz, July 1, 1980.
[35] Yediot Ahronot, June 13, 1986.
[36] Haaretz, February 11, 1987, advertisement of the Government Public Relations Service.
[37] Yediot Anronot, September 17, 1982, Haaretz, August 21, 1984, Maariv, June 12, 1987.
[38] Haaretz, March 26, 1986.
[39] Maariv, May 31, 1979, Maariv, April 7, 1982.
[40] Haaretz, July 3, 1985.

41 Haaretz, November 16, 1972, July 28, 1982, July 24, 1984; Maariv, February 14, 1979.
42 Yediot Ahronot, April 25, 1980; Maariv, April 25, 1980.
43 Maariv, December 13, 1984; Haaretz, December 13, 1984.
44 Haaretz, September 3, 1985.
45 Haaretz, February 5, 1986, Haaretz, May 5, 1987.
46 Haaretz, January 11, 1988.
47 Haaretz, January 10, 1982, February 28, 1986, Kol Ha'Ir, November 18, 1983, Maariv, December 20, 1983, State Comptroller's Report on Paz Co., January 1986.
48 Haaretz, February 5, 1986, May 5, 1987.
49 Ibid.
50 Haaretz, September 19, 1985, September 23, 1985.
51 Hadashot, October 31, 1986, Haaretz, March 26, 1987.
52 Maariv, August 6, 1985.
53 Haaretz, December 20, 1971.
54 Parliamentary Question No. 2167, Haaretz, July 30, 1978, December 18, 1978.
55 Haaretz, July 8, 1980; Maariv, March 19, 1982.
56 Haaretz, December 30, 1975, June 1, 1976.
57 Zvi Weiss, Bank of Israel Survey No. 50, March 1979, 5.
58 Maariv, March 26, 1986.
59 Haaretz, November 19, 1974, February 1, 1975, April 15, 1986; Maariv, Febrary 3, 1987.
60 Dr. M. Rahav, Haaretz, May 8, 1983, July 5, 1985, July 10, 1985, July 12, 1985; Maariv, June 12, 1987; Kesafim, December 27, 1982.
61 Maariv, June 6, 1986.
62 Maariv, August 1, 1975, February 16, 1986.
63 Haaretz, December 2, 1986.
64 Maariv, February 16, 1979.
65 Haaretz, February 30, 1982, Maariv, August 17, 1981, March 26, 1985.
66 White Paper on Transportation Safety, Government of Japan, 1979, Haaretz, September 9, 1981, January 8, 1985.
67 Haaretz, September 4, 1985.
68 Maariv, March 12, 1985.
69 Dr. M. Sela, Haaretz, September 9, 1981, December 8, 1981, January 16, 1986; Yediot Ahronot, February 9, 1979.

70 Report of the State Comptroller No. 31, 1980.
71 Haaretz, January 30, 1976, Maariv, February 8, 1982.
72 Haaretz, January 8, 1984, Globes, January 30, 1985.
73 Haaretz, October 2, 1975, October 22, 1975, October 14, 1986, April 27, 1987, June 19, 1987, June 23, 1987; Maariv, February 17, 1984, January 5, 1987, June 23, 1987.
74 Haaretz, February 8, 1980, February 11, 1980, February 1, 1982, February 7, 1987; Yediot Ahronot, July 19, 1985.
75 Haaretz, February 12, 1980.
76 Haaretz, July 25, 1975.
77 Haaretz, April 30, 1974, April 1, 1983, October 18, 1985; Maariv, November 27, 1984.
78 Maariv, December 23, 1983; Haaretz, July 25, 1975.
79 Haarez, September 5, 1974.
80 Haaretz, June 21, 1974, August 16, 1981, March 16, 1984, August 6, 1984, November 9, 1984.
81 Haaretz, January 19, 1976, Maariv, November 18, 1981, September 3, 1982, October 8, 1982.
82 Haaretz, February 1, 1982, Maariv, July 2, 1984.
83 Haaretz, October 14, 1982, July 3, 1987, Maariv, October 27, 1982, October 29, 1982.
84 Haaretz, June 4, 1980.
85 Haaretz, July 3, 1987.
86 Haaretz, April 19, 1982, May 27, 1982, August 17, 1984; Maariv, October 23, 1984.
87 Maariv, 14, 28, 12, 1984; Haaretz, February 10, 1985, August 13, 1981; Maariv, July 16, 1985.
88 Haaretz, December 17, 1984, June 18, 1985.
89 Haaretz, May 3, 1987, December 17, 1984, June 18, 1985.
90 Haaretz, April 15, 1980, May 5, 1980.
91 Haaretz, September 8, 1986, August 25, 1986.
92 Maariv, May 4, 1982.
93 Haaretz, September 17, 1984.
94 Haaretz, December 19, 1974, June 4, 1980.
95 Haaretz, February 17, 1974.
96 Haaretz, December 25, 1972.
97 Haaretz, January 21, 1973.
98 Haaretz, February 8, 1984, December 16, 1986, Yediot Ahronot, February 24, 1984, Maariv, October 21, 1985.
99 Ibid.

[100] Haaretz, March 10, 1981.
[101] Yediot Ahronot, December 28, 1982.
[102] Haaretz, December 2, 1974, Maariv, April 27, 1984.
[103] Haaretz, February 23, 1983, Maariv, March 21, 1982.
[104] Hadashot, August 8, 1985.
[105] Yediot Ahronot, April 24, 1984.
[106] Haaretz, July 12, 1979, December 16, 1984.
[107] Sha'ar, May 19, 1982, Maariv, August 25, 1983, February 4, 1984.
[108] Haaretz, February 27, 1986.
[109] Maariv, December 19, 1979, June 19, 1981, November 11, 1981.
[110] Maariv, January 27, 1984.
[111] Maariv, August 16, 1985, Yediot Ahronot, October 6, 1985.
[112] Hadashot, August 8, 1985.

Chapter 6 Structure Of The Economy

[1] Haaretz, June 8, 1960.
[2] Haaretz, February 14, 1952.
[3] Haaretz, February 25, 1952.
[4] Haaretz, March 2, 1952.
[5] Haaretz, March 12, 1952.
[6] Haaretz, April 27, 1952.
[7] Haaretz, May 26, 1953.
[8] Haaretz, November 15, 1961.
[9] Yediot Ahronot, May 17, 1962; June 26, 1987.
[10] Kochav, D., and Lifshitz, I., "Defence Expenditure and its Influence on the Economy and Industry," Economics Quarterly, No. 78-79, Sept. 1973.
[11] Maariv, October 18, 1983, Haartez, April 13, 1987.
[12] Ibid.
[13] Haaretz, July 10, 1985, June 19, 1986.
[14] Haaretz, September 20, 1985.
[15] Haaretz, June 20, 1986.
[16] Haaretz, July 15, 1986.
[17] Haaretz, December 25, 1985.
[18] Haaretz, February 7, 1984, June 11, 1987, June 23, 1987.
[19] Haaretz, February 8, 1977.
[20] Haaretz, April 11, 1976.
[21] Yediot Ahronot, March 20, 1984.

22 Haaretz, February 7, 1984; Maariv, April 12, 1983.
23 Yediot Ahronot, June 5, 1984.
24 Haaretz, July 8, 1986.
25 Yediot Ahronot, April 2, 1982, Maariv, April 12, 1985.
26 Yediot Ahronot, February 15, 1984.
27 Haaretz, March 28, 1983.
28 Haaretz, March 28, 1986.
29 Haaretz, March 8, 1984.
30 Haaretz, May 2, 1976.
31 Haaretz, February 7, 1982.
32 Haaretz, October 21, 1985; Maariv, April 9, 1982.
33 Maariv, January 27, 1986.
34 Haaretz, July 11, 1986.
35 Haaretz, August 19, 1985.
36 Haaretz, September 17, 1984.
37 Jerusalem Post, January 16, 1986.
38 Haaretz, November 10, 1982.
39 Yediot Ahronot, January 16, 1981.
40 Yediot Ahronot, November 21, 1982.
41 Maariv, August 2, 1985.
42 Haaretz, September 25, 1984; Maariv, December 24, 1985.
43 Maariv, January 15, 1985.
44 Sha'ar, February 18, 1986.
45 Ha-Mifal, No. 253, April 1982, 106-107.
46 Maariv, April 2, 1985.
47 Maariv, September 5, 1985.
48 Haaretz, February 18, 1983.
49 Haaretz, May 28, 1985.
50 Maariv, May 29, 1985.
51 Haaretz, June 9, 1985; Maariv, June 10, 1985.
52 Maariv, January 8, 1986, January 10, 1986, January 22, 1986.
53 *Foreign Affairs*, Spring 1986.
54 Ibid.
55 Haaretz, August 16, 1983, November 1, 1983, Maariv, January 27, 1987, October 29, 1982, March 11, 1983, June 10, 1983, August 23, 1983, January 24, 1986; Yediot Ahronot, October 25, 1983.
56 Haaretz, July 2, 1986.
57 Haaretz, October 25, 1983, May 10, 1987, April 30, 1987; Maariv, December 28, 1984, April 23, 1987.
58 Haaretz, July 2, 1986.

59 Haaretz, October 25, 1983, May 10, 1987, April 30, 1987, Maariv, December 28, 1984, April 23, 1987.
60 Haaretz, January 24, 1986, August 12, 1986.
61 Memorandum by Tel Aviv Chamber of Commerce, Haaretz, August 20, 1986.
62 Yediot Ahronot, January 23, 1987, December 12, 1986.
63 Haaretz, February 26, 1986; Yediot Ahronot, April 15, 1983, Maariv, October 2, 1981, November 20, 1985, April 1, 1986, November 20, 1986.
64 Haaretz, June 2, 1982, February 26, 1986, June 9, 1987; Maariv, November 19, 1980, August 8, 1986.
65 Globes, October 24, 1984.
66 Haaretz, February 8, 1985, May 25, 1986.
67 Haaretz, July 29, 1982; Maariv, July 21, 1982, August 3, 1982.
68 Haaretz, June 5, 1983; Maariv, June 10, 1983, September 7, 1985.
69 Maariv, September 7, 1985; Haaretz, June 11, 1985, June 6, 1985, December 10, 1984; Maariv, March 26, 1981, August 25, 1981; Yediot Ahronot, May 20, 1986.
70 Haaretz, February 19, 1986, February 5, 1986, August 14, 1984, July 19, 1982; Maariv, November 23, 1984, November 1, 1986.
71 Haaretz, January 30, 1980, June 25, 1980; Maariv, December 15, 1980.
72 Maariv, August 28, 1983; Yediot Ahronot, May 13, 1985, January 28, 1987.
73 Haaretz, July 20, 1982, August 26, 1981, August 14, 1986, July 19, 1982; Maariv, April 22, 1984, December 30, 1984.
74 Haaretz, January 23, 1986, April 9, 1986, February 24, 1986; Yediot Ahronot, May 6, 1982, May 16, 1984.
75 Haaretz, September 21, 1975, June 9, 1976, November 26, 1979, April 18, 1978, December 23, 1980, September 19, 1981, March 6, 1981, August 4, 1982, October 22, 1985, April 25, 1986, February 18, 1986, September 29, 1986; Yediot Ahronot, September 21, 1981, November 2, 1984, May 25, 1982.
76 Haaretz, December 12, 1979.
77 Haaretz, November 19, 1986, November 16, 1986.
78 Yediot Ahronot, August 5, 1983; Maariv, June 25, 1986.
79 Haaretz, April 2, 1979; Maariv, June 10, 1985.

[80] Haaretz, September 1, 1983, November 16, 1984; Maariv, November 17, 1986, July 30, 1985, February 15, 1985; Yediot Ahronot, December 13, 1983, September 16, 1986.

[81] Maariv, January 18, 1984, June 14, 1985, November 20, 1984; Yediot Ahronot, May 13, 1983, September 16, 1986, July 17, 1985, April 20, 1984.

[82] Haaretz, May 18, 1986; Yediot Ahronot, May 10, 1983; Maariv, July 30, 1985, February 15, 1985.

[83] Maariv, April 10, 1986.

[84] H. Ben-Shahar et al., Shocken Publishers, 1973, p. 23.

[85] Maariv, April 30, 1984.

[86] Haaretz, January 20, 1983, December 26, 1983, June 20, 1986; Maariv, February 7, 1984.

[87] Haaretz, March 23, 1983.

[88] Maariv, July 10, 1984.

[89] H. Ben-Shahar, *op.cit.*, 28, 42.

[90] Ibid.

[91] Haaretz, May 20, 1975, August 26, 1975, May 26, 1976, June 3, 1976, November 4, 1982, July 3, 1985; Yediot Ahronot, June 21, 1983; Maariv, August 13, 1986.

[92] Haaretz, April 29, 1986.

[93] Haaretz, February 2, 1986.

[94] Haaretz, April 22, 1986; Maariv, November 11, 1983.

[95] Maariv, November 4, 1983, November 11, 1983, November 18, 1983.

[96] Haaretz, January 12, 1985, January 18, 1985, September 25, 1986.

[97] Haaretz, November 3, 1983.

[98] Haaretz, April 21, 1986, January 14, 1987.

[99] Haaretz, May 27, 1986.

[100] Haaretz, January 9, 1987.

[101] Maariv, October 17, 1986.

[102] Haaretz, February 27, 1976.

[103] Haaretz, November 17, 1972, November 19, 1972.

[104] Yediot Ahronot, November 13, 1972.

[105] Haaretz, June 10, 1976.

[106] Haaretz, June 29, 1984; Maariv, June 25, 1984, November 1, 1984, June 4, 1985; Yediot Ahronot, October 4, 1984; Kol Yerushalayim, June 24, 1983; Maariv, November 25, 1985, November 22, 1985, June 22, 1983.

[107] Haaretz, November 2, 1982.

108 Haaretz, November 7, 1983.
109 Globes, May 30, 1984; Yediot Ahronot, November 13, 1972.
110 Hadashot, October 31, 1986; Maariv, January 6, 1987.
111 Ibid.
112 Ibid.
113 Chairman of Knesset Finance Committee, Israel Broadcasting Authority, December 31, 1981.
114 Haaretz, November 17, 1983.
115 Maariv, September 9, 1986.
116 Maariv, October 7, 1986.
117 Maariv, December 8, 1982, November 12, 1982; Haaretz, November 17, 1983.
118 Haaretz, August 16, 1983; Maariv, November 30, 1982.
119 Haaretz, March 9, 1984.
120 Haaretz, June 30, 1984.
121 Jerusalem Post, June 12, 1984.
122 Maariv, October 4, 1983.
123 Yediot Ahronot, March 28, 1986.
124 Haaretz, January 22, 1987

Chapter 7 **The Bilkers**

1 Maariv, December 13, 1982.
2 Haaretz, September 7, 1984; Yediot Ahronot, May 7, 1982, May 31, 1985.
3 Maariv, March 4, 1981, May 11, 1984.
4 Haaretz, March 8, 1982; Maariv, May 15, 1973, September 21, 1981.
5 Haaretz, April 6, 1976, December 6, 1984; Maariv, March 24, 1982.
6 I. Gabai, *Social Implications of Fiscal Policy*, 1983; Maariv, October 25, 1983, October 28, 1983.
7 Ezra Sohar, Maariv, December 18, 1984.
8 Haaretz, September 12, 1986.
9 Report of the Board of Government Companies, The Treasury, 1985.
10 Haaretz, January 11, 1985.
11 Report of the Board of Government Companies, The Treasury, 1985.
12 Y. Aharoni, *Structure and Behavior of the Israeli Economy* (Manas Publishers, 1966), 84.

13 Report of the Board of Government Companies, The Treasury, 1985.
14 Haaretz, July 28, 1974.
15 Haaretz, September 28, 1986.
16 Haaretz, July 28, 1984.
17 Globes, July 19, 1985; Haaretz, July 18, 1985, December 21, 1984, April 1, 1986.
18 Maariv, April 20, 1984.
19 Maariv, July 24, 1973.
20 Yediot Ahronot, November 27, 1972; Maariv, August 27, 1976.
21 Haaretz, September 17, 1986.
22 Hadashot, August 31, 1986.
23 A. Yakir, and R. Weigert, *Economic Dictionary*, (Hashab Publishers)
24 Haaretz, December 5, 1977, March 25, 1979.
25 Maariv, April 3, 1975.
26 Al-Hamishmar, Economic Supplement, Dec. 1986, 22-26.
27 Haaretz, December 28, 1976.
28 Haaretz, October 16, 1974.
29 Haaretz, February 28, 1986.
30 Haaretz, February 11, 1983.
31 *Economic Quarterly*, No. 124, 12-21.
32 Haaretz, February 27, 1974.
33 M. Atia, and A. Leef, "Subsidies in Export Credit," Lecture at Van Leer Jerusalem Institute, January 13, 1981.
34 Yediot Ahronot, May 3, 1974.
35 Haaretz, May 30, 1986, November 25, 1979; Maariv, October 28, 1983, October 6, 1983; Yediot Ahronot, April 9, 1976.
36 Globes, April 12, 1984.
37 Haaretz, February 18, 1982.
38 Haaretz, May 30, 1986, November 25, 1979; Maariv, October 28, 1983, October 6, 1983; Yediot Ahronot, April 9, 1976.
39 Haaretz, August 22, 1976, November 26, 1985, State Comptroller's Report No.27.
40 Ibid.
41 Kesafim, September 12, 1982.
42 Haaretz, August 13, 1985, December 20, 1985.
43 Haaretz, November 25, 1979, July 3, 1987, Maariv, August 2, 1985.
44 Haaretz, September 12, 1986.
45 New York Times, October 21, 1986.

46 Haaretz, August 13, 1986.
47 Haaretz, November 29, 1983; Maariv, January 17, 1984; Yozma Monthly, January 1984.
48 Maariv, December 27, 1984.
49 Haaretz, February 12, 1985, February 14, 1985.
50 Haaretz, February 14, 1985.
51 Haaretz, August 29, 1985.
52 Haaretz, November 19, 1985, January 21, 1986, December 13, 1985.
53 Maariv, December 25, 1985.
54 Haaretz, July 5, 1984.
55 Haaretz, November 29, 1983; Maariv, January 17, 1984; Yozma Monthly, January 1984.
56 Maariv, April 9, 1985.
57 Maariv, February 11, 1986.
58 Haaretz, August 24, 1975, August 6, 1982, September 4, 1985.
59 Haaretz, August 13, 1986.
60 Haaretz, May 29, 1981.
61 Maariv, February 11, 1986.
62 Haaretz, July 8, 1979

Chapter 8 The Farmers -- Vassals Of The Bureaucracy

1 Maariv, November 24, 1983.
2 Maariv, November 12, 1984.
3 Haaretz, August 11, 1985.
4 Yediot Ahronot, December 25, 1984.
5 Haaretz, September 15, 1982.
6 Maariv, March 2, 1984, January 10, 1986, March 18, 1986, December 1, 1980.
7 Maariv, September 26, 1986.
8 Nutkin, *op.cit.*, 43; Maariv, October 11, 1985.
9 Haaretz, September 8, 1976, September 10, 1976; Maariv, May 14, 1982.
10 Hadashot, March 30, 1984; Haaretz, April 24, 1984; Maariv, May 7, 1982.
11 Haaretz, January 27, 1982, Maariv, April 12, 1983, August 19, 1983 (Jerusalem Supp.)
12 Maariv, September 29, 1986, October 7, 1986.

[13] Haaretz, February 11, 1985; Maariv, August 8, 1983; Haaretz, April 6, 1981; Yediot Ahronot, July 4, 1983.
[14] Haaretz, September 24, 1984.
[15] Haaretz, February 3, 1986.
[16] Haaretz, January 27, 1982; Maariv, April 12, 1983, August 19, 1983.
[17] Haaretz, December 2, 1982, June 29, 1979, Maariv, November 24, 1981, July 17, 1983, August 30, 1983.
[18] Haaretz, August 12, 1982, January 8, 1982, January 21, 1982; Maariv, May 14, 1982.
[19] Haaretz, January 8, 1982; Maariv, June 10, 1983.
[20] Maariv, June 10, 1983.
[21] Haaretz, August 3, 1983.
[22] Haaretz, March 3, 1981.
[23] Haaretz, December 10, 1986; Maariv, September 6, 1983, June 24, 1987.
[24] Ibid.
[25] Yediot Ahronot, September 23, 1983.
[26] Ibid.
[27] Haaretz, 8, July 7, 1985, August 6, 1985, July 5, 1985.
[28] Haaretz, March 6, 1987.
[29] Ezra Sohar, Maariv, December 18, 1984.
[30] Haaretz, June 2, 1982, Sha'ar, February 17, 1982.
[31] Haaretz, August 30, 1982, January 18, 1983; Maariv, August 31, 1983.
[32] Haaretz, April 13, 1986.
[33] Maariv, January 10, 1982.
[34] Ibid.
[35] Haaretz, March 2, 1987.
[36] Maariv, January 8, 1985.
[37] Haaretz, December 11, 1985.
[38] Haaretz, January 11, 1984; Maariv, December 24, 1982, September 6, 1985; Davar, May 25, 1983.
[39] Haaretz, December 31, 1984; Maariv, October 2, 1984

Chapter 9 **Making Israel Work**

[1] Thiel de Sola Pool, "How Powerful is Business?" in R. Hessen (ed.), *Does Big Business Rule America?* (Public Policy Center, Washington D.C., 1982), 24.

[2] Ludwig von Mises, *Socialism* (Liberty Classics, Indianapolis, 1979), 45.
[3] Haaretz, June 21, 1987.
[4] Founding Meeting of the New Liberal Party, Tel Aviv, January 16, 1986.
[5] Haaretz, June 19, 1987; Maariv, June 19, 1987.
[6] Maariv, December 19, 1986.
[7] Haaretz, June 24, 1987.
[8] J. Naisbitt, *The Year Ahead* (Warner Books, New York), 75-86.

INDEX